A LIFE
WORTH
LIVING

A LIFE WORTH LIVING

*The Adventures of a
Passionate Sportsman*

Jack Hemingway

*Edited and with an Introduction by
Geoffrey Norman*

Foreword by Angela Hemingway

THE LYONS PRESS
Guilford, Connecticut
An imprint of The Globe Pequot Press

To Angela—my wife and best friend—

*The woman who threw herself into fly-fishing
with such generosity of spirit,
that she turned what had been for me
mere love for the sport into grand passion.*

"I spent the first fifty years of my life being the son of a famous father and am now spending the last fifty as the father of famous children. There's a lot of truth in that. The only waves I have made have been in the currents of trout and salmon streams, and . . . that's where I propose to continue to make waves."

—Jack Hemingway

Contents

A Note on the Text by Nick Lyons   xi
Foreword by Angela Hemingway   xiii
Introduction by Geoffrey Norman   xvii

ONE
Selections from Misadventures of a Fly Fisherman
I. EARLY YEARS
1 An Angler from the Start   3
2 From Boy to Man   13
II. BEFORE THE WAR
3 Sun Valley   23
4 A Michigan Sojourn   31
5 Yellowstone Country   35
6 Oregon and the Mills   49
7 Back to Paradise . . . Sun Valley   57
III. THE WAR YEARS
8 Abroad with the OSS   67
9 Into Battle . . . Fly Rod in Hand   75
10 Wounded and Captured   87
11 A Prisoner of War   93
IV. AFTER THE WAR
12 Civilian Doldrums   101
13 A Second Hitch   105
14 Another Hitch . . . This One for Life   111
15 Some Hunting Sketches   115
16 Papa's Son Becomes a Papa   123
17 Another Start . . . and a Pact with Papa   127
18 A Bad Ending   135
19 And a New Beginning   139

TWO

A Sportsman's Life

I. SOME WORDS ABOUT FLY FISHING

1 Seasons of the Angler   149

2 Fly Fishing Manners   159

II. SOME MEMORABLE ANGLERS

3 Charles Ritz   169

4 Chez Tolstoi   173

5 Dermot Wilson   177

III. SOME SEDUCTIVE STREAMS

6 The Loue   181

7 North Umpqua   185

8 Irish Rivers   193

9 Icelandic Rivers   199

IV. TRAVELS WITH DAN

10 1944 Revisited   211

V. IN THE FIELD: BIRDS, DOGS, AND GUNS

11 Guns and Shooting   227

12 Snipe Near Cotorro   231

13 A Pre-Castro Cuban Dove Shoot   237

14 Partridge   241

THREE

Some Tributes

A Tribute to Jack Hemingway by Tom Brokaw   247

Eulogy for Jack Hemingway,
December 9, 2000, by Howell Raines   251

One Last Cast A Tribute by Dan Callaghan   257

A Note on the Text

On the Friday before Jack went into the hospital for a heart checkup—which led immediately to open-heart surgery and within days thereafter to his death—we had a long and wide-ranging lunch near my office. We talked fishing, spoke of good friends we had in common, and he told me about a batch of fishing trips he'd booked for the coming year. And we discussed at length this, his last book.

Neither of us thought that *Misadventures of a Fly Fisherman* should be reprinted in its entirety, and we both knew that his new material was not sufficiently complete to make a book of its own. Jack very much wanted the title *A Life Worth Living,* and we both felt that the new pieces did not adequately represent the arc of his life. So we settled on this: we would not make a condensation or a rewritten version of his first book but would take coherent, self-contained excerpts, chiefly centered on his life as a sportsman, and present memorable scenes and events. Much in his first book, he told me, had been said once and needn't be said again; and he wanted this book, which he said would be his last, to focus on his deep passion for the sporting life, not about what he often said was being the son of a famous father and father of famous daughters. The excerpts would become a full section with which to begin the book. They would not tell the whole story, but they would establish the frame of his life, note some of its highlights. Then this would lead into the new material.

Geoffrey Norman, because of his passion for both hunting and fishing and his extensive magazine experience, was my choice for editor of this material, and he has done an excellent job of weaving together and tightening Jack's final book. How I wish Jack was here to laugh that great infectious laugh of his and say, "That's just what I had in mind. Now let's go fishing, Nick." But he isn't—and I can only hope that what we're publishing is what he wanted. I think it is. With its engaging photographs and a final section of recollections by others, this is a compact version of what he liked to call "a life worth living"— scenes from his especially broad-ranging life as a conservationist, sportsman, and, especially, fly fisherman. And I think it is a fine tribute to that life.

—Nick Lyons
New York City
Fall 2001

Foreword

By Angela Hemingway

In the fall of 2000, Jack finished a book called *A Life Worth Living* a few weeks prior to his untimely death. I cannot think of a more appropriate title. Jack approached life like he approached his friendships . . . with unbridled curiosity, a profound sense of humor, and a surprisingly quiet grace. He touched everyone he met, drawing them slowly into the warm embrace of his friendship like a cork is drawn from a fine bottle of wine.

I was pulled into that circle of warmth when I married Jack in 1989. He was my husband, my lover, my fly-fishing instructor, shooting instructor, and—above all—my best friend and confidant. Jack awakened a love of the outdoors in me . . . and he taught me to live a life worth living. He made my life worth living. . . .

Life with Jack was an adventure every day. He brought new dimension to my life. One of the first things he said to me was "I am introducing you to a life of nature, fishing, and shooting. We'll go all over the world and meet wonderful people and share experiences on what I hope will be an unforgettable journey."

When I first met Jack, I was surprised to see that he was without pretense, even though he was the son of a world-renowned father. I discovered someone with an astounding zest for life, freely offering his unconditional friendship. His unaffected manner was refreshing. Jack was true to himself. It couldn't have been easy living in the shadow of his famous father, but he handled his heritage the same way he handled his own life, with a delightful mixture of pride, dignity, grace, and profound humor and enthusiasm. And most important, he was the quintessential gentleman, reflecting his upbringing. His extraordinary life and the vigor with which he lived as Ernest's son embraced his father's style and legacy, yet he never lost the sweet nature he inherited from his mother Hadley.

Jack was bigger than life when he entered a room. You could see that people were captivated by his aura. Since his death, I have been sent countless recollections of those moments from people all over the world, whether they met him at a dinner party, fishing stream, or in the field. He had a great gift for making you feel fortunate to be there with him, as if you were in the presence of an old friend, even though you may have just made his acquaintance.

I learned from Jack how to embrace life and enjoy the outdoors. Realization of this wondrous gift taught me how to live each day as if it were the last. I adopted my husband's philosophy of living and feel blessed with this knowledge.

Jack and I complemented each other. We enjoyed traveling, the nuances of fine dining, evenings at home alone or sharing our time with friends and family, celebrating life with food, wine, music, and an inviting, cozy ambience.

His natural storytelling cadence and abundance of laughter always filled our home whether with friends, family, or just the two of us eating from a tray, watching television. My fondest memories are the many evenings we were alone, whether sharing the events of the day, reading a book or having a quiet moment while we discussed future plans, feeling the comfort and security of our love and ultimate understanding of our relationship.

Jack's generosity knew no bounds. It showed in the way he supported certain charities such as the Nature Conservancy. He was also generous with his time and his affection for friends and family. He was supportive when they stumbled, and grieved when he lost his middle daughter, Margot, in a tragic and untimely death. Jack was also resilient. One of the key elements to his ability to be resilient was his passion for the great outdoors and realizing that *"life is good with Papa"* which he declared at age three during an outing with his father in Paris. His profound ability to deal with difficult times and obstacles in his life was based on what he had learned from the forces of the outdoor life which was, in fact, his natural therapy. A favorite quote from Tully Stroud says it all:

"Man will always seek escapes—special places where troubles are forgotten."

Jack lived a life as big as the whole outdoors. Fly fishing was his passion, and it took him to the far reaches of the planet. Even World War II couldn't dampen this fervor for fishing. In 1944, as an OSS officer, he parachuted into France with a fly rod hidden in his pack. He was eventually captured by the Germans, but not before a few French fish rose to his flies.

Jack poured this passion into preserving one of the country's premier trout streams, Silver Creek, near Sun Valley, Idaho, successfully championing an effort to set aside this pristine paradise. Now a Nature Conservancy Preserve, the clear waters of Silver Creek draw fly fishermen from all over the world. It is a living legacy to a true conservationist.

More than once I heard him say with wry humor that he wanted to see how long a Hemingway could live since both his father and grandfather had taken their own lives. Jack's life ended on December 1, 2000, but not until the age of seventy-seven, due to complications from heart surgery. Perhaps Jack's life should not be measured in years, but in how he lived them.

The son of Ernest Hemingway lived an extraordinary life, in turn enriching the lives of everyone he knew and providing enjoyment to countless others who may not have had the pleasure of meeting him, but have thrilled to the feel of a trout tugging their line from the deep pools of Silver Creek.

Jack titled this book, *A Life Worth Living*, simply because he truly had a life worth living that he wanted to share with others so that they, too, might have a life worth living.

For me and those that knew him, his spirit lives on. Those that read this book and learn about Jack Hemingway's life will find Jack had a secret to making his life worth living. That secret lies within all of us. We just have to find it.

I love you, Jack. I'll always miss you. Thanks for the memories, and giving me a life worth living . . . and an enduring gift of love.

The Long and Various Life of Jack Hemingway

An Introduction by Geoffrey Norman

I t is a mixed blessing, at best, to be the son of a famous father. One believes this, almost intuitively, in spite of the fact that the president of the United States, as this volume goes to the printer, is the son of a former president. Still, George W. Bush no doubt endured the same pressures of high expectations, and the same sense that he might never measure up, that the sons of Winston Churchill and Franklin Roosevelt must have experienced. This comes with the territory, and the territory comes with the name . . . whether you want it or not. Jack Hemingway was never asked if he would like to live his life as the son of the most celebrated writer of the twentieth century. But it was one of the largest facts of his existence and what he had to do, in the current vernacular, was "deal with it."

This he did—ably and cheerfully, though it can't have been easy. It would have been impossible to follow in his father's professional footsteps, which Jack, wisely, never attempted; though it turns out he could write well enough when the spirit moved him. But thousands, if not millions, of would-be writers have been ruined by the example and the challenge Ernest Hemingway established with his unique and magical prose style. Bad enough to be named, say, Ruark and have it said that you write in a style that is third-rate Hemingway. Imagine if your name were Hemingway and you were accused of the same thing.

But it was not merely as a writer—and especially a prose stylist—that Ernest Hemingway set impossibly high standards. He also established a code of conduct, a masculine ethic, and while it is out of fashion now, it was once a pitiless standard by which men were judged and, more importantly judged themselves. President John F. Kennedy wanted to be thought of as someone who demonstrated the Hemingway virtue of "grace under pressure." Hemingway celebrated the courage, stoicism, and the dark humor of bullfighters and soldiers, and a lot of men could never measure up. Even, some might say, Ernest Hemingway himself. Could the standard have been applied any more mercilessly than to the son of the man who established it?

If you were Ernest Hemingway's son, everything from your knowledge of wine to your marksmanship—not to mention your physical courage and your success with women—would be judged not merely against your famous father's example but by a universal code that bore his name.

It is the kind of pressure that makes being the son of a president seem like no big deal.

But in a long and rich life, Jack Hemingway lived with these extraordinary pressures, as well as the normal burdens of celebrity, and did so with a kind of style and humor—a measure of grace—that one hopes his father had the wit to recognize and admire.

Of course, Jack Hemingway had a source of strength and consolation, something to which he could always repair. He was an angler, in the fullest sense of the word. And if fly fishing did not give his life "meaning," exactly, then it certainly gave it music.

Another angler could, of course, understand the importance of fly fishing in Jack Hemingway's life. But not entirely. How many anglers are blessed—if that is the word—with Gertrude Stein and Alice B. Toklas for godparents? How many have grown up with James Joyce, Ezra Pound, Gary Cooper, and Ingrid Bergman—among others—as family acquaintances? Under the malign influence of *People* magazine and the celebrity culture, the life of Jack Hemingway can be made to sound like bliss in a bowl. The Stork Club, the Ritz. Paris, Key West, Sun Valley. The world-famous father and the movie-star daughters. All of the glamour and celebrity that the multitudes are encouraged to lust after with such avidity.

But . . .

The famous father committed suicide and was plainly tormented for years before he put the shotgun in his mouth. And one of the three beautiful daughters also killed herself after Hollywood left her behind. These are unpleasant, messy details in the *People* universe, things to be skipped over in a two-sentence paragraph on the way to the next mention of Marlene Dietrich or some other celebrity in the Hemingway orbit.

But the flesh-and-blood Jack Hemingway—as opposed to the superficial, celebrity-media creation of the same name was acquainted, as we all are, with life's sorrows and he needed, as we all do, some consolations. Anyone who does not understand or appreciate the consolations of angling should read a short story called "Big Two-Hearted River," which is one of the finest things Jack Hemingway's father ever wrote.

While he never wrote anything that magisterial, himself, Jack Hemingway did write about angling with genuine feeling. He understood what Ernest Hemingway didn't have to say explicitly—namely, what Nick Adams was looking for in the burned-out country of Michigan's Upper Peninsula where he camped out and caught trout on grasshoppers. It was a lot more than fish. Like many other passionate anglers, Jack Hemingway visited the Big Two-Hearted River and came away disappointed until his father later informed him that the actual river of the story was the Fox, that he just took the name of the other river for his title as a matter of literary tactics.

Jack Hemingway's first book was called, with customary modesty, *Misadventures of a Fly Fisherman*. It was a guileless memoir in which he wrote about his father without the kind of rancor that would have bought him a few minutes of attention in the circles where literary gossip is a blood sport and you can score big points by tearing down your parents and blaming them for all your woes and shortcomings. But Jack Hemingway plainly loved his father and missed him. This became clear throughout his book and especially in an anecdote about the time when Jack Hemingway was struggling to find his way and having trouble making a living. He went to his father in despair that was, he confessed, approaching suicidal proportions. Ernest helped his son with money, reminded him that he had been a good soldier in the war, and advised him to pick a career and stick with it. Then Ernest Hemingway, whose own father had committed suicide, made his son join him in a pact. "Schatz, the one thing you must promise me you will never do, and I will promise you the same, is that neither one of us will ever shoot himself, like Grandfather. Promise me and then I'll promise you."

When the pact had been sealed, father and son proceeded to drink martinis, shoot buzzards, and watch *Casablanca* together.

This was six years before Ernest Hemingway shot himself.

Jack Hemingway had, indeed, been a good and brave soldier, as his father reminded him. And it was during his service with the Office of Special Services that he made the gesture that more or less summed up his character and his attitude toward life. Because he was raised in Paris, in the time that bred the Lost Generation, he spoke French. So he was sent on a mission into occupied France to make contact with the *Maquis*. When he parachuted into France, at night, Jack Hemingway was carrying a fly rod.

Angling, then, was always at the center of his life. He learned to fish when he was young, and he was never much for the big game fishing that his father found so seductive. For Jack Hemingway, it was all about fly rods and cold, freshwater rivers. And to judge by his writing, he must have fished all of the world's first-class rivers. And relished every minute of it.

Any man who would take his fly rod with him to war, would not let school, work, or family get in the way of fishing. And Jack Hemingway managed to fish Catskill streams when he was in school, the famous Yellowstone rivers when he was on summer vacations, and the great West Coast steelhead rivers when he was working for Merrill Lynch. And while he was undistinguished as both a student and a broker, he became an accomplished angler. In fact, to borrow a phrase, Jack Hemingway made himself into a "complete angler."

He fished well and with style, of course. At Jack Hemingway's funeral, Dan Callaghan remembered, in his eulogy, watching his old friend fish:

> Often, I just sat on the bank and watched you fish. I will always see, especially when I am fishing, the powerful arc in your fly rod, the way you would watch your backcast, the tight, close loop in your fly line and how it would unfold, and just how you would put your hand on your hip when your steelhead drift started. And I remember also the beautiful, rhythmical tempos of your cast when you were dry-fly fishing.

But his skill as an angler went far beyond mere technical competence. When you read Jack Hemingway's essays about fishing, you are struck by how seldom he writes about the big trophy or the big numbers. He catches fish, of course. But he is not so myopic or unimaginative that he believes that is the whole point.

The rivers, of course, are a big part of it and when he died, he was working on a collection of essays about some of the fine streams he had fished. Even a partial list of them is enough to get an angler's blood pumping: the Test, the Grand Cascapedia, the Laerdal, the North Umpqua. These are some of the rivers that he'd fished and gotten around to writing about, and those chapters are included here. Sadly, he had planned to write about Silver Creek and the Little Wood, in his backyard near Ketchum, Idaho, but hadn't gotten around to it. Also the Salmon and the Snake. The Moise. The Aa. The George. The Dean. And others. But he had fished these rivers so you don't grieve too much for the things he'd left undone.

Jack Hemingway's appreciation for the ineluctable properties of a wild river are matched, in his angling essays, by a feeling for his companions. He was, as they say, a "people person." Those who met him did not forget him. The friends he made, he tended to keep. There was no evidence in him of that strain of malice literary biographers have so thoroughly identified in his father. If you never fished with him, you will read his stories and think how much fun he would have been to fish with. Here's Dan Callaghan, again:

> One time, in June, in the Box Canyon on Henry's Fork of the Snake, the salmon flies were everywhere. I was waiting for you on the back of the tailgate. When I heard you whistling, coming up through the trees, I opened the Chilean wine we had. You sat down on the tailgate too, looked down, and said, "I think I will eat one of those salmon flies." You picked one up, and ate all 2½ inches of him. I can still hear the crunch. I handed you a glass of wine, you took a sip, looked at me dead seriously and said, "The wine is wrong."

There is a lot of wine—usually the right one—in Jack Hemingway's angling essays. Also a lot of good food. And he has a touch of his father's remarkable gift for making food and wine come alive on the page.

Finally, there was in Jack Hemingway a deep feeling for the manners, etiquette, and rituals of angling. This is predictable, perhaps, in one for whom angling is something considerably more than a pastime or even a "lifestyle." He felt about the decline of angling's standards the way a devout Catholic a quarter of a century ago would have felt about the loss of the Latin mass and the appearance of hugs in church. He hated anything that diminished what was so important to him, and he expressed his dismay in the most forceful language that ever appears in any of his essays. He is, in fact, harder on angling boors and braggarts than he is on the German soldiers who wounded him and took him prisoner back when he went to war packing his fly rod. They had an excuse, after all.

What makes its way into his writing less, perhaps, than it should is the way in which he gave something back to the calling that nourished him and provided him with such deep satisfactions. But, then, Jack Hemingway was a gentleman of the old school and a gentleman does not boast any more than he hogs a steelhead pool when other anglers are waiting to fish or breaks into the rotation on a salmon river. He was a dedicated and practicing conservationist who served as head of the Idaho Fish and Wildlife Commission and made it his mission to get hatchery trout out of the first-class rivers and the catch-and-release ethic written into the state game laws. He was successful on both counts. He was a longtime member of the Atlantic Salmon Federation, the Nature Conservancy, and the North Atlantic Salmon Fund and was willing to use his celebrity, which he did not otherwise treat with any great regard, to advance the cause.

"An ardent outdoorsman and respected salmon conservationist, Jack gave willingly and generously of himself to draw attention to the serious decline of the world's wild Atlantic salmon populations," Donal C. O'Brien Jr., chairman of the federation (and Audubon) said when he announced the creation of the Jack Hemingway Memorial Fund to help end salmon netting in the North Atlantic.

Jack Hemingway was an enthusiast who enjoyed life. That is what his many friends remember about him. He had the gift for laughter and for friendship, and angling was at the center of things for him. It was entirely in character for him to use the self-deprecating title *Misadventures of a Fly Fisherman* for his first book, but the working title for the unfinished volume he left behind more accurately sums up the man and his seventy-seven very full years. He was calling that book *A Life Worth Living,* and the finished chapters are included in this volume along with some selections from his first book to round out the self-portrait of a man whose love of angling no doubt helped him through a destiny that came with his name and which he did not choose but nevertheless navigated with uncommon grace.

—Dorset, Vermont
June 2001

ONE

Selections from

MISADVENTURES OF A FLY FISHERMAN

I

EARLY YEARS

1
An Angler from the Start

My first experience of fishing—which was to become a life-long passion—was strictly as a spectator sport. There was always fishing of some sort going on along the quai-sides and embankments of the Seine. Whenever I went there with Papa to visit the bookstalls, or with Tonton, my nurse's husband, a retired soldier who worked in the French civil service, we would stop and watch the fishermen of the Seine. They were, and still are, a breed that's unique. These men with weatherbeaten faces and shabby clothes, wielding long bamboo poles with goose-quill bobbers, seemed as rooted in the landscape as the ancient trees.

In the late twenties and early thirties, the great river was perhaps not so polluted as it is now, but it was by no means clean. It ran full of rich, organic sewage. Today, the sources of pollution are far more dangerous, being composed of insoluble inorganic chemical compounds. But the Seine fishermen are unchanging and eternal.

At any rate, the fishermen did seem to catch greater quantities of fish as well as more highly prized fish for the table then than now. The degree of sophistication in tackle has changed greatly, but essentially a Seine fisherman was and is a skillful and a very patient man who is never without hope no matter how unappealing the weather or the river conditions.

You need to watch longer now to see an angler on the Seine catch a fish than you did in those bygone times. Some in the old days were successful enough to be able to sell their catches of whitebait to the small specialty restaurants which deep-fried them for finger eating. They were a great treat and a great favorite of my father's and mine.

We sometimes took the paper-wrapped fries to a bench on the Henry IV Bridge. After our feast, we often tried our skill at spitting from the bridge into the funnels of the *bateaux-mouches* excursion boats that plied the current of the Seine from dawn till dusk every day of the year, except in times of serious flooding. A successful spit into a moving funnel was rare and resulted in the reward of a beer or an aperitif for Papa and a grenadine or an ice for me at one of the nearby cafes. Just watching the fishermen made me want to try to fish someday, but I never dreamed how soon it would become possible.

It was during a long weekend at the Mowrer villa in Crécyen-Brie that I could restrain myself no longer. Paul Mowrer, a fine newspaperman from Chicago, my mother and some friends had gone for a long walk as was their custom on a Sunday afternoon. I was left alone with fat Madame Fouk, the cook, and Kimi, the fat black cat. Kimi had often followed me down to the lower end of the garden before, where we would slip out of the gate in the high old stucco-covered stone wall to the river bank. The Grand-Morin, a placid little French river with deep weed beds and a nearby mill dam, provided Paul with an ideal spot to swim and to enjoy his beloved sport of canoeing. The canoe was kept upside down on the bank next to the path and against the wall, and locked to the post with a chain and padlock.

There was a small dock extending into the water. From its outer edge I could watch the different kinds of minnows swimming in the current and among the waving strands of water weed. On this particular day I had fashioned a hook from the proverbial bent pin with pliers and a small hammer. Using some of the strong black thread Paul used to perform his marionette tricks for a fishing line, I fastened the line and the hook to a three-foot piece of willow shoot. With some of Madame Fouk's bread—the part inside the crust—I rolled some tiny dough balls and impaled one on the barbless hook. I had a difficult time fastening the thread to the pin, but somehow I managed.

I had no bobber but the water was so clear I could see the minnows attacking my baited hook as it drifted in the current. I tried to imitate the style of the Seine fishermen I had seen. It worked. Not often, but often enough to excite and encourage me. I was able to time a strike *cum* heave and found a shiny minnow flipping and squirming on the dock beside me. Kimi took advantage of me and rounded out his already rotund shape even further with a feast of minnows, but I did manage to get some back to the kitchen in my pockets.

They were well received, and after Madame Fouk had taught me how to snip their bellies with a small pair of sewing scissors to remove the guts, they were eaten as a special treat that night along with the regular dinner—although I was later admonished for using my pockets for a creel. Thereafter, I was provided with a cloth flour sack and my fishing forays became a regular feature of our Crécy weekends. I didn't know it, but a radical change had taken place in my life. I had become a fisherman and would never ever be quite the same again.

In the years following my parents' divorce until my mother and Paul Mowrer were married, when we moved back to the States permanently, I had practically become a trans-Atlantic commuter. I spent the greater part of every summer with Papa and Pauline, and though they kept an apartment in Paris and used it periodically, their principal residence was in Key West, at the very tip of the Florida Keys.

Sometimes I traveled alone under the supervision of the ship's personnel, but usually I went with a friend or relative who would deliver me into Papa's safekeeping at the docks in New York.

The first of these expeditions to New York stands out especially because the memory was heightened by an unusual incident. After leaving the docks and the cab ride to Scribner's on Fifth Avenue, there was a pleasant visit with Max Perkins followed by a restaurant lunch where I listened with fascination to Papa and Perkins' men's talk.

Next to Papa's burly figure, Mr. Perkins seemed a reed of a man, with a schoolmasterish bearing and a total lack of egotism. I remember his calm, low voice—quite a contrast to Papa's—as they talked of books and writers, though what they said was beyond my understanding.

Afterward, I took a bus ride on the open top of a double-decker Fifth Avenue bus to within a couple blocks of the Perkins' brownstone where I was left for the rest of a very pleasant afternoon with Mrs. Perkins and had the run of the garden while the sun still shone, then took my customary nap.

That evening, Perkins accompanied us down to the train at Penn Station where we boarded the Pullman bound for Miami and the Florida Keys. At Trenton, a bit before Philadelphia, the conductor delivered a telegram to Papa. Papa explained to me that Grandfather Hemingway was dead and that he must go to the funeral and take care of things for the family. I had nothing to worry about since I would be left in the care of the Pullman porter, who would see that I got my meals and went to bed on time and would see me safely to Key West where Pauline would be waiting. I was, as yet, unacquainted with death, and these events didn't seem to me, an experienced world traveler of five, at all unusual. Papa did not tell me then that Grandfather had shot himself in the head with his old Civil War pistol.

After a few months in Key West, we all returned to France via Havana and Spain; but when summer came, off I went again to Key West: this time for what was to be the first of many car trips west with Papa. After traveling via Piggott, Arkansas, to visit Pauline's family, the Pfeiffers, where I was taken in with great kindness, love, and affection, we took the Model A Ford coupe, with its running boards and rumble seat, west through the center of the country into the Rocky Mountains and on to the L-T Ranch near Cooke City, Montana.

Lawrence Nordquist's L-T Ranch was situated on the south side of the valley of the Clark's Fork. Now it is reached by crossing a wooden bridge after coming off the Cooke City/Red Lodge Highway and then crossing a series of broad meadow pastures and fields of oats to the ranch house, with its cluster of log cabins scattered through the grove of lodgepole pine.

That first year we arrived via the "old" road, which crossed the stream by a ford in its shallow headwaters close to Cooke City and skirted myriad swamps, rock falls, and finally ended crossing the sagebrush flat beyond One Mile Creek near the ranch. The main building was typical Western guest ranch—very simple but clean and piney, with a big living room with lots of chairs, and books left by former guests. The lodge had a couch or two and a big dining room where overabundant but delicious meals were served. I was alone, that trip, with Papa and Pauline and had a little room of my own in their cabin. The Franklin stove was in their room, and my first job in the morning was to put some of the kerosene-soaked sawdust and a few small logs on the fire to get the cabin warmed up.

After breakfast at the main lodge, Papa and Pauline would get their fishing tackle ready and, after getting the horses saddled, they would take off with a pack lunch to some point on the river, usually several miles downstream. I was left pretty much to my own devices, and the ranch was well organized for kids.

On the days that Papa worked, Pauline would sometimes go on the trail rides. This was my cue to stay home. Not because I didn't want to be with Pauline, but because I knew that Papa would go fishing near the ranch by himself when he was through work. I knew he really wanted to be alone, but, on the other hand, I really wanted to learn about trout fishing. He knew I was just hanging around waiting to be asked to join him so he could teach me how to cast and all the other great mysteries. He didn't, so I tried sneaking up to the river where he would be wading in his chest-waders in the fast, clear, green-tinged water.

He spotted me right off and came over to the bank.

"You know, Schatz, trout spook awfully easily—"

"I'm sorry, Papa. I only wanted—"

"If you really want to watch, just stay back a little from the bank. You mustn't move around until I go further down. Then move very slowly and stay low."

"Yes, Papa!"

"That way the trout won't spook."

I tried to become a part of the shadows along the streamside.

I had to settle for this role for the rest of our stay that year, except for the last few days when I was rewarded with an opportunity to fish with Pauline's already set-up outfit with a single hook, which was an old, work fly that Papa trimmed the dressing off so I could impale a grasshopper and fish it in the swirling back eddies that Papa pretty much ignored while he was fishing his two- or three-fly wet-fly rig through the riffles.

My purported patience during the endless periods of being a watcher had been a sham. I had darn near died of impatience to have a real go at it myself, and the trout that Papa caught were so beautiful compared to my Grand Morin minnows that my desire to capture one became an obsession.

Nevertheless, I learned a lot about casting and about playing fish once they were hooked. Papa was a pretty straightforward wet-fly fisherman. He used Hardy tackle and his leaders were already made up with three flies. His favorites were a McGinty for the top, a *cock-y-bohdhu* for the middle, and a woodcock green and yellow for the tail fly. He sometimes fished with single-eyed flies and added a dropper. At the ranch, for these, he preferred Hardy's worm fly and the shrimp fly.

Ninety percent of the time, Papa was an across and downstream caster whose team of flies swam or skittered across the current so that a taking fish pretty much hooked himself. He played the fish gently and well and with the necessary calm that eliminates hurrying a fish too fast or playing it too long, which is just as great a sin.

He seldom failed to land his trout except for the rare double-header when one or both fish were often lost. He taught me how to clean them and insisted that the part along the backbone which looks like coagulated blood, which ought to be the aorta but is in reality the trout's kidney, be left if the fish weren't to be kept too long before eating. He said this improved the flavor.

He used a woven grass basket rather like a shopping bag from Hardy's for a creel and laid the trout in it on fresh leaves of grass or branches of fern. The creel was dampened in the river and the evaporation kept the fish cool. "Never waste fish, Schatz, it's criminal to kill anything you aren't going to eat," Papa told me. Then he impressed on me how important it was never to waste fish or game by not taking proper care of it.

The trout Papa caught were seldom cooked in the ranch house kitchen. He preferred to cook them himself, usually for breakfast, on top of the stove in the cabin in a frying pan with lots of butter and lemon and salt and pepper. He always added the lemon while the fish were frying, claiming this gave them a better taste.

My immediate problem, now that I was rod in hand with a six-foot leader and the hopper impaled on the fly hook, was that the grasshopper wouldn't sink, because of its natural buoyancy. I had no idea then about floating flies, nor did I know about lead split shot used for sinking a bait or a fly. With just the leader and hardly any line extending beyond the rod tip, I flipped the hopper out toward the center of the whirlpool, and then it was pulled under into the vortex and I immediately saw my line twitch, and I gave a powerful yank and, unlike the minnows which had flown out of the water in the same circumstances, I found myself with a bent rod tip and a very active, strong, living creature doing its best to get to the middle of the stream.

I tried to emulate what I had watched Papa do, and with luck on my side, I finally landed the most beautiful fish I had ever seen. It was a rainbow cutthroat hybrid about eleven inches long and looked enormous to me as I pounced on it on the sandy backwater shore.

It's hard to imagine what a miracle that first trout seemed to me. Everything about it was perfect, and after the long weeks of watching in frustration as my father fished, it truly seemed the ultimate reward. That trout was consumed in its entirety by me at the ranch house that night, amidst much ado. It was the first of many from that lovely river, although the next few days were filled with various frustrations, some of which were overcome.

I just continued to fish places exactly like the one where I had had my initial success. Experiments in different types of water were unsuccessful, but the seed had been well planted and it had grown into an overwhelming desire to fish for trout—a desire which remains just as strong to this day.

I sometimes wonder if I'd have retained my enthusiasm to such a degree, or at all, if my father had followed the usual path of providing me with all the necessaries and plying me with detailed instructions and supervision. I know he wanted me to love fishing and hunting, and I believe that he deliberately set about to make me really want to do it on my own initiative. Tennis parents and stage mothers should take note. The kid has got to want to do it, not just to please the parent, but for himself.

The winter following the first summer at the ranch was filled with dreams of trout streams . . .

Chicago

I had trouble with math at Latin School, and Papa came up with the solution of having me spend the balance of the first Chicago winter down in Key West, where his poet friend Evan Shipman would tutor me in math.

Evan was a kindly, thin, pale man, the seeming epitome of a poet. It was hard to equate his passionate love of trotting horses and the betting on them that made him such a good math tutor. Even less likely was his later role as a Loyalist machine gunner badly wounded on a Spanish battlefield.

I went for three hours every day to his room at the Colonial Hotel, and he taught me basic principles he'd acquired by being an odds-maker—principles which served me well most of the way through high school.

I also learned a lot more about fishing that winter. The years at Chicago Latin School went by swiftly with the usual summer formula of visiting Key West for a month, followed by the drive out West to the ranch, with the exception of two summers we spent in Bimini and the Bahamas, where I was exposed to a lot of saltwater fishing; which I hated because I became seasick every time we went out.

Nevertheless, I learned a lot about fishing the flats by going out with the local boys—all black except for the commissioner's son—and fishing for whatever came along. We'd dive for conchs and eat them raw with limes instead of taking a sandwich along. We'd see and stalk bonefish but had no tackle to catch them, but we did get one with a bait-casting outfit and a piece of shrimp while fishing for snappers.

The nights were the best. Papa would let me take one of the old, light saltwater rods and a medium-sized reel with a woven wire leader and a big 12/0 hook. We'd take a barracuda and cut him into big chunks for bait and chum. Then we'd fish right from the beach where everyone swam in the daytime. It sometimes took a little while, but usually not more than twenty minutes at the most before we'd feel a pull at the bait, and then it would be dropped and a little while later there would be another pick-up and, finally, one of the sharks would swallow the bait and head out for the blue of the Gulf Stream. That was real excitement!

Sometimes it took up to an hour to land one of the big ones, and we'd leave it there until the next morning when one of the locals would come around in his skiff and take whatever they wanted of the shark and then haul the rest out into the current to be eaten, presumably, by its brethren.

The boys also introduced me to sex. There was quite a bit of promiscuity among the young blacks, and quite often girls would come down with us for fishing and to build a fire, and maybe sneak some beer and try smoking if someone had cigarettes. I was crazy about the hotel keeper's daughter, who was a year older than I. Naturally, she would have nothing to do with me, so I gave in to the temptations on the beach with the sister of one of my black pals, who encouraged me to do so. All I can say about it was that I liked it immensely, and the experiment was repeated a number of times.

During these years, the gap in ages between my two younger brothers and me seemed a gigantic gulf and, while I was fond of them and we shared many interests in common, I always felt a separateness which was abetted by Ada Stearns, Gregory's nurse, who also served us all as surrogate mother and housekeeper much of the time. After she departed the scene much later on, I came to know both boys much more closely and to appreciate the qualities each had. Greg was the natural athlete with a flair for the handling of money which won him the nickname of "The Irish Jew" from Papa. Patrick was always viewed as the intellectual, and Papa sometimes joked of a time when the three of us would be put to work to support him in his old age. Patrick would write the books, Gig would handle the money, and I was to act in the subsequent screenplays.

Apparently, my lack of interest in the deep-sea trolling which so captivated my father was a disappointment to him, but I caught the largest amberjack of the year in Key West, and when I was ten I was the youngest ever to catch a marlin on rod and reel off Havana. I think that first summer of fishing in Cuba is what put me off. There was an epidemic of polio, and I had to stay on the boat the whole time in the harbor so as to avoid exposure. The harbor stank at night in the heat of the summer and with no breeze at our mooring. The greasy food and the long days out on the water, and my adolescent stomach which wasn't catching up to the quick growth of the rest of me, made for seasickness almost every day, and even my love of reading could not dispel it. In fact, whenever I tried to read for long, the motion sickened me even more. Not until I was full-grown did I stop being seasick, and now I can enjoy fishing from a boat on the ocean. Nonetheless, I think I shall always have a strong preference for the fishing of rivers and lakes by wading with both feet firmly planted on solid bottom.

I like the feeling of being fixed in one place and having the water move by me, pressing in against my legs, either wet against my skin or through the thick fabric of chest-high waders. It is only one but an important element in what makes fishing important to me.

2
From Boy
to Man

Lake Forest High was the first school I had attended with girls since kindergarten, and to say that I found it distracting would be a gross understatement. My grades took a tumble, and the following year, after a wonderful summer at Holm Lodge (also called the Crossed Sabers Ranch) on the Shoshone River, where my fishing improved remarkably, I was sent off to boarding school back East.

Storm King School was on a spur of Storm King Mountain in the Hudson Highlands just north of West Point. The Albee family, who had been artist friends of my mother's in Paris, had sent their sons there and the two youngest, Jack, who was my age, and his youngest brother, Ed, were students there when I arrived. The Albees had strongly recommended the school to Mother and Paul and I was delighted to know the boys would be there. I was even more pleased to find two natural new friends in the Sanchez brothers, Bernabe and Fernando, who were the nephews of Papa's old Cuban pals, Thorwald and Julio Sanchez.

It was an ideal school for an outdoor-loving boy. Set on the edge of the Black Rock Forest, which was a fourteen-mile square right in the middle of the best and the wildest of the highlands, the land was owned by a member of the Stillman family, who was also a trustee of the school, which gave us access to small lakes and ponds scattered throughout this paradise. Most of the ponds had small streams entering and leaving them, and each led to larger streams down in the populated valleys outside the forest. The ponds boasted eastern-chain pickerel, small-mouth bass, long-eared sunfish, and perch. A few of them held brook trout, and all the streams had brookies in the upper stretches and brown trout in the lower parts. Several had rainbows, which had recently been introduced. Needless to say, when I began to learn these secrets during my three years spent there, I spent more and more time exploring and fishing.

During the Storm King years, Papa came to New York on numerous occasions, and I had several opportunities to spend weekends with him. He started me taking boxing lessons from George Brown, and we often went to the fights together. Once he even arranged through *Esquire* magazine for me to fly from Chicago to New York to see the second Louis/Schmeling fight. I was with David Smart—Arnold Gingrich's co-publisher—in the best possible ringside seats and, since we arrived too late to see the prelims, I had the great treat of seeing the great Schmeling completely demolished by an unsmiling Louis in two minutes and eighteen seconds of the first round! That night, returning to the hotel through Harlem was a frightening experience, with blacks climbing all over the stranded cars and taxis in the snarled traffic. Had Schmeling won, it might have proved tragic.

On one occasion, after attending the Lee Savold/Billy Conn fight, a real stand-up boxing classic between two great light heavies, won by Conn on a close decision, we all went to the Stork Club where Sherman Billingsley led us to my father's favorite table, where we met Donald Friede who gave Papa a check for $100,000. It was the first color, imprinted check I had ever seen, and Papa, who was soon feeling very little pain, called Sherman over to the table and asked if he could cash the check. Of course, all banks were closed, but Sherman made every effort to cash the check, calling all over town to every connection he had, since it would be a real coup to be able to come up with $100,000 in cash at that time of night. The Stork Club was, as usual, full of gossip columnists who would have made a big thing of it; unfortunately, he was unable to do it. But I, for one, will never forget that check, which Papa called the "Technicolor check" and was from Paramount for the movie rights to *For Whom the Bell Tolls*. Nor will I forget that celebration at the Stork Club. By the way, my father's official biography has a vastly different account of this incident, which I can assure you is inaccurate.

It was during one of those weekends from school with Papa that I first met Martha Gellhorn. The occasion was the opening of the documentary movie, *The Spanish Earth*, which Papa had been responsible for producing and which he narrated. I was to meet him at the theater and came directly from the Weehawken Ferry terminal by cab to the theater, off Broadway, where the film was being shown to critics. When I alighted under the marquee, a gorgeous blonde lady rushed up to me and said, "You must be Bumby; I'm Marty."

Of course, I knew about her but had no idea what a beauty she was, and I did not know for sure that Papa was going to leave Pauline to first live with Marty, then marry her. After seeing her, I was overwhelmed by this marvelous creature who could say the "F" word so naturally that it didn't sound dirty and, otherwise, talk like a trooper or a high-born lady, whichever suited the circumstances.

I was her immediate captive and just accepted Papa's behavior as completely natural. After all, they had been together for many months on end in the Spanish Civil War, under combat conditions at times (I had wanted more than anything to go there with Papa but was too young).

The summer of 1939 was a key one for me. I was allowed by Paul and Mother to drive alone out to Wyoming to meet them at Holm Lodge. I enjoyed the long drive alone, and to give myself time for exploring, I drove straight through without sleep and spent time in Yellowstone

Park fishing places I had never had the chance to try before. It was the beginning of a long love affair with the area.

I was particularly entranced by the Madison drainage and spent most of my time right around the big Madison meadows below the junction of the Firehole and the Gibbon. I was starting to get a feel for dry-fly fishing, though I had very little savvy about insect types and recognition of species that might be hatching. The fish, while relatively sophisticated in comparison with the Shoshone River trout, were reasonably catchable, and I managed to land a fair number, though few over a pound.

At that time, my largest trout had been a four-pound rainbow caught on a worm in the Muskegon River, on a float trip in Michigan from Hardy Dam to Newaygo. I had caught no outsized fish on the fly as yet and considered anything above twelve inches very special and was delighted with a one-pound trout.

To add to the information I had gleaned about Yellowstone from chapters on the area in Bergman's *Trout*, I bought a small book at the park by Howard Back called *Waters of Yellowstone*. It was very well written and detailed, with stories of trout much bigger than those I had managed to connect with to date. One of the places it mentioned that intrigued me was Grebe Lake.

To get to the lake, you had to go to the end of a fire trail by car then hike in about two miles. There was a large population of grayling, a lovely troutlike species with a beautifully spotted dorsal fin that smells like wild thyme when first taken from the water. The clincher for me was that around the lily pads at the opposite side of the round lake from where the trail approached, there were supposed to be some very large cutthroat rainbow hybrid trout which could be enticed with flies on rare occasions.

That first time on Grebe Lake I worked my way around the right side of the lake, first crossing the little inlet stream that had the vestiges of an old fish trap where the Park Service presumably took eggs from grayling to distribute in other waters. Nice grayling were to be caught on wet flies and nymphs all the way around the lake, but when I arrived at the sandy point where a second small feeder entered the lake, just a little way from the outlet bay where the lily pads grew in profusion, I started to connect with more trout than grayling, and I started catching some very fine rainbows up to about two pounds.

In my lexicon of fish at that time, these were pretty spectacular fish, and they fought magnificently, and I was lucky to be able to land any of them on the light gut leaders I was using in those days. They were willing takers, but my skills were limited and I lost most of them.

As I worked my way around the point and almost reached the edge of the lily pads, I saw a cruising fish that had me shaking with the awesome size of him. To my untrained eye, he looked three feet long. In retrospect, he was probably a little over twenty inches and would have weighed close to four pounds if he were in equal condition to the fish I'd taken so far. I crouched low and waited until he was headed across and away from me before getting out a good cast well in front of his nose. The fly settled slowly in the water, and I waited until the fish was within five or six feet of it and started a slow hand twist retrieve. That lumbering trout turned slightly and came right for the fly. I saw its mouth open and show white, and I set the hook.

The fish panicked and came right out of the water, looking even bigger in the air, and fell back with an enormous splash, heading directly for the lily pads and was off within two seconds, escaping with my fly. He jumped again, twice, and I saw the fly. He looked so big I damned near cried. That was not the last time for me at Grebe Lake, it goes without saying.

Later in the summer when Paul and Mother were at the lodge, we all took a fine pack trip together with Diana Jane Mowrer, Paul's niece. We went over the range bounding the south side of the upper Shoshone Valley, following Fishhawk Creek and crossing into Timber Creek, which we followed down to the upper edge of Yellowstone Lake, far from any roads. From there, we followed the shoreline south to the inlet of the upper Yellowstone River and up its valley to a beautiful lake just a stone's throw from the river called Bridger, after the famous early scout and explorer, Jim Bridger.

We made our second night's camp there and enjoyed some of the finest and, I must say, easiest fishing for trout I had ever encountered.

You could see them cruising around easily, and no matter what fly you put anywhere near them, they would take without hesitation.

Compared to rainbows, the fight was disappointing, though it still felt good to have such hefty fish on the end of your outfit. Some of these fish would go 2½ pounds, but most of them were about 1¾, and almost none were smaller than 1½. They were fat and healthy, and marvelous eating.

Diana Jane was only a year, possibly two, older than I, but she was easily ten times as smart. She was not only better read than I, but she was erudite in German, French, and Italian. She was also very competitive, and it was the first time I allowed fishing to become competitive, as I felt I had to be better at something to protect my masculine ego. But that was a mistake. She took to the fishing very well and quickly, indeed, and it was always a pretty close thing, though the old ego managed to survive somehow. Fortunately she decided the constant pursuit of fish with a fly rod was not to be the main interest in her life, and we went on to become good, close friends for many years.

I was scheduled to go to the L-T Ranch to spend the last days of the summer with Papa and my younger brothers. Pauline had gone to Europe with a friend. From the L-T, I would be put on the train to return to school.

Before I left, I wanted to show Mother and Paul Grebe Lake. Neither had ever caught grayling, and they both loved to hike. We stopped for a quick go at Yellowstone Lake on the way, but mother got a fly hook caught in her eyelid when a sudden gust of wind caught her line. Paul saved the day by slicing the hook out and Mother never flinched, so great was her trust in him. We continued the hike to Grebe Lake and both of them caught grayling and a few rainbows, then we headed back along the trail toward the car while I went through my usual routine of "just one more cast," which would sometimes last a half-hour or more, though I was confident I would be able to catch up with them.

When I did, I was delighted by the sight of Papa, Paul, and Mother sitting on the edge of the trail talking animatedly. Papa had phoned the lodge and was told where we would be. He parked at the end of the fire trail, where we had left the car, and headed in after listening to the news on the radio. It was September 1, and the news was about the invasion of Poland by Germany and the consequent, imminent declarations of war by Britain and France.

By the time I arrived, they had finished their discussions of my progress in school and any plans relating to me, and were deeply involved in discussing the probable events and calamities which would most likely follow in the wake of the day's events.

Both my father and Paul felt that there would be a long period of war and that we Americans would inevitably be drawn into it, despite the strength of the isolationists in both houses of Congress. It was wonderful for me to see my mother, my father, and Paul all together talking like that. They had maintained a regular correspondence, of course, because of the details of managing my education and travels back and forth, but this was the first time since the Paris days that they had been together, and, as it turned out, it was the last time ever.

Paul and Mother took their leave at the car to drive back to Holm Lodge to pack for their return to Chicago. Papa and I drove around the north end of the park and out the northeast entrance through Cooke City to the ranch. Papa was pleased to see how well my mother looked and how happy she obviously was with Paul. Though I never saw it in that light, it may have helped relieve his conscience.

On the way, we stopped to talk to two bears, one a cinnamon and the other black with a white blaze on its chest. Papa liked talking to bears, and it did appear that they reacted to the tone of his voice, either appearing cheerful and alert when he spoke kindly to them— "Hey Bear, you're looking awful damn fat. Must've had a good summer, eh?"—or seeming to cower and look aside in embarrassment when he chided them—"Bear, you dumb son of a bitch, aren't you ashamed of yourself begging when other bears are out making an honest living, working? Bear, you're just no damn good." I tried it, but my voice was ignored by the bears, who seemed to know which of us in the car was the figure of authority and, possibly, a fellow bear.

When we got to the ranch, there was word that Pauline would be arriving shortly, and I saw her for a bit before I had to leave for school.

She had a bad cold, so the boys and I spent our time shooting ground squirrels, fishing, and riding to nearby lakes and streams. After I left that year, Papa didn't stay for his usual fall hunt. Pauline took the boys back to Key West, and shortly thereafter Papa left to rendezvous with Marty and head over to Idaho and their first look at Sun Valley.

I guess this was the definitive rift with Pauline, for after the fall in Idaho, Papa and she were definitely separated, and she was living in her apartment in New York while he went to Key West and moved out to the new home he and Marty had bought near Havana, on a hill overlooking the city and the sea. Marty had gone directly from Sun Valley on an assignment for *Collier's* magazine to cover the Russo-Finnish War. When she returned, there remained only the divorce proceedings to keep her and Papa from marrying right away.

That summer I received a tantalizing letter from Papa along with several glossy eight-by-ten photos which whetted my appetite for a visit to Idaho and, particularly, Sun Valley. The letter described their fine reception there, the great bird shooting, and Papa told about floating down Silver Creek in a canoe. "You'll love it here, Schatz . . . There's a stream called Silver Creek where we shoot ducks from canoe . . . Saw more big trout rising than have ever seen . . . Just like English chalk streams . . . We'll fish it together next year . . .," he wrote. "If money OK we'll spend the whole fall." He sent some photos including some of parties at Trail Creek. I was already hooked by the mention of English chalk streams. These were the ultimate in crystal clear meandering spring-fed rivers flowing through the chalk downs of Hampshire, where dry fly fishing had got its start.

The photos included one of him with several beautiful, fat rainbows he'd caught in the lower cottonwoods stretch of the Big Wood River, where he wrote, "The part fished was hundred feet wide, and shallow, and only hundred yards downstream flowed into narrow lava gorge three feet wide and hundred feet deep!"

The spot still exists, by the way, but the gorge has mostly filled in with gravel, and that stretch of the river runs dry during most of the irrigation season. In agricultural Idaho, crops take precedence over nature, which remains in the local ethic as something to be conquered and used and not to be "wasted" by "preservation."

Another photo found a prominent place on my dresser at school, as it featured a bar top in Slavey's Saloon in Ketchum, Idaho. Behind the bar was a comely lass, the bartendress, and lying in state in front of her was a gigantic trout, which the caption said weighed eighteen and a half pounds. To one side of the fish stood the angler, whom I later came to know well. He was Austin Lightfoot, a well-known guide who could, and would, use any means, not necessarily the most sporting, to catch his prey. Austin was, however, highly respected and, along with Taylor Williams, Sun Valley's head guide, had as wide-ranging and diversified a knowledge of the hunting and fishing within reach of Sun Valley as anyone I have ever known. The comely lass, alas, I never got to know. However, she was a true indicator of the great possibilities inherent in the beautiful women of Idaho. In a sense, I was looking at my distant future.

II

BEFORE THE WAR

3
Sun
Valley

Sun Valley was like paradise found. Papa's letter of the previous fall had in no way exaggerated. Papa and Marty stayed in a suite at the lodge while my brothers and I had adjoining rooms sharing a bathroom at the inn. We could charge by using our room number anywhere within the confines of Sun Valley proper. This new temptation was the ruin of my youngest brother, Gregory. He went completely berserk and charged unbelievable quantities of any and everything from the drugstore, restaurants, bowling alleys, stables, ice-skating rink, the photo shop, tackle shop, and the trap and skeet ranges. The figure on the room bill would have been enough with our legitimate charges, but the number with Greg's signature was nothing short of astronomical, and Papa was furious. Thanks to Sun Valley's publicity department, run by Steve Hannagan, which had invited Papa and Marty the year before, the rooms were complimentary, but they didn't pick up the tab for extraneous expenses. By the time the smoke cleared, needless to say, Gigi had gained a whole new respect for the idea of credit.

Comping our rooms was not a bad deal at all for Sun Valley since it was no secret that Papa was just finishing work on the galleys for *For Whom the Bell Tolls*, and that there would be a lot of publicity forthcoming and, with any luck, Sun Valley would be prominently mentioned. Later that fall it was, of course.

I had gone back to school and Bob Capa, Papa's *Life* photographer friend from the Spanish Civil War, was assigned to do a feature story on "Hemingway in Sun Valley" with some great shots of Papa with Gary Cooper and my kid brothers hunting as well as partying at the lodge and at Trail Creek Cabin. . . .

Quite apart from the glamorous side of Sun Valley itself, for me the exploration of the fishing possibilities was the primary consideration. I would not be able to stay long enough to take part in that fall's hunting, but there were about two weeks in which to check the Big Wood River and Silver Creek. Both had received some publicity in *Field & Stream* in an article by Ray and Dan Holland concerning the making of a film on dry-fly fishing called *Silver Rainbows*. Both rivers were apparently every bit as difficult and demanding as the greatest English chalk streams on the Hampshire Downs.

Clayton Stuart took me down to Silver Creek for my first try at it. We drove the thirty-odd miles with me peppering Stu, who was in his early twenties, very little older than I, with every question imaginable about the potential size of the fish, which flies to use, leader length, and tippet size. He was in his first year as a guide for Taylor Williams, and he had the natural fine manners of a real Westerner, which was ideal for dealing with anxious city sportsmen who really needed to be put at their ease so as to avoid becoming competitive in their fishing, so they could settle down, relax, and enjoy the pure magnificence of it.

What puzzled me was that the entire trout population of Silver Creek was composed of rainbows. There were no brown trout, and yet I had read time and again that the truly difficult fish are browns, and that rainbows are relatively easy to deceive. I was to learn over the years just how difficult big rainbow trout can be, especially in the right circumstances. These were the circumstances on Silver Creek.

Located in a broad, pastoral valley with little incline, but surrounded by high, humpbacked, sagebrush-covered hills on both north and south, with the north hills backed by great mountain ranges, Silver Creek is formed by the confluence of a number of small tributary spring feeders into three prime tributary creeks, all of which join together on a property which belonged to the Union Pacific Railroad—owners, at the time, of Sun Valley. It was called the Sun Valley Ranch and was composed of about 780 acres.

In those days, the tributaries were all closed to fishing, and there was no farming of any importance in the whole valley. The valley was devoted almost entirely to grazing, and even that was relatively light. There was no agricultural activity on the ranch at all. As a consequence, the creek was almost crystal clear at all times. There was a luxuriant growth of a wide diversity of aquatic plants, all of which made for ideal conditions for a great profusion of aquatic insects, scuds, shrimp, and snails. Such, then, was Silver Creek when Stu took me down that first time.

We crossed the sagebrush flat in our waders toward the inside bank of an acute horseshoe bend. At the top of the downstream leg of the horseshoe, a wooden stake was impaled in the creek bed, and it had trapped a line of weeds which streamed for ten feet below it. Stu cautioned me to stay low, and then we sat on the bank with our legs in the water about thirty feet below the post and waited for the hatch, which he said was due to start at any time now.

It was a perfect day with a few scattered high clouds, and soon I saw the first rise. It was slow and deliberate, showing the head and then the dorsal fin of the fish as the pale-colored mayfly disappeared in the swirl. Stu suggested I put on a #16 ginger quill, one of the patterns we had stocked up on at Lane's shop at the valley. I had on a 4X gut leader of nine feet.

Repeated casts—which seemed perfect to me—to that fish and to others which started rising regularly in two lines along either side of the weed line and ahead of the post, produced absolutely nothing, though I did manage to avoid putting them off their feeding by frightening them. We tried other patterns to no avail until, finally, a very small rainbow of about seven inches engulfed a Woodruff and was promptly released because it was too small. When we left, after two hours of frustration, I was thoroughly humbled, and Stu kindly assured me that it was that way quite a lot of the time, and that there were times when the fish seemed to be easier and would take more freely. I was certain there was a solution to the problem, but I sure as hell didn't know enough to solve it yet. As we drove back, I was determined to figure it out and learn to succeed regularly when the fish were so obviously feeding.

I returned to Silver Creek alone several times but only improved my success very modestly, using the small, more delicate patterns I had had some success with in Yellowstone. I suspected there was something going on that I simply didn't understand, and it wasn't until many years later that I would gain a real understanding of the great variety of things going on under my very eyes that, at that moment, I hadn't the knowledge, capacity, or understanding to recognize and differentiate.

I had my best success when there was really no particular hatch taking place, and the only fish of any respectable size I caught were those waiting for targets of opportunity, such as insects blown into the stream from the banks. Such fish were not so particular so long as I didn't scare them by a careless approach or a sloppy cast.

Big Wood River was altogether another matter. I had no trouble catching decent fish in the stretches of the river close to Ketchum and Hailey. After Silver Creek, it was duck soup. When they were feeding, the fish rose freely to my flies, and when there was no surface activity, I simply fished wet flies and continued to catch the occasional fish.

But what I really wanted a go at was the place where that monster in the picture with the comely bartendress was caught. Austin Lightfoot wasn't around because he was guiding some fishermen up by Sunbeam Dam on the Salmon River, so Taylor Williams arranged for one of the finest big fish fishermen in South Idaho at the time, Art Wood, to take me down to the Big Wood, down below Magic Dam in a narrow basalt canyon only three miles long, before the diversion dam siphoned off a considerable portion for a big irrigation canal.

Art was a big man in every sense. He looked to be about six-foot-four and he had the meat on his bones to go with it. It was said he could wade any river in the state. At sixteen, I was already five-eleven and heavy-boned and long in the legs, so I was a pretty good wader, or thought so until that day.

After an hour's drive across the desert country to the south, we arrived at the edge of the canyon above the very pool where Austin had caught the monster the year before. It was called the Wagon Wheel Hole, and we put on our waders and set out rods with line and leader but without putting them together so we could go through the maze of wild rose thickets and willows along the sides of the canyon.

We climbed carefully down a short stretch of black basalt cliff, being exceedingly careful about where we stepped or put our hands since two shed rattlesnake skins on the rocks were proof enough that we were in snake country. The rest of the way down was over a steep slope of fallen, black boulders to the bottom, where we tried to stay along a scarcely visible path through the heavy brush until we had progressed, sweating through the oppressive heat of the bake-oven canyon, about two hundred yards upstream.

We broke out into the open on a small sandy shelf above a heavy current that looked about a foot deep but proved to be more like two and a half feet deep when we were standing in it. We put the rods together, and I had an ungreased silk line on with a nine-foot leader to 0X, and I put on one of the big, heavily dressed wet renegades that Art handed me.

He rigged up a six-foot leader and an Andy Reeker flasher spoon with a 2/0 siwash single hook. He didn't bother to fish at first but spent his time showing me where to wade and which currents the fish were likely to be lying in. It wasn't fast and furious fishing, but every few yards as we worked our way along an unseen path down the middle of the river—a path which Art seemed to have perfectly mapped—there would be a jolting strike usually just as the big wet fly started to come off its natural downstream drift and headed cross-current toward a point directly below me.

The fish were fat and active and very strong in the heavy current, and most were twelve to fourteen inches, with one or two up to sixteen inches. Their condition factor was excellent, and they were deep and heavy with the small heads of young fish that have grown disproportionately fast. The bottom was of coarse gravel, all covered with a dark, brownish-green moss, like algae, which was an indicator of the tremendous food-producing capacity of the water. There were parts where Art literally had to hold me down to keep the current from sweeping me away, and my felt-soled waders were no great advantage. Art was wearing old, hobnailed brogues which seemed to cut through the algae to the rock and hold better, which was another lesson for me.

The fishing tapered off as we came to the middle, deepest part of the pool, and we wended our way back toward the shore behind us. At this point, Art started fishing his Reeker, just letting it out on a medium long line and letting it work its wobbly action in the deep cut that was gaining strength toward the tailout of the pool on our side. He directed me out onto the shallowing wide apron of the tail-out and told me to fish it all carefully and work my way all the way down through the shallow riffle leading into the top of the Wagon Wheel.

Art hooked several nice fish which were all bigger than mine, and he lost a fine fish of over three pounds, which threw the Reeker as it cartwheeled in the air. The sun was below the canyon rim, and while my fly was traveling through what appeared to be the shallowest part of the riffle, there was a huge boil behind my fly, and then a torpedo line toward it and I was suddenly hooked up to the biggest trout of my lifetime. It jumped clear of the water before tearing the hook free as it surged toward the shelter of the deep pool below.

Art yelled, "That was a real 'ne, Jack. Mebbe six pounds. If you hook another like him, let him get on the reel so's he can run. You can't hold a fish like that!"

"I guess not," I returned, sadly, though I don't think he heard me above the rush of water around our legs.

I finished out the riffle and the head of the pool where the tongue of heavy current dipped over the lip into the deep water, but no further action was forthcoming. Art came over to where I'd ended up and practically hauled me up through the riffle and through the heavy cut where he'd hooked his fish, and we clambered out and carefully climbed out of the canyon to the car. Going home that evening, Art, who wasn't known for gushing off at the mouth, finally said:

"Jack, you cast like hell, and if you keep fishing that stretch of water you're gonna end up with one hell of a fish someday." A gracious compliment.

"Art," I answered, "if I could wade that water like you, I'd be down there every day 'til I have to leave."

"Son, you just keep eatin' heavy and don't worry. You'll make 'er one of these days."

It was hard to leave Sun Valley to return to Chicago for a few days before my return to Storm King. Papa had been in good form, and we'd had great times with Rocky and Gary Cooper, Howard and Slim Hawks, and our new local friends. I got to know Howard and Slim from sessions at the skeet range. He was a skillful and enthusiastic shotgunner, then on the top of his directing career. Both he and Slim were fit sporting types on the lean side. Slim was a great beauty, though despite my liking her open manner she didn't have the sort of beauty which at that time appealed to me. They were the sort of looks which endure, however, and to this day she is a knockout. We shot together later again for doves in Cuba, and I was somewhat surprised when Slim later went on to become Mrs. Leland Hayward.

Rocky Cooper liked shotgun shooting as well and was a friendly, easy person to get to know despite her tough veneer. It was a long time before I felt comfortable around Coop; my own fault I suppose. I was simply too shy around his fame. I didn't yet know how shy he himself was.

What was especially difficult, though, was having to leave Sun Valley while Pat and Greg, known then as Mouse and Gigi, got to stay on through the hunting season. Still, since then I've more than made up for it.

4
A Michigan Sojourn

Graduation was full of excitement. Paul and Mother drove all the way from Chicago in their new Pontiac and planned to take the train back from New York City, leaving me to drive the car back to Chicago along with a couple of friends, Bernabe Sanchez and Hilary Maher—Hilary was the younger brother of my old pal, Boolie, who was graduating from Milton Academy.

It was to be our first drive across the eastern states into the Midwest, and when we got to Lake Bluff we had about a week to kill before two other friends, Al Millet and the elder Maher, would be ready to leave. Mrs. Maher, who had been divorced from her architect husband a couple of years, had a good friend who owned the Hines Lumber Company with a big mill out in Oregon, just outside Burns in just about the geographic center of the state. She was able to arrange for Boolie, Al, and me to get jobs in the mill starting the latter part of July as "lumber students." This was a sort of industry training program which allowed us to work in the mill without having to be union members, as it was supposed to be the preliminary stage of an executive training program.

31

We decided to drive my old '37 Pontiac sedan, which had re-placed the '35 coupe, up to the Upper Peninsula of Michigan.

On June 15, Al Millet, Bernabe Sanchez, and I took off from Chicago headed north with the objective a new one for all of us—the Big Two-Hearted River in the Upper Peninsula of Michigan. Al had been clos-est to it since he had spent many summers with his family at the Huron Mountain Club. He assured us it would not be good because it held only a spring run of lake-dwelling rainbows, but I insisted that it must have fish in the swampy section my father had described in his short story, "Big Two-Hearted River," that we had all read in school.

We passed a lot of likely looking water on the way north but re-mained firm in our objective. The road across the Upper Peninsula was not promising and the country looked less trouty by the mile. It was alternately rolling, flat, dusty, and sparsely wooded, and I was starting to lose faith in my conviction. On the way to Newberry, we did cross one fine looking stream, the Fox.

When we finally arrived at our destination, it was hard not to give in to abject disappointment. The place where we hit the river, which was really a pretty small stream on that hot June day, was dis-enchanting, to say the least. We were prepared for the tea-colored water, but the pure sand bottom, the marginally warm temperature, and the featureless straight-away from the edge of the sand dunes where the stream made its long shot parallel to the shore before fi-nally emptying into Superior, were not calculated to raise our hopes of catching trout.

Where it wound in sharp bends through the dunes, things ap-peared to be somewhat better. There was at least some kind of cover in the form of snags, stunted trees of varied kinds, and most of all there were blueberries. We set up camp—just our sleeping bags, a tarp and cooking gear—and then put up our rods. We took the car and followed a track which looked well worn and then left it to be closer to the stream. That was our fatal error, though we weren't to find out about it until the next day.

We fished different stretches of the river. I headed up, skipping a long stretch, to try to find the swamp. I found an approximation of a swamp where, to no avail, I fished blind to every indication of possible cover or depression in the sandy bottom. I never saw a single rise form nor any sudden movement across the light covered bottom and, hoping for better things with the cooling advent of the evening, I gave in to the berries. The picking, hoarding, and eating of blueberries can be a fascinating pastime when nothing else is going on. I loaded up and then fished my way down toward our camp, where I arrived at dusk with not even a pull on the wet flies I had used. I found my friends in the same straits. Not a sign of a fish seen or felt by either of them. We decided after a heated canned dinner that we would get the hell out of there first thing in the morning and find us a real trout stream.

The next morning reality struck with a vengeance in the form of our inability to get the car through the seemingly short hundred or so feet back to the track without sinking up to the hubs in sand. We had no shovel and didn't want to sacrifice our new sleeping bags as mats as we had saved all winter for them. Hell, we were just plain stuck. I was elected to walk out and somehow get to the nearest town for help. Help was much closer than I expected in the form of a berry-picking camp about two miles along the track. I asked the man in charge if he could help us, and he replied that he could and it would cost us ten dollars. I knew we barely had that among us and it would have to go for gas to get us home. I told him we were close to broke, and he said we could work for it by picking berries. If we stayed at it all day, we could make it in two days. He said if we were regular pickers, we could do it a lot faster; but since we were new, it would take two days for sure.

I got the boys and we went to work. Ever since then I've sympathized with the Chicanos who bend over all day picking fruit and vegetables. Man, it's a killer, especially if you have been stuffing yourself with berries and have to hit the bushes every two hours.

Well, we finally made the two days, and the boss got his rig into where our car was and got us out. We decided we were short on time and low on money and headed back to Chicago. But I still love blue-berries and I still love trout fishing. I have not, however, set foot in Upper Michigan since.

Years later I told my father about the trip, and he said the Big Two-Hearted never was much of a year-round trout stream after the logging and the fires. He had loved the name but fished another place. I could have used the information a lot sooner.

5
Yellowstone Country

The trip to the Upper Peninsula taught us, at least, that we could all four fit into the old Pontiac with all our gear, after eliminating a few unnecessary items. It had been a proper shake-down cruise, even if a little hard on our morale, but we were, if anything, resilient and looking forward to our great adventure in the West.

I was the only one who had been before; Bernabe had never even set foot west of the Hudson. Phil and I had taken a week's bicycle trip up in Wisconsin once when we were thirteen. At the beginning of the trip, we had been on the best of terms, but by the end of it, when we were staying at a fishing lodge on Ghost Lake and got cabin fever from too much of each other's company, we were hardly speaking. In the meantime, we'd gotten over those difficulties and become fast friends again.

Phil knew Al Millet better than I did, but Al's mother was a close friend of my mother's and of Paul's, and I could vouch for his deep enthusiasm for fly fishing. Phil had fished with him at the Huron Mountain Club, and they both knew what they were doing. Bernabe loved fishing and, after I had introduced him to fly fishing in the Black Rock Forest, he experimented with it, fishing for bass on his family's cattle ranch in Camagüey province in Cuba He had read all the fishing books that I had with me at school and was dying to have a really serious go at trout. You might say we were, all of us, trout crazy and that fly fishing for these fish was the real enthusiasm of our young lives—taking precedence even over chasing young ladies.

We had each been given enough money by our parents to handle our bare necessities, and no one had more than anyone else. We'd planned the trip very carefully, and there wasn't much room for extras. We could have telegraphed for money in case of emergency, but I think our pride would have prevented our doing so except under the gravest of circumstances. We pooled our resources and ate the same, or at least the same-priced, food when we were on the road and, of course, when we were cooking in camp. On the road, there wasn't much of a problem since we all had hamburgers, french fries, and milk shake appetites. After the routine of school food, these were true luxuries, and we seldom tired of them. Also, it was our common opinion that the quality of these American basics varied greatly, and, moreover, they improved the further west we traveled. This was apparently true up to a point, but more about that later.

We all took turns driving and, since there was room enough to sit three-abreast in the front seat, one of us could always be napping on the back seat. We were so impatient to reach the Yellowstone country that we just kept driving right through, stopping only for meals and to relieve ourselves and freshen up at gas stations. It was a wonder the old Pontiac put up with such a grueling ordeal. It never did get a rest until we'd reached the east entrance of Yellowstone Park. We avoided the temptation of stopping in the beautiful Bighorns of east central Wyoming even though Ten Sleep Creek, coming down the west slope of the range, looked fishable, though still a little bit high from a late runoff. We were all of one mind: get to Yellowstone.

The weather being good, we camped in our sleeping bags one night outside the park entrance, at Pahaska, and the next morning proceeded into the park. We couldn't resist Sylvan Lake, the first one we came to, which was small and which I had tried once before with some success. It was surrounded by trees right to the bank, so it was necessary to wade out into dead trees that had fallen into the quickly deepening water to be able to cast properly. All of us managed to get into at least one or two of the many small cutthroat trout in the lake by fishing ungreased silk lines and letting our nymphs sink slowly to the bottom before starting a slow hand twist retrieve. The boys were delighted, but I hurried them away from there since I felt that we wanted to get to some of the areas where we would have a chance of bigger and more difficult fish.

We had decided to use the Madison Junction campground as base headquarters for our extended stay in the park, but, first I wanted them to have a look at the park as a whole so they'd have a better idea of the topography and the possible choices. All of us had read Howard Back's *Waters of Yellowstone* and Ray Bergman's *Trout*, so even the first-timers had preconceived ideas about where they wanted to concentrate their activities.

Actually seeing what you've read about in a book or magazine article can be quite a shock, since we tend to construct our own image of what we expect to see from the author's words. I thought both Howard Back and Ray Bergman had done splendid jobs of describing the places they fished and particularly enjoyed, but I was a poor judge, since I had already seen most of the places they described before reading their work. My friends had built images from the writing without having seen any of it, and I was anxious to see if they would be surprised, disappointed, or pleased by the actuality.

After leaving the little lake, we descended toward Yellowstone Lake and followed its shore north and west to Lake Junction where we started north on the upper loop of the figure-eight road which delimits travel within the park.

It's always a pleasure to take an appreciative audience through a magnificent piece of country such as Yellowstone. We made the whole inner circuit that first day and there was enthusiasm about everything from the geyser basins to the magnificent Yellowstone River, its Grand Canyon and its Great Falls, and farther down river, Tower Falls. We had no cameras with us, but some of these sights remain indelibly in the memory and require no camera to bring them back.

We made the high ridge to Norris Junction and then down the Gibbon drainage to Madison Junction where we established our semipermanent campsite. Even though Madison Junction campground was relatively uncrowded in those days, it was, nonetheless, crowded from our point of view. With our primitive arrangements, and just a tarp instead of a tent, it was unpleasant having people's dogs, which were supposed to be muzzled and leashed in the park at all times, come around sniffing us in our sleeping bags, or, as sometimes happened, chasing a bear through the camp when the bear was only doing its regular rounds of the garbage cans.

A lot of people stayed in that campground most of the summer, and they had fancy tents or trailers, which were just starting to come into vogue. They were mostly retirees, and they would go into West Yellowstone to buy supplies periodically, and most of them didn't even fish but just lazed around and gossiped among one another. They were friendly to us and gave us helpful hints about where to stop and what foodstuffs would last without going bad too fast. It was dangerous to keep food even in your car, let alone in the camp, because of the bears who could, and sometimes actually did, open up a locked car if the aromas emanating from it were sufficiently tantalizing. They could open it with a swipe of their paws just like a can opener and it was awesome to see a car they'd broken into. It gave you, so to speak, food for thought.

We found that West Yellowstone had the best tackle stores and, at that time, both Pat Barnes and Don Martinez had the fly business all sewed up between them. We were inclined to overspend our budgets when we went into their shops. The problem was that they had really well-tied flies which were successful patterns in the area and, though we brought tying equipment with us, our materials were limited in scope.

I had learned tying from the son of the British consul in Chicago, Peter Bernays, and then, through a connection of Paul's on the Chicago *Daily News*, I had the opportunity to spend a couple of days at Paul Stroud's operation in Arlington Heights, just outside Chicago, where he had a bevy of ladies tying for him. He was a good commercial tyer and took the trouble to teach me lots of shortcuts and tricks of the trade, including tying his standard hair wing patterns very sparse so they could be fished upstream and would sink quickly. The tendency in those days was for commercial tyers to overdo the materials because people thought they were getting more for their money, while, in fact, they were receiving inferior goods which didn't become effective until they were half worn out. Most importantly, watching the ladies tie was an eye-opener in the art of neatness and organization, and it was there that I learned to make small neat heads on my flies.

Paul Stroud kindly gave me some sample nylon leaders and tippet material which he had dyed brown with silver nitrate. The brown was useful for the Wisconsin and Michigan streams, where he and his customers did most of their fishing, and where the water was, often as not, of varying shades of brown due to the acidy bogs through which they flowed. Several streams in the Madison drainage, including the Madison itself, have the same tint to a lesser degree, but for different reasons, I believe.

The nylon leaders were a huge success, but it was hard to share them equitably, I must admit, there is a fine feeling in having a bit of an edge over the other guys in the matter of tackle. The leaders made it possible to land larger fish on lighter tippets and, while they tended to float, unlike their soaked-gut counterparts, it didn't seem to make much difference, though all the authorities used to insist that the fly in dry-fly fishing should float but that the leader should be completely submerged while the line floated. It was not often that even a highly skilled angler managed to get it all together, and it usually didn't last long when he did. So it was a real pleasure just to forget about trying to sink the leader altogether and to have the results better than they had been heretofore.

The month in Yellowstone was a memorable one for all of us. We each had our favorite places and we moved around a lot, but because of its convenience and the transportation problems, we concentrated heavily on the Madison drainage, which includes the Gibbon and Firehole rivers, and the Madison itself, which is formed by the juncture of the other two. This was, by all odds, the most challenging fishing and it enabled us to be easily distributed at various points in a relatively small area, to be picked up later by whoever took the car.

Each of us had our particular high points, and I had three that stand out still as benchmarks of that trip, and milestones in my fishing progress.

The first was an incident late in the evening after a long and frustrating day on the Madison, where I had frightened each and every big fish I had tried to approach. We were all tired and it was someone else's turn to cook. I decided to walk up across Firehole Road and fish for the last half hour of light in the grass meadow of the last quarter mile of the Gibbon just before it flowed under the bridge to join the Firehole a few hundred yards downstream. I had an English Hardy Brothers tied #16 blue-winged olive with double-duck quill wings dyed dark slate blue and a quill body dyed olive with dark olive hackle and tail. As I approached the stream across the meadow, I heard the *plunk* rise of a big fish and could only guess at the exact location next to the overhanging grass along the opposite bank. I knew I could not get a long drag-free drift and just hoped I had guessed right about the location.

I had, and I heard the slurp of the fish taking my fly and tightened carefully into a fine fish that didn't fight spectacularly at all but was my biggest brown trout to date when he came to the net and I could admire all nineteen inches of him and his beautiful red spots and butter yellow lower flanks.

I didn't then realize the importance of not killing a fine fish such as this one, and I quickly dispatched him and took him back into camp, where he was admired and quickly cooked and consumed. He was the first one we'd had to cut in half in order to fit into our large frying pan. I cleaned the dishes willingly that night and slept soundly through any bear invasions that may have occurred.

The second highlight was also on the Gibbon but way up at the top end of Gibbon Meadows, above the falls and some ten miles from camp where Phil and Al had remained to fish the Madison while Bernabe and I explored the upper Gibbon. It was afternoon and

Bernabe started at the lower end of the big meadow while I went into it some two hundred yards above, where it wound around out of the lodgepole pine woods and where its meanders were a nightmare filled with deadfalls all the way from the foot of the Virginia Cascades.

The first two hundred yards in the open meadow yielded only tiny brook trout, though a few torpedo-like wakes appeared from unlikely spots in the slick water side of undercut bends as large trout were surprised in their hunting of smaller trout and minnows in the shallows when I approached from below, directing my casts to the more obvious deep currents running against the undercuts. It was starting to get late, and that strange time when there seems to be very little activity if any was upon us. I had almost reached the edge of the woods, and there was a log lying in the stream with its root system upstream and about twenty feet of tree extending downstream alongside the edge of the bank close to the road, and invisible from the road.

The tangle of roots was at the top end of a straightaway just below a sharp bend, and the current above the bend flowed almost directly into the top of the roots where it was then deflected to the right and down along the edge of the log. It was a natural place for a big trout because the current had gouged out a deep spot under the log and just ahead of it. The current was slow, and there was no rushing water by the log but just an easy flow with an occasional bubble.

I saw no rises along the log but couldn't resist it anyway, so I worked my casts up very carefully and gradually, each cast landing just a bit farther upstream than the one before. I was using the same blue-winged olive from Hardy's that had done the damage with the nineteen-inch brown on the lower meadow in the evening. I had changed from the lighter-colored flies I'd used lower in the meadow, as the small brookies had demolished them. I was totally unprepared for what happened next.

I was so certain there was a big fish along that log that when the fly disappeared in a tiny bubble I didn't even bother to strike, as I was sure a small fish had taken it again and I didn't want to frighten the big one by having a baby thrashing around as I pulled it out to free the hook. Unfortunately, my fly had apparently been snagged on an underwater protrusion or a weed when the small fish took it under, and I applied pressure to release it as carefully as possible.

That's when the "fit hit the shan," as Dr. Spooner was wont to say. It hadn't been a small trout at all but a very large rainbow who'd simply sipped the tiny morsel from the surface making hardly any disturbance at all, save for the single bubble. He'd held the fly in his mouth totally undisturbed or frightened until I set the hook thinking I was releasing from a snag. He came right out of the water and I was lucky he didn't reenter on the other side of the log or in the tangle of roots. He then headed out across the current and rushed down past me and tore line from the reel before jumping again, two or three more times. After that it was just a dogged resistance with a couple of short runs, and finally he lay on his side in the shallows about twenty-five yards downstream, where I shakily tried to get him into my net, which was too small except when I got him bent almost in half.

He was the most beautiful rainbow I'd ever seen and was in excellent condition. He measured twenty-two inches, exactly. I laid him out on the grassy bank after dispatching him and just sat there admiring him for about ten minutes until Bernabe came slogging up in his water-filled waders. He had taken a dunking farther downstream but had stung a good fish, and otherwise, had had the same experience of tiny brook trout that I had. He was as ecstatic over the big rainbow as I was and suggested that we get it to West Yellowstone the next morning first thing and have it shipped with dry ice to my mother and Paul in Lake Bluff.

He came into town with me the next day, and we got if off all right, but what was received at home was quite another matter. There had been some delays in the train schedules and the delivery to the house, and that notable fish arrived a rotting mess, though we didn't find out about it until much later.

I was very lucky with that fish, and it taught me several important lessons which I try not to forget. A quiet bubble rise is very often the rise of a truly large trout in slow water. Art Wood's advice about fighting the fish directly on the reel, instead of hand-lining him, if he's big, is the only sound way to proceed if you're to avoid trouble. And, finally, luck is important.

The last week of our time in the park we decided to do a real backpack-type hike into an area totally unknown to us, where we would be completely away from it all for a couple of days. It was to be our grand finale as a complete group because Bernabe had to leave us to go back to Cuba for the balance of the summer where he would be working on the Camagüey ranch. Our proposed destination was Heart Lake, one of the sources of the South Fork of the Snake River, which runs out of the south end of Yellowstone through Jackson Lake and Teton National Park to its eventual destination in southeast Idaho.

The trek to Heart Lake is a grinding eight-mile hike over a hump lined with geysers and hot springs on the downhill side, dropping down to the lake. We did not, in fact, have any backpacks but simply rolled what we needed into our sleeping bags, which we rigged as horseshoe rolls and slung over our shoulders with pots and pans jangling from our belts and rods and reels in our hands. We left our waders behind in the locked car at the trailhead. The weather was unusually warm, and we were hot, sweaty, tired, and hungry when we got to the lake shore. We didn't bother making camp properly because our first action was to take off all our clothes and run and dive into the lake for a bracing swim. Then, of course, instead of getting things organized, we all decided to have a go at the fishing around the stream mouth where the flow of many small, cold streams and the hot springs we had passed made an alluvial fan out into the lake, which otherwise appeared to be quite deep around its shores.

The fan should have been a natural feeding place for big trout, since it was a gathering place for minnows, and big fish can corner and catch minnows more easily in shallow water where the schools panic when they are chased against the shore, falling easy prey to the attackers. Such was not the case in this instance, and we kept doggedly fishing until it was pitch dark and not one of us had had a strike.

As it turned out, we should have fished all night, even if we caught nothing. When we quit and went back to the pile of sleeping bags and organized some food, we ate quickly and, being bone tired, just left the cooking mess, the dirty tin plates, and the frying pan with its thick film of grease to clean in the morning. We would never have been so sloppy around our permanent camp at Madison Junction because of the bears, but we had been led to believe that all the bears in the park were concentrated near the roads, campgrounds, and garbage dumps where the pickings were easy.

Our sleeping bags were rolled out in a line, each about two feet away from the next. Mine was on one end near the doused-out campfire. We all fell into a deep sleep with no difficulty at all, and we were glad we'd left the big tarp we'd used for rain shelter back at the car, since the weather was so fine and warm.

I awakened to a distinctly unpleasant odor and the sound of rattling metal very close. I didn't want to open my eyes, but I did and looking straight up could see nothing at all of the clear night sky. There was a heavy grunt right above me and, instinctively, I tried to shrink into the smallest possible form I could, which provoked an instant reflex action from our visitor, who swiped at the offending form under it and then went on calmly licking away at the greasy frying pan and the leavings of our meal, not to mention the rest of the food we had planned for the next day.

I had distinctly felt a sharp blow at the moment of the swipe, and I was frozen with fear. The bear, for such it was, moved over a few yards to get better purchase, I presume, on one of our cans, and I finally ventured an arm out of the bag to touch Phil who was on my right. He groaned, and I pushed insistently until he rolled over and asked what was up.

"Look behind me," I said. "What do you see?"

He got up on one elbow and immediately scrunched back into his bag muttering, "Oh, God!"

I heard the bear scrounging around for what seemed forever before it finally left. I didn't get out of the bag to check it out, I can assure you, and finally went back to sleep, though how, I don't know.

The following morning, bright and early, we had damage assessment. Phil just thought he had had a bad dream until I showed him the rip in the top of my sleeping bag and the very faint scratch marks across my chest. Our eating and cooking utensils were a mess, and the other two wanted to know why we didn't wake them. We readily admitted that we were too damned scared. I know I was, and the tear in the bag, and the scratches, faint as they were, demonstrated what a truly close call I'd had. We all kidded about it on the hike back out, which we started right away since the next two days of fishing had to be aborted, but I can assure you that I never slept completely without some foreboding in the western wilds ever again, even if only subconscious. Also, I think all of us learned never to leave food around a campsite, whatever the circumstances.

We decided to try the famous Widow's Preserve for our last expedition together with Bernabe. Its real name is Culver Springs, but in those days it was still the property of the two sons of the widow who had established her home on a knoll overlooking the head of the long spring pond. The greatest volume of spring flow came into the pond right there at the head in a beautiful shallow pool with a light-colored bottom punctuated by patches of bright green water weeds. The spring was about an hour's drive out of West Yellowstone over a summit into Idaho and around Henry's Lake to another small dirt road over a small divide into the upper end of the Centennial Valley.

We followed the directions in Howard Back's book and found the brothers' cabin without difficulty, and there was no one else fishing there. The brother we talked to said that we could go ahead and fish but that we would have to come by the house afterward and have the fish weighed and pay forty cents a pound for them cleaned. With our slim budget, we agreed among ourselves that we would only keep a couple of fish each to eat, and release the others.

We went right down to the springhead to start fishing, distributing ourselves around it. We were considerate of each other and could all fish a small area like this in a cooperative fashion without causing too much of a ruckus and frightening fish. Over the course of the trip, we'd learned not to tear our fly lines out of the water to start the next cast, but to finish out the retrieve and lift out lines as gently as conditions permitted, avoiding false casting as much as possible when we were fishing wet, and learning to shoot line accurately.

From a mechanical point of view, we had become accomplished fly fishermen, all of us. We acquired a lot of know-how, but mostly, we made up in enthusiasm and energy for what we lacked in knowledge. The latter would come only with the passage of time spent on streams, ponds, and lakes over a lifetime. I know that at this juncture we thought of ourselves as being pretty hot stuff, and, of course, we were headed for our comeuppance. We all caught very nice brook trout from a pound to three pounds fishing nymphs crawling very slowly along the bottom. They were gorgeous fish with their glorious color array at its brightest in the perfect water of the springhead.

We had heard that there were giant rainbow in the pond farther down and that there were some unusually big brook trout as well, Reputedly, rainbows had been caught weighing close to twenty pounds and brookies of six to eight pounds were supposed to be a distinct possibility. Whether or not this was true, one thing was certain. This secret hideaway contained some of the biggest fish we had encountered so far, and they seemed to be lacking in sophistication to an extent that would enable us to come away from there with the fish of our lifetimes.

No one had mentioned to us that there were a lot of very large grayling in the long pond as well as rainbow and brook trout. As we worked our ways separately around the pond, the first surprise for all of us was seeing rising fish that seemed fairly large and, from the look of it, were apparently feeding on emerging and adult damselflies—the long-bodied kind we often called "darning needles." We didn't then know that the nymphs would probably be the most effective for the larger fish, and besides, we didn't know what damselfly nymphs looked like.

We all found our own solutions, and mine was to find the largest spent-winged dry flies I had in my box, which happened to be spent mayflies that Paul Stroud's ladies had tied to imitate the Michigan mayfly, or *hexagenia*. It filled the bill, and I started catching very large grayling that were twice the size of anything I'd run across in Grebe Lake. I kept one that was unusually large, measuring twenty-three inches. Farther down the lake, I saw some more rising going on in a small bay, where I had to wade out through a tangle of water moss of the water buttercup family of *ranunculus*. By the time I reached a point where I was at the edge of the weed bed and could reach relatively open and clear water, I had waded almost to the top of my waders, which reached about halfway between my belt and arm pits. It was awkward casting, but from the heavy look of the rises which were not within reach, it would be more than worth it.

I thoroughly dried the big spent mayfly and soaked it in the floatant we used in those days, which was a mix of cleaning fluid and candle wax which dissolved if we kept the bottle in a pocket against our body, and left a light film of wax on the fly. When we shook the fly in the capped open-mouthed bottle, the solution cleaned off the slime from any fish it had caught previously. It had the slight disadvantage of changing the color of the fly to some extent, but we didn't let that bother us, and it apparently didn't bother the fish.

It did seem important, however, to flick the excess fluid off thoroughly by casting and completely drying the fly before casting to a fish. Otherwise, the fluid left an ugly coating on the surface of the water like oil or gasoline. The fish would consistently refuse such a fly almost as if it were a repellent. This certainly wasn't the case in the little moss-filled bay. The very first cast when the fly alighted on the surface brought a vigorous rise and solid take. I didn't even have to strike or tighten up. The fish simply took the fly and dove for the bottom, which was apparently lined with more of the moss, because I was suddenly tangled in some kind of growth and, naturally, lost the fly trying to retrieve it.

I had about a half dozen of the big spent-wing hexes. Before putting on another, I retrieved everything and shortened the leader from nine feet to 3X by removing the last eighteen inches of tippet and fastening the fly directly to the heavier 2X. After the full procedure of dressing with floatant and drying, I cast out again and once again had a firm take in a big boil of a rise, and the fish dove once more into the moss and was lost.

I'm fairly sure they were big brook trout. I never really did find out, though, because I never managed to land one of the damned things, even when I was down to three feet of butt section, which must have tested about ten pounds, at least. At that point I was determined to hold the fish out of the moss at any cost. I cast little more than six feet of line and the short leader and fly, and when the inevitable take came, I held on as hard as I could, and I'm no weakling. The fish dove like an irresistible force, and the hook straightened out and came free. I was thoroughly beaten.

I left the little bay and had a hell of a time getting out, as I'd been sinking in deeper and deeper the longer I stood on the mucky bottom. When I reached shore, I'd been over the wader tops and was soaked to the skin and in a foul mood. I couldn't take the beating I'd been given by a bunch of dumb fish. They had to be dumb or they wouldn't have been fooled by the fly on such a short, heavy leader.

They beat me, anyway, and I shudder to think what would have happened it I'd hooked one of the big rainbows. These brook trout must have been well over five pounds to exert so much power, though I can't swear to it. It's still nice to think about, though, and to wonder how I'd solve the problem now if I had it to do over again in the same place.

My companions had had similar experiences, but all different in their own way. One of them did have a hookup with a big rainbow that took off on a power run and jumped off. Bernabe showed the good sense to stick with the springhead pool and its edges and caught many more fine brook trout and some of the big grayling. We had all kept our two fish; each of us had one grayling and one brookie.

When we checked out at the cabin, we had just over twenty pounds of fish between us, and it cost us a little over eight dollars—a lot more than we'd expected. On the other hand, each of us had broken his personal best on brook trout, including Al who had fished for coasters (the big brook trout of the Great Lakes) in the river mouth at the Huron Mountain Club.

I returned to Culver Springs many years after the war and found it was government property and part of a federal migratory waterfowl refuge. If the big brookies are still there, they are not in evidence, and there are no longer any grayling. There was a large feed-storage tank for the waterfowl, and the tracks of many anglers as well as trash. I've never bothered to go back again.

6
Oregon and
the Mills

Monday morning the paymaster took us to the mill and put us in the charge of our foreman, Leo, who turned out to be one of the nicest men I've ever had the good fortune to work for.

The mill was awesome in size, and we were told it was the largest completely covered mill in the world. All the lumber cut in the forests, twenty to fifty miles to the north, was shipped in on a private rail line and kiln-dried there. It was all ponderosa pine, Leo told us, generally of high quality and in great demand in the Midwest, where the Hines company had its principal distribution area.

Leo separated us from each other for good tactical reasons. He put each of us with an experienced man on the lumber chain, and we were introduced to the art of "pulling lumber." . . . Each of us along the chain had from two to five different grades to pull as the lumber came by. We had to keep each in distinct piles, perfectly aligned, and when the stacks reached a certain number of layers, cross pieces were put in to start a new stack. We built each stack to the maximum height a forklift could carry; then they were moved out to storage or shipping areas, and we started a new stack.

The first few days were real back-breakers. At first we were using nothing but muscle power and were, of course, totally exhausted and sore the entire first week. As we got the hang of it, we expended less and less energy. Leo allowed as how he was proud of us and asked if we would like to go to a movie with him Saturday night. I can't remember the name of the film, but I knew it wasn't the one showing at the local theater. Leo proceeded to drive us all the way to the town of Bend, over 120 miles away, to see the movie, have a few beers, then head back to Hines—a two-hundred-forty-mile round trip for an evening's entertainment. These Oregonians seemed to have no sense of distance.

When we passed the two-man town of Brothers, where there was a slight bend in the otherwise straight road, Leo told us, "Those two guys make a living off'n the drunks that don't make'er through the bend and drive off through the sagebrush. They got car repair all locked up for miles around!"

Our five weeks at the mill were a combination nightmare and circus. It was the hardest any of us had ever worked, and after our easygoing pace on the fishing trip, the change was especially startling to our physical and nervous systems. There was also another problem: a certain resentment from some of the crew members who viewed us as spoiled brats with our eastern accents and privileged assignments. They were always on the lookout for opportunities to pick a flight . . .

Phil, Al, and I managed to get beered up one night at the tavern and, on the way out, we were accosted by a couple of thoroughly drunk crew members who thought we needed taking down a notch or two. As it turned out, the three of us were a match for the two of them, though we quickly found out there were no rules. We settled it outside and, with only a few marks to show for it, wound up drinking with our opponents until we were almost as inebriated as they were. I ended up getting my first-ever ticket, for driving without any lights on the way back to the mill. I was lucky the deputy didn't haul me in for drunken driving.

*   *   *

One Sunday Leo, who was also a fisherman, offered to take us to see the best trout stream in those parts. It turned out to be two streams, the Donner and the Blitzen, which joined together where they came out of their respective canyons to form a single stream called, oddly enough, the Donner and Blitzen, then continued, after being robbed of a considerable part of its flow by pasture irrigation, across the flat bottom of the Harney basin to Malheur Lake, the swampy remnant of the once great lake which now serves as a duck-breeding area.

Like the ride to the movies, it turned out to be much farther than it appeared, and the lower part of the stream was disappointing. Over what passed for a road, we went as far as the forks, and my friends stayed and fished down the main stream, which was reasonably trouty-looking, while I headed up the right canyon, fishing my way along with a grasshopper imitation. I picked up the occasional fish and missed some impressive takes from the surprise of seeing large fish boil to my fly in such a relatively small stream. I was in the stream the whole time and had moved well up into the canyon. I had finally hooked and landed one of the larger fish that came to my fly. It was a brightly colored rainbow with some cutthroat markings, and I later learned that it may have been a distinctive species native to the area, known as the red-banded trout, which is now near extinction.

I was delighted by this twenty-two-inch specimen that put up a fight worthy of any rainbow. Needing to relieve myself, I stepped up on the bank and proceeded to do so. Suddenly I heard a rattling buzz like a rapidly shaken gourd full of seeds. I stared at the coiled rattler and heard another to one side, then another. The whole area was absolutely infested with rattlesnakes, and I could see them everywhere along the banks. I had been so taken with the fishing that I never noticed them. Now that I had, it was hard to keep from total panic. As it was, I felt real fear and, finally gathering my energies, I made a near-record standing broad jump into the water and made my way downstream without so much as another cast.

As I came out of the canyon, I saw snake after snake along the bank, and I couldn't believe I hadn't noticed. I also understood why there were so many large fish in that stream. Only a fool would fish there.

Leo was the first to notice me when I arrived back at the pickup. "See any snakes?" he asked.

"Too goddamned many!" I yelped.

He was surprised that I had gone in so far and fished for so long. "Most guys go in there and head right back out when they see all the rattlers."

I showed him my big fish and told him it was almost worth it, but that I didn't think I'd go back in there, even for a twenty-four-incher.

Leo said he thought there were fish that large in the stream but they were pretty safe from most fishermen. I couldn't have agreed more.

When we headed west again, there was just a week left before Phil and Al had to return home to prepare for their first terms at college. We agreed that the word "lumber," or the name of any other wood product, would no longer be a part of our vocabulary. But before the last hurrah, I persuaded the others that we should have a one-day shot at fishing the famous North Umpqua River we had read about in Ray Bergman's book, *Trout*.

The drive to Diamond Lake wasn't bad, but from there on down the "unimproved track" was truly something else. We left the volcanic barrens and the high ponderosa forest on the eastern slope and wound down a narrow, twisting road through dense forests of rhododendrons, vine maple, and enormous towering Douglas firs. It was very steep and, suddenly, we came to a stretch where no track could be seen at all. There was simply a large expanse of bare, black rock. There were no tracks on a rock, so we got out and crossed to the other side where the forest started once again, and the track picked up, wandering through the trees even more steeply downward into the canyon, where we could just hear the first roaring sounds of the new river far below in the gorge.

Altogether, from Diamond Lake to Steamboat, our destination, there were six hours of driving. (Today it's a forty-minute drive at moderately high speed.) When we finally came within sight of the river we stopped and looked down from high above and saw two large fish lying in the tail-out of the big, deep pool below. They were larger than anything we'd ever seen in fresh water and, in retrospect, they may have been salmon rather than steelhead, as we thought then. In any case, we put together our rods and clambered down the cliff to the head of the pool.

Phil drew the big pool, so Al went one pool up and I went to the next one downstream. We spent about an hour, and I tried a wet royal coachman because it was the only big wet fly I had that was bright enough. I had on a gut leader, since we had long since run out of Paul Stroud's miracle dyed nylon. The heaviest gut leader I possessed was a 3X and, soaked, it probably didn't test more than a pound and a half, if that.

The pool I was fishing had not been visible from above because of a large outcrop overhanging the head of the pool, and where I set up looked deep and strong and limpid, though I couldn't see the bottom due to the turbulence. Because of the overhang, I had to use the steeple cast I had learned so long ago from Leander McCormick. This enabled me to direct my backcast perpendicularly behind me before extending it forward to its target. With it I was able to do a creditable job of covering the pool with my casts, but nothing happened until I reached the lower end with a full extension of the line.

The fly skimmed across the water just in front of the tail-out where it sped into a chute that dropped to the rapids below then entered another pool out of view. As the fly sped across the lip, there was a giant bulge in the water just behind it and a splash, and I saw, for a frozen instant in time, the maw of an enormous fish reach for the fly and miss. Anyway, I thought it missed, for I felt nothing and my rod didn't double up, as they say in the big fish stories; nor did my reel scream. I just stood there aghast, and started to try a cast to the same spot again as soon as I stopped trembling. Then I realized there was no longer a fly on the end of my leader. As it turned out, the last section of the leader was also missing and, doubtless, trailing from the jaw of the steelhead. Even though we hadn't done battle, and had barely touched gloves, I felt in no way cheated. There was pure exhilaration in the sure knowledge that I had found something entirely new to me, and which was going to stimulate endless interest, anticipation, and excitement from then on.

Phil and Al had each fished out their respective pools without result and were yelling at me to get back to the car. The thought of the river down below in the famous stretches we had read about was compelling enough to get me up the cliff to the narrow ledge, and off we went, with me spouting off about "the one that got away," about which there was a lot of playful kidding.

It was nearly dark by the time we arrived at the junction of Steamboat Creek and the main river and, though the road was an improvement over the high parts, it was still narrow and winding and dangerous because of the constant temptation to look at the river. We passed the Mott Bridge a couple of hundred yards before the Steamboat Creek Bridge and decided to camp on the point just upstream where we found some fine, soft fir needles beneath the majestic trees. It was as soft and comfortable a spot as we had found to sleep on our whole trip, and we slept soundly with the perfume of pine and ripening blackberries in the air.

The next morning, after a quick breakfast, we did a bit of arranging with whatever leaders we had, and each of us ended up with a nine-foot gut leader to 1X, and our biggest squirrel tails on #8 hooks from Paul Stroud's. First we walked up to the Mott Bridge, where we could see what the river really looked like from above, but the light was not right yet to have a clear view of the long pool below, so we split up, with Al on the right side going down and me on the left, fishing it a little above the bridge downstream, foot by foot. Phil opted for the junction, which we later learned was called the station pool, though Bergman referred to it as the plank pool, as there was a plank set up from the bank to a rocky reef where the middle and lower parts could be covered easily by even the most inadequate caster.

I was fishing faster than Al and reached the lower part of the pool, which is called the Upper Sawtooth, where two distinct reefs project up into the pool and cause the first turbulence in the two-hundred-yard length of water. The reef point closest to my side lay a bit down-stream of the one on Al's side, and the near side of his reef was the ob-vious target of choice for a thorough working-over. That looked like the ideal holding spot for any big fish that might have just moved into the pool from below.

I remembered that Bergman had fished this pool from the oppo-site side and wrote of having hooked a fish just above the reef. This time I was somewhat prepared for what might happen, but when it did, I was just as shocked and excited as the first time. The only im-provement was my immediate reaction of letting go of the line in my left hand. I would eventually learn not to hold it at all when fishing for steelhead or Atlantic salmon because of the great possibility of their breaking away immediately if they can't take line directly off the reel.

The Sawtooth fish took the fly and, as I let go, he turned sharply and ran down into the chute on my side, which was pure luck, then the leader snapped. Once again I was left with nothing, though I did see the fish jump in the run below. Shakily, I retrieved my line and leader. My reel had made a funny noise and seized. It was dry and should have been oiled but, beside that, if the fish had kept on going he'd have broken away anyway because none of us had any backing on our small trout reels—just the thirty yards of fly line which we had always thought would be adequate for any situation.

We had all been taught the usual homily that a fly reel was just a place for storing one's line out of the way. We had at least progressed to the point of recognizing that a smooth click on a reel not only stopped overrunning, but also served as a means of slowing down a stronger-than-usual fish. We were not, however, prepared for what fish the size of steelhead could do, and do so quickly.

I sat on the bank and waited for Al to fish out the pool on the other side. Just as he was about to reach the hot spot, from which he would be able to cover the front tip of the reef, I heard a voice behind me and looked around to see a state trooper.

"Hello," he said politely, then asked to see my license. I took it from my shirt pocket and showed it to him. After looking it over he asked, "Is the young fellow fishing up on Steamboat Creek with you?"

I said that he was, and so was the other fellow across the river. He motioned for Al to join us at the bridge, and as we walked up the road to where his pickup was parked he told me he'd issued Phil a citation for fishing without a proper license.

Since we'd never been checked before, Phil thought it was worth the risk to purchase a local license instead of the more expensive non-resident license. As much as we would have liked to, we couldn't lie for him, and we were all together in a car with Illinois plates. Phil was sitting dejectedly at the Steamboat Bridge; his rod and reel had been confiscated by the patrolman. The only way to get it back would be to appear in court and pay the fine. When asked, the patrolman opined that since Phil was from out-of-state, this particular judge was likely to impose a stiff fine and that it might be better to give up the rod. After we'd gone back to the Mott Bridge to check Al's license, we were free to go, but without Phil's precious rod. It was a hard lesson but one that made a permanent impression on all of us. The temptation to lie about our place of residence had been great because of the disparity in price between the two licenses; in retrospect, not so great a price after all.

That pretty well wrapped up the summer for us. That was the last fishing stop, and we couldn't very well go on fishing with Phil just looking on. He was unhappy enough as it was. We decided to get on our way down to Roseburg and to the main highway south to San Francisco, where Pauline would put us up for a couple of days before Phil and Al caught their train back to Chicago.

7
Back to
Paradise . . .
Sun Valley

My fishing highlight that fall was going out with Pop Marks, an old-time guide. Using my old car, we drove down to Bellevue and crossed over what we used to call Muldoon Summit, going high up then descending into the upper Little Wood River above Carey Reservoir. . . .

It was my birthday, the tenth of October, that Pop showed me the way over there. We stopped some distance away from the stream because it was in a sandy bottom where it would be easy to get stuck, and we walked out across the willow flats. Pop had kept this spot pretty much a secret, and it didn't get hit much, if at all, even by the local fishermen.

Pop knew I preferred to fish dry-fly so he picked a spot about halfway into the good fishing area, and I headed upstream while he fished down, with the agreement that we meet back at the car by 3:30 to give us plenty of time to get back over the hill in time to clean up for my birthday party, which was scheduled to be held at The Ram.

Pop favored wet flies and didn't mind the old Andy Reeker which his cohort, Art Wood, preferred. He went for the Reeker right away, which was a big surprise to me since the stream couldn't have been over ten feet wide in the broad spots and was seldom over eighteen inches deep. I had already developed a strong penchant for the Adams, especially the version called the Lady Adams, which had a yellow egg sack at the end of the grey fur body and was the latest hot fly from Michigan, according to *Field & Stream*. These, and their variants, were my current favorites, and they had produced well all fall everywhere but on Silver Creek, a place where there were seldom any easy solutions.

So I put on a Lady Adams and went to work within talking distance of Pop for a little while. The main flat of the long, narrow pool, between the gravel banks and willow thickets, was shallow and featureless and the water was just a little off-color from a rain shower the night before. I got no action until I arrived within range of the faster and deeper current at the head of the pool, where there was a snag of willow roots in the water. Very much like the log pool on the Gibbon, the first fish that took did so so quietly that all I detected was the disappearance of my fly underwater just as if I had forgotten to put the floatant on it and it had sunk. There was, however, a slight dimpling of the water, and I tightened gently into a good fish of some seventeen inches with a fine deep belly. The fish jumped immediately and came tearing back down the creek toward me and went on past. Pop turned around when I yelled and saw the second and third spectacular leaps. I played the fish carefully then brought it in and put it into the grass creel where it would soon be joined by half a dozen others nearly the same size, plus one gorgeous fish of twenty-three inches. Pop was delighted by the success of the dry fly, whose effectiveness he had admittedly doubted and was especially surprised that our largest fish came to a dry and not to the Andy Reeker spoon.

My birthday party at The Rams that night was a great success and, much to my surprise, Pop Marks had arranged for the trout to be arrayed on a serving tray brought in from the cafeteria to show to the guests. Pappy Arnold, the Sun Valley photographer who accompanied us on many of our hunts and other expeditions in the area, took some photos with his Speed Graphic which still show as pretty a mess of trout as you could want to see. In those days there wasn't, as yet, any ethic about returning fish to be caught another day. As a matter of fact, quite the opposite was true, and one took pride in the number and size of fish killed. We had no idea then that one day there would be so many fishermen that the wild resources we cherished so much would be threatened by even small limits, and that it would become praiseworthy to limit killing nearly altogether except in unusual circumstances. Still, turning eighteen had been a splendid occasion in every way.

Before Pat and Greg left for school, we went with Papa and Marty, and a visiting sport from California, to the Pahsimeroi Valley for a historic antelope hunt. The whole retinue came along with Taylor Williams as head guide, Lloyd Arnold for pictures, some of the horse wranglers, and a camp cook. The drive over Trail Creek Summit, and then the Big Lost Valley and Lost River Range via Double Springs Pass, was spectacular. The valley of the Pahsimeroi, itself, was almost treeless except for a few willows in the bottoms, where the spring-fed creek flowed, and the aspen grew in the rolling foothills. There were evergreens on the high flanks of the valley, and there were already whiffs of new snow on the upper ranges. Nights had a bite to them that made leaving the cozy warmth of the sleeping bag difficult in the dawn hours which seem so much a part of the world of hunting.

There is still a photo, somewhere, that shows our hunting party with a group of hanging antelope, all of us in a line and big grins on our faces. There is only one incongruity that becomes apparent on closer inspection. One young man is not wearing jeans, chaps, and boots like the others, but waders. That nonconformist is me; I had been much more intrigued by the idea of an unfished spring creek with giant rainbows than by the idea of pursuing the elusive antelope. As a result, two things happened. In one instance, I missed seeing Papa achieve what Taylor Williams said was one of the finest pieces of rifle shooting he had ever seen, when Papa, after a grueling uphill stalk, made a particularly difficult running shot on an antelope at a considerable distance, using, as he always did, open sights. The incident was written as a short piece called "The Shot" and has been reprinted many times. I will say, though, that I certainly heard the story enough times during the next few days that I don't believe I really missed anything. In the meantime, I had some fine dry-fly fishing for smallish trout in as pretty a weed-and-cress-filled meadow stream as I had ever seen, and I kept the camp larder filled with fresh breakfast trout to accompany the enormous feasts of hot cakes, biscuits, and eggs that our cook provided every dawn. My younger brothers were both hunters by inclination and spent the long days afield in the everlasting antelope chase as well as hunting deer, which were open then and plentiful in the area.

My curiosity about the outlet of the river into the always-turbid waters of the Salmon River overcame me. The mouth of the Pahsimeroi was only a few miles away from our camp, and I had brought my own car, so I drove down the dirt road to Ellis, where there was a small post office serving the area. I started wading the creek upstream a few hundred yards, with a small streamer, and I took some fish very much the size of those I had been catching all along—in the seven- to twelve-inch range. There was a solid willow cover on both sides and I could hardly get out even though I would have preferred to walk along the bank. I hadn't learned my lesson well enough on the North Umpqua that summer because I didn't think to change to a heavy leader when I got close to the mouth. I was fishing 3X, which would have been strong enough to hold a fish up to two or three pounds, but the last thing in the world I was thinking of was the possibility of a steelhead. Their presence in the Middle Fork was well-known, but they were thought to have been nearly wiped out by the mining pollution in the main Salmon. The fact of the matter is that there simply weren't that many people fishing the wilds of Idaho in those days, and no one really knew what was there and what wasn't.

My sense of anticipation was keen when I arrived at the junction of the two currents. I extended my casts gradually and covered the clear water tongue as it extended into the main river. I had a relatively short line out, maybe thirty feet plus leader, when the little light-winged streamer coursed across the slick of clear water with my eyes glued to it. My memory of that sight is as clear today as it was then, and what comes up is the ultimate monster of the deep rising deliberately under that fly and suddenly opening its jaws to engulf the fly, then returning back down into the depths. Fortunately, I was too paralyzed to strike and the enormous fish was on—one should never strike when the line is extended below, the fish will break the leader—though I doubt if the fish knew it. I exerted a little pressure and it turned and headed for the Pacific Ocean some six hundred river miles away.

My reel was properly oiled, and nothing went wrong except that when the end of the line was reached there was a pop and the whole line went sliding out the guides on the rod, and I watched as the silver and pink crescent arched out of the water almost out of sight with my whole outfit still fastened to it. I'm certain they parted company at that instant, but my fishing was over for the day, and for the trip, since I had no replacement fly line.

I had the shakes for a few minutes until I gathered myself together for the climb up the bank and the walk back up the Pahsimeroi Road to the car. At the time, I had thought the fish was a salmon because of its size, but I'm certain now that it was, indeed, a steelhead, and possibly one of the thirty-pounders the river used to be known for before commercial netting of salmon became so concentrated that the truly big steelhead were all too often taken in the nets intended for salmon and sold as such, and called "incidental catch."

That was the day Papa shot his second antelope, and a big mule deer as well, and we decided that we would return to Sun Valley the following day, but not without a celebration in the little "cowboy" *cum* "mining town" of Patterson that night. It was a rough evening with fistfights and a near-stomping, and even guns were pulled in a threatening gesture, but I missed most of the action because, after a couple of beers, I went back to the car and conked out.

I heard the whole story in detail on the way back to camp and then the next day when it was repeated for Pat and Greg's sake. It was repeated again when we got back to Sun Valley and had assumed epic proportions when relayed to Marty. Patterson was a real fighting town in those days. The cowboys, who had a union called "The Turls," came into town Saturday night when the local miners were also in town on a tear. Miners and cowboys don't get along very well after a few drinks—maybe even before—and they went at it every week. Papa had simply walked into the local social event of the week and, because he was tough, became embroiled with a gigantic miner in stomping boots who, fortunately, finally went down under a barrage of Papa's special left hooks to the head.

Soon after our return to Sun Valley, my brothers left to go back to school. Both duck and pheasant season had arrived. We had prepared for the birds by several rabbit drives, one of which would have attracted the attention of a Cleveland Amory, had such a creature existed in those days. Papa was the general who deployed all of us, including any visiting guests of the moment, in a skirmish line along the property line of a farmer whom we knew to be having terrible problems with crop losses to the hordes of jackrabbits that lived in the sage-covered lands surrounding his farm near Dietrich.

John Frieze and his two sons, who were farming this new area, would bring up the rear guard with a pickup truck and gather dead rabbits as we advanced through the sagebrush toward an irrigation canal, where the rabbits would be trapped. When the animals tried to escape by coming back through our advancing line, it literally looked as though the earth were moving, so plentiful were the long-eared predators. This was one of the great peaks of their population cycle, and the Friezes collected over seventeen hundred rabbits on that one drive.

Meanwhile, we had done a lot of shooting, and Gary Cooper, who preferred rifles to shotguns, sat on a hillock at the edge of the drive and shot rabbits at long range. It was economically unsound. The rabbits were worth less than the bullets Coop fired, which were all hand-loaded for his 2200 Lovell. But it was fun for him and good practice for the upcoming bird shoots, and it certainly helped solve the Friezes' rabbit predation problems. When they had skinned the rabbits, the farmers collected about five cents apiece for the skins from the dealers, which was a good piece of change at the time.

Our pheasant opener that fall was on Tom Gooding's farm near the town of the same name. It was a fine hunt but was marred by one bad incident when one of the gunners, John Boettiger, who was along with his wife, Ann Roosevelt Boettiger, inadvertently shot one of the Labrador retrievers, through a careless error. He felt very badly about it, but we all took it pretty hard, and Papa was most unforgiving and forever afterward had little good to say about the president's son-in-law.

It was characteristic of Papa in that he did not easily suffer fools or stupid behavior, particularly in those who should know better. Usually, though, he was more forgiving of human frailty, and Boettiger's mistake was one of carelessness and certainly not malicious in any way. Boettiger felt terrible about it and even expressed the thought aloud that anyone who did such a thing ought to be shot. Unfortunately, Papa agreed, which caused an amusing incident the following day when I came up to his room to bring the morning newspapers.

It was about seven o'clock, and there was a high, heavy, overcast sky. Papa answered my knock and, while he glanced at the headlines, I walked over to the window and stepped out onto the terrace overlooking what was then a small pond with some ducks and Canada geese with pinioned wings. There had always been six geese, but I noticed there were now ten.

I said, "Papa, there's ten geese out there."

He immediately put his finger to his lips and motioned me back into the room. Marty was still in the bedroom. He took his model 12 pump from its soft case and quickly shucked three shells into it. Then he ran to the window and out onto the terrace overlooking the pond and four of the geese took flight. One was a giant and Papa poured all three shots at it. It was hit, albeit with lighter loads than one would normally use for geese.

At that point Marty called from the bedroom in a startled voice, "My God, Ernest, you didn't shoot John Boettiger did you?"

The big lead bird was obviously in trouble and, instead of gaining altitude as it would have normally, it headed for Sun Valley Lake a quarter mile away. We couldn't see it from the terrace but we knew it had to go down and roughly where it must go down, and there was a good possibility the other three geese had followed it. Papa called Taylor Williams, who called Pappy Arnold and others of the troops, and we all foregathered in the lobby of the lodge.

Papa and Taylor assigned the positions for surrounding the lake and retrieving the wounded bird, and possibly taking another for our Thanksgiving feast. I was with Papa and no geese came over us, but the three smaller birds flew over Taylor and his group and they got two of them. The big bird was floating dead on the water where one of the big black Labs Averell Harriman had first brought to Sun Valley retrieved it. There was much rejoicing, and the birds were beautifully prepared by the cooks at The Ram for our Thanksgiving dinner. The big goose weighed thirteen pounds dressed, and the smaller ones about eight to ten pounds. We were sure there was no better bird to roast for such a festive occasion.

After some successful pheasant shoots down at the Friezes', and some jump shoots on Silver Creek with Papa and me changing ends of the canoe to take turns shooting, the tail end of fall brushed past and winter took over. On the last canoe shoot with Papa, we had gone farther down the creek than ever before—all the way past the "stutter man's" place. He must have been away, for this once he didn't come out yelling, "Ggg-get offa mmmy ppplace!" threatening to shoot us, as he usually did.

The creek narrowed perceptibly in this last stretch, and we weren't prepared for what awaited us around the narrow bend where the willows crowded the banks. Papa was in the stern so I was the first to see the water pipe with its wooden housing stretching across the creek. By the time I reacted, it was only a few lengths away and the current was too strong to dodge it or, much less, paddle back upstream. As I reached forward to grab the housing, the rear of the canoe slammed around to the right. Papa reached out to steady his end, but the current's force against the wide beam of the canoe forced the upstream thwart under and we were unceremoniously dumped into the frigid water along with our guns and the birds we'd shot.

The way was clear beyond the pipe so we had no trouble getting out, but we were soaked, cold, and gunless. The canoe had run aground at the next bend, so, after setting it aright, we took off our clothes, wrung them out as best we could, and hiked as fast as we could out to the road and back to Picabo, where Chuck Atkinson's store was located and we recovered from our mishap with the aid of a little bit of the stuff that killed Dr. McWalsey. Taylor and I recovered the guns the next day and, fortunately, there was no damage or rust on them. I learned then, for the first time, that things completely underwater rust more slowly than those exposed to air.

I shot fairly consistently with the shotgun for the first time that autumn. Up until then, I had always been the rifle-shooting member of the family. The two tend not to be compatible unless you are careful to separate them completely in your mind, keeping the natural instinctiveness of shotgun shooting, in the one instance, while exercising the precision and carefully controlled breathing of the rifleman, in the other. Except for the skeet lessons Carl Bradshire had given all of us boys and Marty the summer of 1940, I really had no idea what I was trying to accomplish with the shotgun, other than to get certain leads at certain angles. By dint of doing more shooting, more often, and cutting down slightly on my fishing, I was starting to do the right thing, instinctively, more often.

But there was little doubt that fishing was my specialty and my first love. I was reminded of it every time Papa and I floated down the creek shooting ducks and occasionally frightened a big trout off a waving weed bed. When it warmed in the midafternoon, we'd see the big rainbows rising to small flies drifting on the surface. Just the sight of them sent a shiver through me, and as much as I enjoyed shooting with Papa, I knew I'd rather be casting to those rises and testing my skills on those elegant, canny creatures of the streams.

Considering his increasingly imperfect eyesight, Papa was a first-class wingshot. As long as it was game being shot at and not clay targets, he could outshoot just about anyone around, and he seemed to thrive on competitive situations such as the live pigeon-shooting in

Spain and in Cuba. The best shot amongst us, however, was Gigi. He used his little single shot .410 to deadly effect, and the following winter would be runner-up in the World Live Pigeon Shooting Championship, which was held in Havana that year because of the war in Europe. He was a natural. At age eleven, he did not feel the pressure of the competition as severely as others. Patrick was already a good rifle shot and had made a clean kill of his first mule deer the previous fall after my return to school. It was a near-record head and presaged his later career as a successful white hunter in east Africa.

It has been an altogether fantastic fall . . .

III

THE WAR YEARS

8
Abroad with the OSS

When the Japanese bombed Pearl Harbor, Jack wanted to join the war effort immediately. He was frustrated by bad eyesight when he tried to become a Navy pilot. Then the Army assigned him to MP duty. But because of who he was and because he spoke French, he was able to transfer, eventually to the Office of Special Services. The OSS was a clandestine outfit that was the precursor of the CIA, and its ranks included many well-connected privileged men of talent. The joke, among insiders, was that the letters "OSS" actually stood for "Oh So Social." Jack was right at home.—GN

The OSS training camp at Chréa, Algeria, was as beautiful a setting as could be imagined. Located atop the highest point of the minor range of mountains immediately behind the provincial city of Blida, in a regal forest of blue cedars, the camp had a few small Quonset huts and a number of tents. On one side, the little resort village provided limited services for a small community of summer villas of the very wealthy who came to the 6,000-foot mountaintop to escape the summer heat of Algiers and the Mitidja Plain.

67

"Jumbo" Wilson, the British commander of allied forces in the Mediterranean since Eisenhower's departure to London, had a week-end retreat there guarded by the roughest contingent of soldiers imaginable. There were twelve of them, Scots Guards, all of whom had at least seven wound stripes acquired as desert rats in Egypt and Libya. Not only was their vocabulary limited to variations of the "F" word, used as noun, pronoun, adjective, verb, adverb, interjection, or preposition, but they were always cheerfully spoiling for a fight at every opportunity. If you wanted to test your toughness, these fellows would oblige, and you'd better be good and willing to take as well as dish out.

The road up the mountain from the edge of Blida was narrow and winding and had the usual low stone walls on the outer edge, like French mountain roads. It wound first through small hillside vine-yards, small farm patches, and sheep and goat pastures. Then the foliage became semitropical with lush vines and creepers until it entered spreads of live oak and scrub brush. At that point, the view of the valley below was unhindered, and the whole of the plain could be seen stretching to the sea in the north, rimmed on the west by the coastal range, and off to the right by the rising heights of Algiers and the bay. Blida, below, was the site of a busy military airport where both British and U.S. bombers were based—the latter as part of the U.S. Twenty-fifth Air Force.

Driving down the mountain one morning at dawn for a field exercise, I was captivated by the sight of the whole plain below covered by dense fog. We were well above it looking down on the cloudlike surface when, as if by some sorcerer's incantation, B-24 bombers began emerging from the cottony blanket, rising in ever higher circles to form up together, then accelerating off toward a distant bombing mission somewhere in Europe. With the rays of the rising sun glinting off their cockpits and gun turrets, they were a stirring sight. The roar of all those engines filled the air space around and before us until the massive squadron reached altitude where, forming up, they lumbered on their way.

The camp itself was used for training both French and American personnel. There were courses being given in every conceivable type of weapon, including the enemy's. There was map work, demolitions and sabotage, use of radios such as "agent sets" in small valises, encoding and decoding, special devices, unarmed combat, and what has come to be known as "agent trade craft." I was assigned as part of the permanent staff, though I attended all the different classes when I was not teaching weapons to the French joes. I'm not quite sure where the name "joes" came from, but it was certainly not used in a pejorative sense.

The other instructors were a mixed lot. All were older than I, and many had been in the field prior to being assigned to teaching duties. Security was excellent and, while many tales were told to illustrate points, the specifics of who, where, and when were left out. Everyone understood that the less any one person knew outside what he absolutely needed to know, the better off he would be in case of capture or torture.

Certainly I learned a lot more than I was teaching, and after a few weeks my commanding officer permitted me to assist in the instruction of some of the other subjects. The people who came to take the courses were given a first name when they arrived, and they were never called anything else. It was forbidden to discuss one's own background or to question others about theirs. All soon understood that it was for their own safety, since these were all people preparing to go on missions in enemy-occupied territory.

In addition to the French joes, I was involved in training other special operatives. The school had a diversity of students, including Operational Groups (OGs), who were trained for disrupting rear areas in enemy territory by sabotage of railroads, roads, and communications, and by attacks on enemy units using hit-and-run tactics. There were also SI agents, though rarely, who needed some brushing up on weapons or map work in communications. Their job was Secret Intelligence and all the ramifications of obtaining it and communicating it back by radio or other means. Occasionally Jedburghs used the camp,

I was told. These teams were trained in Scotland and were comprised of three men from the three nationalities: U.S., French, and British. Usually two were officers and one an NCO (noncommissioned officer) radio operator, and their function was to provide staff leadership to existing resistance forces and to help coordinate their activities.

Among the teaching staff was a number of very tough, young men. They had all been to the OSS training schools in the States, and some of them had been through training in England as well. One of them impressed me especially. He was the only one of the younger men who had been in the field, and his toughness was not put on. In some ways he was crude. He was not particularly well educated, but you could sense his innate intelligence through the rough exterior. He did not talk about his prior missions, and they only came out to illustrate points he was trying to teach. I was to get to know him as well as anyone ever would, and I eventually learned that he had already made three jumps behind enemy lines prior to the assignment at Chréa; once in North Africa, once in Italy, and once in Sardinia. He had been commissioned in the field and, being several years older than I, he filled the spot one always has for a hero figure. His name was Jim Russell. . . .

Jim was the complete antithesis of the OSS staff person. In fact, he abhorred them. In his view they were nothing; only field men counted, and the tougher the better. I'm afraid I couldn't come up to the standards he set in that regard. However, the day he took me aside and told me the two of us would be going on a mission together I realized he had decided to accept me, if only for my ability to speak French. Jim's knowledge of French, or any other foreign language for that matter, was rudimentary at best. I remember, though, his getting results with the ladies using the phrase, *"Voulez-vous promenade avec moi dans les buissons?"* I think it was the twinkle in his eyes that got results, not the words, which ought to have put any girl with sense off.

I knew that Jim must have approved of me or he would not have been told about the possible mission before I was. He was quite blunt about the circumstances surrounding our mission. He found out that one of his despised staff men, a full colonel, was supposed to have commanded the mission but had begged off for some obscure reason. It seemed that I outranked Jim by a month or two, having been promoted to first lieutenant just before we went overseas. As a result, I was to be in command, theoretically at least. I knew perfectly well that Jim would be the one calling the shots and that's the way it worked out, though we agreed in advance we'd be in joint command.

The mission, as first outlined to me by the briefing officer, was to parachute into occupied France in the northwest part of the Hérault department. The purpose of the mission was to establish and take over existing information networks in the area with a view to transmitting all available information regarding enemy force dispositions in the area, with particular emphasis on enemy defenses around the Port of Sète as well as the movements of the Eleventh Panzer Division. The Eleventh Panzer had the nickname, "The Ghost Division," and was scattered over a wide area of southern France, where it was resting and reorganizing after a severe mauling on the Russian front, where it had distinguished itself valiantly and acquired a formidable reputation. The briefing officer confirmed the rumors we had heard that there would be a southern France landing but said that the time and place had not yet been chosen and that the information we would gather and transmit would determine whether the landing would take place to the east or to the west of the Rhône River mouth.

Although Jim Russell was a competent radio operator and had "ham" experience, we were assigned two French radio operators, both non-coms, to free the two of us for action. Tall and lean, Julien had the rolling, heavily accented speech of the Toulouse area and the energetic cheerfulness of the Midi. Henri seemed more timid, though cheerful, and was short and pudgy. They were a sort of Mutt and Jeff team, but their role was invaluable.

A second aspect of our mission involved arming and training the local resistance and helping them in any action to impede German movements in the area. A concomitant of the latter aspect would be showing the presence of U.S. military personnel in the area which, it was presumed, would benefit the morale of local resistance groups.

With my agreement, it was decided to skip my jumping training. With time so short, it seemed illogical to risk injury in practice. The sort of jump we would be doing was relatively simple and straightforward and didn't require the skills inherent in jumping out a door with a stick of troops. We would be going out the round hole in the floor of a B-17 whose belly gun turret had been removed for the purpose. There would be two planes, each with a load of containers full of arms, ammunition, explosives, and our radio equipment. Jim and I would jump with our personal armament, map case, compass, and the precious crystals for the agent set which would be our contact with base. Different crystals were to be plugged in for transmission at different scheduled times, making it possible to avoid operating on a single wave length for very long. These transmission schedules were memorized by both of us.

I spent hours at a time at the safe house where we were isolated, memorizing the maps of the area of the drop as well as our contacts and all available information about the area. There had never been an allied mission there before and the nearest ones were some distance to the north in the Correze and to the west-southwest near Mazamet, with the famous *Corps Franc de la Montagne Noire*. It was not a place of strategic importance in itself and had little industrial base of any kind except for a marginal iron mine and ore processing plant. The country was essentially poor, rough, and sparsely populated by French standards. The rail line running down from the *Massif Central* to the north followed canyon beds along streambanks except where it tunneled from one drainage to another or passed through short tunnels making shortcuts through rock outcroppings. It might become important to German troop movement out of the south after a successful landing in southern France, though to rely on a line so easily cut would have been a foolhardy decision by any German commander and would likely be undertaken only under extreme circumstances.

Since I was forfeiting jump school, the briefing officer decided that I should participate in the last-minute preparations for several agent drops originating from Blida Airdrome in order to become familiar with the process. In each of these instances, the agents were not among those we had trained at the school. The organization involved with the last-minute processing and on-field briefing seemed most efficient, though I had reason to wonder later on just how efficient it really was.

I was impressed with the fact that one agent was a girl and another a one-armed man. What was done at the briefing hut at the airfield was really a checklist operation to see that nothing had been forgotten. The briefing officer was British and supervised the equipment of the joes to see that nothing went with them that could give them away, and also that nothing vital was overlooked. His crew was expert at exuding confidence and helping the agents on with their striptease suit, and warm rubber outer garment which covered their clothing, and the foam-rubber-lined helmet to protect their head and, then, their single, British-made parachute.

Having seen this last-minute preparation, I began to fret about how I was going to get away with bringing along my fly rod, reel, and box of flies. I had managed to keep them with me ever since I had become an officer, and I was damned if I was going to leave them behind. It might even be bad luck. Jim suggested I lie a little, and that's exactly what I decided to do.

9
Into Battle . . . Fly Rod in Hand

For me the tension was mounting by the moment. It was almost a relief when we were finally at the briefing hut checking equipment and being dressed and harnessed. When the British officer saw the fly rod in the cloth case he exclaimed, "I say. You can't take THAT with you, you know." To which I replied, "Oh, it's only a special antenna. Just looks like a fly rod."

"I say. THAT's clever!"

I was relieved. I had twenty feet of line in my map case to fasten to the end of the rod just before the jump so I could drop it and have it hanging from me when I hit the ground, to avoid the possibility of injuring myself with the rod. Of course, there was always the chance I might land on the rod and break it, but that was a risk I had to take. My reel, leader case, and fly box were in the map case as well.

Jim had rechecked the containers and the packages in which our radios and other gear were packed, and we were ready to go. A late addition to our party, who we were told would be dropped in another area after us, went in the first plane with Julien and Henri. Once he'd boarded, Jim and I got aboard and settled in a small space near the belly hatch. The containers were loaded in the bomb bays, but the smaller packages with our gear were in the hull of the plane, on the floor behind us. The section of flooring covering the hole through which we would exit the plane was in place to keep out the noise and the cold. Although it was August, the air at altitude was frigid.

As we crossed the Mediterranean, the dispatcher and his assistant brought us sandwiches and coffee. I wasn't hungry but the coffee tasted good. Jim said to eat. It might be a while before we got to again. I chewed and swallowed without tasting. Then the pilot came back and chatted for a bit, and I remember him pointing out the bright lights in the distance to our left. "Barcelona," he said. "No blackout." It struck me as strange that Spain, where it all started, was at peace.

We lapsed into silence, each with our own thoughts. As we came over land again we could feel the turbulence. Jim reminded me to be sure to keep my head up until the chute opened in order to avoid either knocking myself out against the edge of the hole on the way out or starting to tumble, which might cause my chute to malfunction.

It was considered very bad luck to wish anyone luck, so we followed the injunction all the French joes used, *"Mille fois merde!"* I managed a smile and the dispatcher removed the hatch cover and the two of them prepared the packages around the hole for the second pass, fastening each one's static line to D rings on the floor. I huddled out of the way and Jim stood above the hole watching for the signal fires and the code letter flashed by the head of the reception committee on the ground. Proper identification was imperative. There had been a number of incidents of jumps into false reception committees with tragic consequences.

Both the rush of air and the noise of the engines was deafening. The signal checked out to both the navigator's and Jim's satisfaction. We slowed and turned, dropping altitude. The second plane made its pass first to drop its containers and packages, then we followed as the dispatcher and his helper frantically shoved packages out. We could feel the plane jump as it lightened from the drop of containers from the bomb bays. We made a circle while the other plane made its second pass to drop Julien and Henri, then Jim and I sat on the edge of the hole with our legs hanging down, our feet just above the airstream, and our static lines fastened to the D rings.

I grasped my fly rod by the center in my right hand, prepared to bring it parallel to my rigid body as I readied myself to stand at attention going out the hole. The red light was on and I couldn't help tensing. It switched to green and the dispatcher hit Jim's shoulder and, as soon as he was out, mine, and I was gone.

Never have I felt a greater sense of jubilation. After a short moment of total disorientation, the chute had opened with a snap and I was alive in what seemed total silence as the sound of the engines faded away.

"God damn, that was great!" I shouted without thinking, only to be admonished with a "Shush!" from Jim.

We'd been dropped from way too high, about fourteen hundred feet above the DZ (drop zone), because the rough terrain had made the pilots nervous about going as low as they should have. For the moment it seemed wonderful to me but we would have to pay a price. Jim realized immediately that the wind was taking us away from the signal fires of the drop zone and he slipped away below me to try to land as close to them as possible. I followed as best I could but, suddenly, I was below the horizon and, an instant later, trying to fight the impulse to reach for the invisible ground with straight legs, the rod line went slack and I was tumbling through a thicket of bushes to the bottom of what proved to be a deep gulch. I had landed in France, whether safely or not remained to be seen.

I was unhurt, save for some bumping around on the rocks. Moreover, the rod was unbroken. After hiding the chute and striptease in some bushes and covering them with stones, I started climbing up the steep slope of the deep ravine. It was a hell of a climb, about three hundred feet through brush and thorn thickets to the crest of the ridge between me and the reception area. The night was moonless with a clear starlit sky, as planned. That was just as well because it was practically the only thing that did go according to plan.

When I finally made it to the reception area, after three bad spills coming down the hill from the ridge, Jim was there covering the reception committee with his Thompson submachine gun. I got everything sorted out quickly. It seemed the Frenchmen had not given any password, much less the right one, and since Jim's French was so limited he wasn't taking any chances. It turned out they hadn't received any information about a personnel drop and weren't expecting people, and certainly not Americans. Someone in Algiers had fouled up royally. They had been expecting a supply drop, nothing more.

They were, however, ecstatic that *les américains* had arrived; but first things first. We asked if they had seen Julien and Henri. They hadn't, so finding the joes and gathering up all the supply chutes before dawn became our first order of business. The maquisards had posted watchers on the ridges to mark the location of the falling chutes, but the country was so rough it was still a difficult and time-consuming operation. Although our personnel chutes were camouflage silk, the package and container chutes were bright and varicolored and would be spotted easily by the German observation planes that flew patrol over the area early each morning. Shortly after landing, we had heard small arms and machinegun fire in the distance; it turned out a German armored patrol was trying to wipe out an ill-conceived resistance effort at the ore refinery in Le Bousquet d'Orb. While that action had nothing to do with the *"parachutage,"* as it was called, discovery of chutes in the area would certainly bring a German attack force into the area. We found out later that the German retaliation at Le Bousquet had brought plenty of force with it.

The next news we heard was catastrophic. Both Julien and Henri were badly hurt in the jump. Little Henri had landed hard in a live oak tree, and the handle of his entrenching tool gouged out an eye. Julien had suffered a broken femur. Both required a doctor's help and would have to be treated by the local sawbones and hidden in the nearby town of Lunas. The nearest reliable doctor was in Le Bousquet and would have to be fetched.

The metal containers were scattered to hell and gone, and when each was recovered, men and oxen were needed to bring them back, though the first priority was still to get the bright parachutes out of sight. The latter task was completed, thankfully, before dawn, and about half the containers and all the packages were brought to the drop zone then loaded on an ox cart and trucked down a dirt track to an old, stone farmhouse where they were hidden under the hay. Jim and I, and our contact whom we called Robert, settled in a manger with a pile of hay in one corner and exchanged information. Robert had a bottle of rough country red and some *pays* cheese, the poor man's Roquefort, plus a half loaf of coarse country bread, which he shared with us. It tasted wonderful. . . .

There were many lulls during the mission to France. During one of them, Jack decided—perhaps unwisely—to do some fishing.—GN

I decided to explore the stream down in the valley below the settlement. I hadn't had a chance to put the rod to work yet, and this was my chance to fish in occupied France. Everyone was working at something, and I had nothing to do. It was about twelve hundred vertical feet down to the valley floor where the Verene, a small tributary of the Orb, flowed north to south in a deep canyon along a stretch of the rail line between tunnels. This area had never supported agriculture and, consequently, there were no ancient terraces along the valley walls as there were at Lunas. It was just rough country with steep pitches, broken by small, meadowed flats.

The surrounding country was solid limestone, and I had high hopes for the stream. Limestone means rich aquatic life and healthy, well-fed trout. I was in khaki, a civilian garb not uncommon at the time, but wore no cap and there was a U.S. flag sewn to my right shoulder, but no insignia on the left. I wore the shoulder holster and a .38 inside my OD shirt. I fastened the reel onto the rod butt, left the rod case behind, and stuck the fly box and leader damping case inside my shirt beneath the pistol. I allowed myself the whole day and started down toward the stream while it was still cool. I had barely broken a sweat by the time I got there. Nervous at first, I had finally been overcome by the joy of going fishing. Despite the incongruity of the circumstances, I broke into a wild, leaping run down the mountainside, totally oblivious to the risk to life and limb.

I didn't even bother to study the stream carefully as I should have but stepped right into the water, which, at low summer level, reached only to my knees at the deepest part of the run. The cold was at once shocking and delightful. I set up the rod and jam-knotted the leader on, fastening a wet leadwing coachman on the 3X tip. I had jumped into what was the best-looking water around and, of course, had completely ruined any chance at a trout, if such there were. The railway tracks were some forty yards away, above and to my left as I faced downstream. I started casting across, letting the fly swim down and across the current in classic wet-fly style. Nothing hit, but I saw fish below me dart away at my approach and knew they were trout by their speed and the manner of their movement. I had to be more cautious, get lower, and move more slowly, since the water was crystalline and the fish spooky.

I hunkered down and kept my casts horizontal, to fish out the tail of the pool where the water roughened a bit before leaving the pool for a short series of chutes down to the next deep water. I had become totally concentrated on thoroughly covering the last few yards of possible holding water when I heard a most unwelcome and frightening sound, that of marching boots close by. With the sound of the stream through the nearby riffles, I had been caught completely unaware. I looked up and, marching at route step with rifles and machine pistols at sling arms, was a patrol in German uniform. They were all looking toward me and making what sounded like derisive, joking comments as they went along.

For the first time in my life I made a silent wish that came as close to a real prayer as I had ever come. Above all, I wished not to hook a fish at that moment. If I had, the whole patrol would have halted to watch. Then there would have been conversation and, if I had turned to any degree, the U.S. flag would have been visible. The powers above were with me; I hooked nothing, and the Germans kept on marching down the track. I started to shake, but with far better reason than I had when I lost the big steelhead on the Pahsimeroi. I got the hell out of there and started the long climb back up the *causse*.

A few hundred feet up, at the first flat ground above the level of the tracks, I stopped and scanned the valley bottom. The foot patrol was out of sight around the bend, but I spotted a figure wading in the stream a quarter mile downstream. I watched curiously as he waded slowly upstream, stopping periodically to lean down and reach under stones, then put whatever he'd got into the willow creel hung over his shoulder. He was too far away for me to see exactly what he was doing, and it wasn't until I asked Robert about it that I found out what the fellow was doing. He was a professional trout fisherman who fished for the local inn at Avènes, which still served the occasional meal for a price. He walked slowly up the current of the long, shallow pools and spotted the surprised trout shooting off their feeding locations to hide under a rock. He then calmly approached the rock and put his hand in the water for a moment to let the water cool his skin then reached under the rock skillfully and grabbed the trout around the middle and lifted it, immobilized, into his creel. The manner of grabbing around the middle was obviously a much-practiced skill, but it seemed so deliberate it gave the impression of utter simplicity. The fisherman was well-known for his skills, and few others could come even close to filling a creel with lively trout for the trade as he could. I had heard about tickling trout before but had never thought it could be done in so seemingly easy a fashion.

The war news kept getting better. Apparently the landings on the south coast had been a huge success and the consequent rapid advance toward Toulon and Marseilles, and up the Rhône valley, was pulling all, or most, of the German forces out of southern and southwest France toward the northeast, to avoid entrapment. Paris had been liberated by the Allies, and German armies were in full retreat on every front.

We were still unable to get a message out and, by this time, must have been considered lost by our headquarters in Algiers. It seemed the best we could do now was to arm as many men as possible and try to prevent, or at least slow down, any attempt by German forces to evacuate through the area under our control. We decided to move down into Le Bousquet d'Orb where we could hear in advance of anything coming up the valley from Bédarieux or Lamalou toward us.

Jim, Robert, and I settled into an empty apartment above a corner pharmacy which gave us a good vantage point overlooking the southern approach into town, where the firefight had taken place on the night of our jump. We were invited to eat at the inn at Avènes, where there was a low weir across the Orb and some inviting weedy water where I caught several trout on dry flies. We ate crayfish *à l'américaine*, a great but messy delicacy, followed by trout doubtless caught by the hand fisherman. The old grandfather of the family was in the bedroom listening to the personal notices on the BBC and suddenly burst into the dining room with tears in his eyes, crying out, *"J'ai pleuré de joie! J'ai pleuré de joie!"* It was the personal message which meant that the following night there would be a parachute supply drop in our sector.

The *"parachutage"* turned into a great social occasion. Gone was any semblance of security, and the whole population of the valley seemed to know about it and had apparently turned out to help with the work. These people quite evidently felt that the war was over for them, what with the presence of Americans in uniform and the Germans not in evidence for some time. We had sentries posted all the way down the valley to warn of any danger. Even Jim let down his guard and there was quite a lot of wine consumed by all present, and the ladies were flirtatious. We kept our heads in that regard, however, because the worst possible thing we could do would be to fool around with some local girl and create internal problems with the resistance people. We would await a better chance somewhere else for any catting around.

Everything went off perfectly except that there was no message for us from base and no replacement radio. We came to the conclusion that they must have written us off completely.

The following night I was awakened by Robert shaking me. The guard had reported that an enemy column was headed up the valley and would reach the edge of town shortly. Our dispositions, in such an eventuality were already planned and we gave the necessary instructions. No one was to open fire until Jim and I did.

The point man in the German column carried a Schmeisser machine pistol at the ready and marched up the middle of the street until he was opposite Jim and me. We opened fire with our Thompson guns. He went down without firing a shot and the second man, fifty yards behind, threw down his weapon and put his hands in the air. Unexpectedly, there was no firing from below where the main body of the column should have been. It turned out there were only three men and they had been trying to bluff their way through by pretending to be the point scouts of a larger formation. Word sped to us that that was all there was, and our sentry had been carried away in his first report. We brought the wounded German into the pharmacy where he was made comfortable, though his wounds were in the gut and he had little chance of survival. Amazingly, no one had fired at the second and third men, who threw down their weapons and surrendered; they became our first prisoners and were put into the jail where they were the sole occupants. All were very young and I had fired my first shots in anger, and I didn't feel all that good about it. The wounded youngster died the next day.

By now we were known to all and sundry as the lieutenants Jimi and Jacques *le fou*. I had my first fly-caught trout in France, and on a dry at that. Robert was wild to engage the enemy and Jim was coming close to having a functioning transmitter. Robert had managed to requisition some gas at gunpoint somewhere and was in control of an *onze cheveaux traction avant*, the first Citroën with front-wheel drive. The FFI had commandeered one of these admirable vehicles before our arrival, but it had been shot up the night we landed and barely made it to Les Pascals farm before collapsing permanently. We had pushed it down into the ravine where it lies rusting to this day.

While we had no knowledge of other Allied missions in the area, it was common knowledge among the FFI that there were Americans with the Corps Franc de la Montagne Noire near Mazamet. Robert thought we might be able to contact them and perhaps solve our communications problem. Jim decided to stay at work on his set while Robert and I set off in the *traction avant* for a thriller-chiller of a ride down the valley through Bédarieux, Lamalou, and along the base of the Espinousse Mountains through St. Pons to Mazamet. The windshield was open, and I sat on the passenger side with the Thompson submachine gun sticking out the front. Robert drove like a madman and, luckily, we encountered nothing on the road until just outside St. Pons, where a German jeep with four men in it sat parked by the side of the road just as we came around a turn. Robert floored it and I let go a couple of bursts at the jeep and we went flying through the winding streets of the town and out the other side with no pursuit behind us.

We made it all the way into the town square at Mazamet without further incident. Robert may have been wild but he was good, and the *traction avant* really held the road well on the curves, though it had a distressing tendency for the rear end to drift, which I wasn't used to, and that action scared the hell out of me.

Mazamet was celebrating its official liberation, and the square was crowded with people yelling, laughing, and drinking. We stopped the car and put it under guard at the city hall and went in. The mayor and the local resistance chiefs greeted us but told us the Americans had left. We'd missed them. With little hesitation, we circled around the square and headed back the way we'd come and, this time, encountered nothing at all. At Mazamet, we had heard that the Germans were still around Montpellier, and we decided to head down there with two cars armed and see if we could help. This time Jim didn't want to miss out on the action so he came along.

Robert drove the lead car filled with armed men and Jim drove the second car with me at the gun beside him. Three of our guys were crowded in the rear. Jim couldn't believe what Robert was doing in the front vehicle: we barely managed to keep within sight. We headed toward Béziers and cut across the back roads to Pézenas, where the people told us the Germans had all pulled out toward Montpellier. So we drove along the road to the coast, where we saw the hillock of Sete across the lagoon, then drove along back roads inland parallel to the national highway number 115 until we were approaching a crossroads just outside Montpellier.

There was a new burned-out panther tank in the crossroads, and small arms fire coming from close by. We conferred and decided to bypass to another entrance to the city which Robert said he knew. We ended up following a maze of small streets all the way to the central square, where we were told the German forces were evacuating to the northeast and only fighting rear guard actions to protect their convoy. At that point we realized we were out of our league and called a halt. People were just starting to come out of their houses, aware that the hated occupiers were indeed gone. Spirits soared with every hour that there was no sign of a return by the Germans.

Since it was late, we decided to spend the night at Montpellier. Everyone was on his own and we agreed to meet in the square the following morning. Robert stashed the cars with a cousin then joined the celebration. There was no danger of any problem with the local populace. We joined the throng and were soon accompanied happily by some very attractive local ladies and, since the mood was one of such complete abandon, we just allowed matters to take their own appointed course.

The next morning, badly hungover, our little group joined forces in the square where we satisfied our need for a hair of the dog that bit us. We sat at an outdoor café watching the crowds when, suddenly, a great cheer went up. We heard the roar of tank engines, then watched as the lead elements of the French Armored Division clattered heavily into the city with General De Lattre de Tassigny in the lead tank waving to the multitudes and being cheered in return. It was a historic occasion I would recall with some amusement several years later when attending a diplomatic reception in Washington, D.C. A young Frenchman told me about being an aide to De Lattre and when I questioned him about what battles or campaigns he'd participated in he told me about the battle of Montpellier. I was unable to refrain from laughing as I told him of having been sitting in the place when he arrived. It did not amuse him, I'm afraid.

Without further ado, we headed home to Le Bousquet, where Jim finally got his jerry-rigged radio to function with our crystals. Transmitting at one of the scheduled times, he actually made contact with Algiers. We were told to stand by, and after a long wait, we received a message of congratulations on our survival and were ordered to proceed forthwith to Headquarters SSS (Strategic Services Section) Seventh Army, at the beachhead at St. Maxime.

10
Wounded and Captured

O
n the 28th of October 1944, Captain Justin Greene, who commanded the OSS team with the Thirty-sixth Infantry Division on our northern flank, had a problem. He needed to put an agent in the field in an area which was on the very edge of the Third Division sector. The location was important because there was a house that he had used in the past for a letter drop. It was a place where he could pick up important information and, at the same time, be assured of help for the agent he needed to infiltrate. Because of some slight readjustment in the division sectors, it appeared that the exact location, or the best approach to the house, was through the northern edge of Third Division's sector.

I was pleased to give any assistance I could and went over the operations map very carefully with Greene to try to find the best possible route. We drove north along the west bank of the Moselle River to Poueux Fort d'Arches, where we crossed and headed northeast on Departmental Highway D44 to Bruyères. On the way, we saw considerable air support activity from P-47s dropping bombs along the horizon ahead of us in support of a U.S. attack through the *Forèt de*

Champs toward St. Dié. We could hear the bombs over the noise of the jeep and see the dark smoke rising from the explosions. Everything to the right of the road was Third Division territory; to the left was Thirty-sixth Division's.

Bruyères is a fair-sized old town in rolling foothill country not nearly as precipitous as the mountains east of Remiremont. Units of the Thirty-sixth Division were in the town but just east of it and to the north were Third Division troops. I believe we made our first mistake at that juncture. We did not check in with either battalion or regiment but just asked any troop commander on the spot what his assessment of the situation was. Granted, it would have been awkward to make a long detour to observe the rules, but it might have been well worthwhile.

At any rate, we tried several approaches before ending up in a small valley where a Third Division aid station was receiving a large number of fresh casualties from a firefight a few hundred meters up a gully behind Belmont-sur-Buffant, a tiny hamlet on the edge of the forest. The officer there told us that the troops on his left flank had advanced much farther and that we could go that way without encountering resistance. We climbed over a high hump of open wooded hillside until we were suddenly right in the middle of a forward platoon of Nisei from the 442nd regimental combat team which was attached to the Thirty-sixth Division.

As I remember it, we tried to question them about the situation ahead and the ones we questioned, who were regular GIs, couldn't tell us anything. Again, we didn't take the time to check with their commander or higher headquarters, but now that we were definitely in Thirty-sixth Division territory, I was just along for the ride. Any purpose I could have served from that point on was clearly ended. The French joe who was with us never spoke a word and was clearly spooked.

We were now on the forward slope of the hill and could see that there was a long, narrow clearing in the hollow ahead and to the left of us. The place we were trying to reach was called Grébéfosse, another cluster of three or four houses a few hundred meters up the hollow from the *Commune de Bois de Champs*, which was not much bigger. The people who lived here were woodcutters whose families kept a small kitchen garden and a few chickens. Justin said he was fairly certain this was the spot and that the letter-drop farmhouse would be just a little farther down the hollow to the left.

We stayed in the woods going to the left around a turn until we suddenly saw an American light tank hunkered down on the opposite side of the clearing. The big gun was facing left, positioned on a track running along the bottom of the opposite wooded hillside. Justin wanted the joe to cross over and, using the tank for cover, to proceed along the track to the left for another hundred meters until he came to Grébéfosse. The letter-drop house, he said, lay back in a little cul-de-sac at the bottom of the opposite hillside. We held a whispered conference with him, and the joe refused to go on alone. Justin then asked me what I thought we could do, since his man wouldn't go on alone. Like a damn fool, I went along with the suggestion that we take him ourselves. With the tank there covering our approach, the path looked clear.

Justin hid something under some tree roots—which he later told me was incriminating stuff—and then we edged to a point just opposite the tank, and all three ran across the thirty-five or so yards of open ground into the shadow of the rear of the tank. The joe and I stayed hidden there for a minute while Justin climbed straight up into the woods above us where he thought he heard some voices. Meanwhile, a closer look at the rear of the tank revealed a clean two-inch hole made by a Panzerfaust anti-tank shape-charge grenade. The tank was dead. We should have been suspicious that it had remained in position so long without even moving its turret, but by that time Justin had stepped right into a hornet's nest and awakened the hornets.

It was hard to believe, but there was a whole unit of *Alpin-jaeger* mountain troops digging positions along a sunken road about six or seven yards up the slope in the thick forest and, experienced though they were, they had not posted sentries and had not even noticed us crossing the open ground. Justin reacted as quickly as if he'd stepped on a snake and came crashing back down the slope with small arms fire popping all around him. The joe panicked and broke for the other side of the tank only to have a grenade explode right in front of him, tearing out his guts. I hit the ditch at the foot of the slope and scrunched down as small as I could get while Justin went down, followed by more grenade explosions and small arms fire.

Two soldiers came down, and I tried to open fire with my M3 submachine gun but was hit immediately by a single round from above. I let out a cry and tried to hide in the ditch again. Within seconds someone above me fired several more times, hitting me in the right arm and shoulder each time. I felt no pain but was conscious of being sprayed with grenade fragments along the right side. My right arm and shoulder were the only parts exposed to the firing from above. At that point I figured there wasn't a whole hell of a lot that could be done to save this situation and joined Justin in crying out, *"Kamerade!"* German for, "I surrender, dear!"

We were both disarmed and helped up to the road where, dazed, we were given rudimentary first aid. I remember the aid man cutting off the right sleeve of my tanker jacket and emptying it of at least a pint of jello-textured blood, then applying several large patches of bandage, which he wrapped with a long, wide strip of gauze. They injected us with the morphine ampules from our own first aid pouches to relieve the pain which still hadn't cut through the shock. One of the men laughed and pointed at a new type of carbine they had been using, and kept repeating, *"Schiessen, Schiessen,"* over and over again, pointing first to the carbine and then to my wounds. Justin had been hit in the foot and they had his boot off with some difficulty and, though it bled almost not at all, you could see bone. He had also had a bullet hit his helmet and follow the helmet liner before exiting without so much as scratching him. Then they blindfolded us and half led, half dragged us to their company CP which, Justin told me later when we could talk, was the very house we had been trying to get to.

The fatally wounded joe was brought in, too, and I could hear him groaning outside in the hall where he died within the hour. Justin and I were taken right into the room where the company commander, an *Oberleutnant,* was seated at a table. I was having a hard time staying alert because of blood loss, but I heard him questioning Justin through an interpreter and Justin's explanation seemed to be something about our being with a French guide who was taking us to catch a Frenchman who was collaborating with the Germans. I was wearing my military police insignia, so the story made some sense and appeared to pass muster with the officer. Then Justin was taken into a bedroom, and I was seated before the *Oberleutnant*.

Through the interpreter, he asked my name, rank, and serial number, which I gave him. He looked at me quizzically and asked to see my dog tags. I pulled them out with my good left hand, and he read them carefully and asked in German if I spoke German. I answered, *"Nein."*

He then asked in French if I spoke French, to which I replied in the affirmative. Then, in French, he asked if I had ever been in Schruns.

I answered that I had, long ago as a child. He asked me the name of my nurse. I told him she was called Tiddy. He broke into a broad grin and said in French, "We drink a toast to Tiddy. She is my girlfriend!"

11
A Prisoner
of War

There were no organized prisoner activities in the camp. There was insufficient food. Red Cross parcels were seen arriving but were never distributed. There was no fuel for the single stove in each of the leaky wooden barracks. The straw-filled ticks on the wooden slats of the triple-decker bunks were filthy and lousy and were never changed. Officers were filthy and unshaved, and no shaving gear of any kind was made available. Between the two roll calls each day, prisoners spent the whole day in their bunks trying to keep warm with thin blankets and suffering through their private thoughts. I believe I saw one book the whole time at Hammelburg, but much later. The only reading material when we arrived consisted of OKW *(Oberkommando die Wehrmacht)*, bulletins recounting the glorious German victories as the Nazis continued to consolidate their fronts, and an occasional copy of a German publication much like *Life* magazine.

A "man of confidence" represented each barracks. Ours was a chaplain from the 106th. It did little for our religious zeal when we caught him stealing food for himself from the common supply, which it was his duty to pick up and distribute to the men in the barracks. At that point, he lost his job and was ostracized. For a time at Ludwigsburg, when Justin was very ill, I had been senior American officer and, as such, had been requested by a French army priest to perform certain functions in his stead in the likely event of one young American Catholic boy dying before the priest's next visit. He instructed me and, understanding that my faith was not deep, he confided that if I made a sincere effort the effect would be the same. The young soldier, having been assured by the priest that I was okay, didn't mind.

If one spends a lot of time alone with one's thoughts during a prolonged period of cold and hunger, thought patterns can be very revealing. At one point I dreamed of a small paradise on earth that I had seen once with Papa. It was down in the Snake River canyon close to Twin Falls, Idaho, and had bountiful clear-flowing springs alive with trout and cress beds and was surrounded by the high black lava walls and the dry desert. He and Gary Cooper were planning to buy this place, and I visualized myself as the permanent guardian of this paradise. I think everyone dreamed of a somewhere that would never be short of food. Strangely, the lack of food took such high precedence that sexual thoughts, even if deliberately entertained, simply had no substance. The planning of menus was a much more popular pastime.

Many things about this period are not at all clear in my memory, though I do remember one incident which I found frightening. One day after morning roll call formation, my name was blared out on the loudspeaker with the order to report to the *Oberleutnant* who called roll each day. As I crossed the parade ground I remembered, with some trepidation, the comments my father had written in *Men at War* suggesting that SS officers should be castrated.

I felt some relief in noting that this was not an SS man, but I was nervous nonetheless and would have preferred total anonymity. The *Oberleutnant* was a well-fed, clerkish-looking fellow who wore Himmler-style pince-nez glasses. I reported properly and was told, in perfect English, to stand at ease. He hesitated, then asked if I were by any chance related to the writer Ernest Hemingway. I acknowledged that I was, upon which he went on to tell me that he was a great admirer of my father's work and had taught about his writing as a university lecturer in American literature. He smiled broadly, shook my hand, and that was that.

An incident occurred later which profoundly affected everyone in the camp. The German commandant, a colonel *(Oberst)*, made the announcement at roll-call that, henceforth, a new set of rules was going into effect. Previously, no one had been permitted to leave the barracks to go to the latrine during the air raid alarms, which could often last a long time. It had been decided, the *Oberst* told us, that in the interest of sanitation one man at a time could go from the barracks to the latrine during the *Voralarm*, but if the full alarm should sound while in the latrine he would have to remain there until the all-clear was sounded. That was good news. The only problem was that the *Oberst* hadn't bothered to inform the guards.

That night there was a *Voralarm* about eleven o'clock. Several guys leaped from their beds and headed for the latrine, each trying to be first since only one could go at a time. In fact they all had to stop since an officer from another barracks had beat them to it. But, suddenly, a long burst of machinegun fire shattered the night. We crowded around the door to see what had happened; a body lay crumpled twenty feet from the latrine building. There was shouting and anger throughout the camp, but we had to wait for the all-clear before recovering the body. The young man we discovered there was a lieutenant, and lawyer in civilian life, who had been well liked by all who knew him.

We were permitted to hold a funeral procession through the compound. During the procession, a platoon of German officer candidates marched by on the outside of the fence singing the Horst Wessel song in their full, proud Germanic voices. I believe every man in that compound felt hatred stirring in his guts. There was never any apology for the "incident," only the cursory explanation that there had been a "misunderstanding."

It was early March before there was a real change for the better. It came about as the result of the arrival of a large contingent of prisoners from the East: American officers of mixed branches who had been captured earlier on and been sent to the Offlag at Schuben, Poland. They arrived after a long march of hundreds of kilometers across central Germany brought about by the evacuation of their camp before the Russian advance. In this latter stage of the war, the value of American prisoners as bargaining chips was increasing daily.

Pop Goode, Colonel, U.S. Army, had commanded an infantry regiment of the First Infantry Division in Normandy. He had been assigned to the division before the Normandy landings straight from Camp Hale, Colorado, where he was a regimental commander in the Tenth Mountain Division before the unit was shipped out to Italy. At the time, he claimed to be the senior colonel in the U.S. Army, and I'll tell you he was some kind of fine soldier. His capture in Normandy may have hurt his career chances, but we all soon became grateful he was among us. Within twenty-four hours of his arrival, the American officers' compound underwent a total change. The way I heard it from one of his staff, Pop Goode reported to the camp commandant and faced him down, refusing to accept any order from him since the Commandant was junior in date-of-rank. He demanded and got all the items necessary to clean house: razor blades, distribution of Red Cross parcels, coal for the stoves in the barracks, a new commandant, this time a brigadier general, all within a week.

Suddenly we all ceased being slovenly, despairing, and dejected. Leadership made all the difference. Classes were organized, some of them serving as cover for committees on subjects from weapons procurement to escape. Hope made its appearance, and soon even the weather started showing signs of improvement.

Col. Goode's executive officer in the camp was Lt. Col. John Waters, who happened to be General George Patton's son-in-law. He had been taken prisoner during the North African campaign in Tunisia, foreshortening what would doubtless have been a brilliant military career. A fine-looking, soldierly officer, his flair helped bring a quick resolution to a tricky situation during the event of our first, but false, liberation.

The incident took place in the early afternoon of a spring day in late March. It was the first in a rapidly unfolding series of events which are still nightmarish in retrospect, over forty years later. We had been hearing the distant thunder of artillery fire for several days, but on this day it seemed to be getting closer. Beyond the wire on our side of the camp, we could see a partially cleared hillside on the edge of the woods. Farther to the right, where the Serbian general staff was quartered with most of its entire officer corps, were the administrative buildings of the POW complex. A dramatic increase in the noise, and the clank of armored vehicles approaching, drew many of us to the wire facing the clearing on the hillside. We could see a haystack on the hill, which burst suddenly into flames, and the sound of 50-caliber machine guns and 20mm cannon fire rent the air as the horizon was filled with the dark shapes of American light tanks, half-tracks, and tank destroyers.

The U.S. Army had arrived, or so we thought. The guards all disappeared from the towers and their walking posts. Word reached us to get inside and down under the bunks, which we did immediately. The camp commandant apparently was prepared to turn over the camp to Col. Goode but, as I heard it afterward, another German unit housed at the camp refused to go along. Lt. Col. Waters was wounded trying to assure the turnover of the camp without unnecessary casualties or bloodshed. The U.S. forces held back while the Germans withdrew and then came roaring to the edge of the camp, several tanks penetrating the wire by the simple expedient of driving their tanks through it.

Next we were ordered to assemble and Col. Goode explained to us the risks involved in trying to make it out with the armored task force. It seems the armored unit had blasted its way fifty miles behind enemy lines in a planned breakthrough with the express purpose of liberating the U.S. officers in the camp. The problem was, their intelligence reports had been mistaken, and there were ten times the number of prisoners they had expected. There was a total of only twenty-three vehicles in the task force, over half of which were lightly armored half-tracks intended to carry out POWs. They had taken casualties in several firefights during the day and had managed to reach Hammelburg only because of the close fighter support, which would not be available if the evacuation continued into the hours of darkness. Furthermore, their last functioning radio to call for tactical air support had been knocked out.

The time lost by the confusion and the unexpected numbers at the camp delayed the departure sufficiently to make a return to Allied territory the same day impossible, especially now that the element of surprise was no longer in their favor. By now, German forces were fully alerted to the armored incursion and would be mounting an organized counterattack.

Even though all of this wasn't spelled out at the time, we knew that the odds were poor for those who chose to go with the armored column, and Col. Goode gave us the choice. The result was that everyone who felt up to it boarded the half-tracks, and others, including me, crawled up on the tanks, hanging on wherever we could. Even Justin Greene, with his bad foot, got aboard one of the tanks.

It was already almost dusk when the task force leader gave the signal to start back. He had selected a different route than they had followed to Hammelburg; unfortunately, that route turned out to be through an area used by the German Army for maneuvers and artillery practice. They knew it, literally, as well as their own backyards.

As we started out, the atmosphere was one of great exuberance. Everyone thought the war was finally over for them. Some of the tankers had liberated some hooch, giving some to the prisoners. You can imagine the effect: noise, cheering, pandemonium where there should have been discipline, silence, and attention. Ray Saigh and Dewey Stuart had come to Hammelburg, and I was with them behind the turret of the lead tank.

The first attack hit us just as darkness settled over the area. We were moving along a narrow defile beside a hedgerow. The hedgerow concealed a platoon of attackers who fired several *Panzerfaus* projectiles at the tanks. This German version of the bazooka was a one-shot, hand-held shape-charge, which had to be loosed at its target from close range to be effective. The hedgerow was hardly three yards from our vehicles, plenty close enough, and the first hits threw us rudely off the tanks. The tracks on the lead tank were blown away and we clambered aboard another tank, just barely hanging on as it worked its way around the first tank and the armored infantrymen cleared the hedgerow with automatic weapons. By midnight there had been several more attacks of the same nature, and the column had made precious little progress when the commander decided to halt for the night and set up a defensive position and await the return of close air support at dawn.

The area where we set up was in rolling country with scrub woods, where the road wound in a horseshoe deep into the fold of a hill. I had become separated from my friends during the shuffling; everyone was either asleep in the vehicles or camped on the ground nearby. Sentries had been posted on all sides.

Another fellow and I decided it wasn't a healthy spot and, about an hour before dawn, we decided to part company with the column and try to make it across country on our own. We reported our intentions to the commander, who did not try to discourage us. We then started up through the woods toward the top of the hill where we felt we could see what went on and case the country ahead to the west where eventual safety lay.

It turned out we weren't the only ones with the same idea, and we ran into some other prisoners on the way. We must have been a half mile away from the column when it became light enough to see the column in the fold of the hill stretched out like a snake that had been cut into pieces. Within minutes we heard the ominous roar of heavy tanks and the clangor heightened sharply as, one after another, six Tiger tanks appeared around the bend in the road from a distant hill. It was too late for the column to take defensive action, and they were fired upon by the overwhelmingly superior guns of the Tigers.

The sound was deafening and most of the vehicles of the column, tanks as well as half-tracks, were totally demolished within minutes. We heard later that casualties were not so heavy as it appeared from our vantage point. The survivors dispersed, and we headed out as quickly as we could to avoid the inevitable roundup by German infantry.

Our main priority was to stay as far away from other prisoners as possible, so long as we were headed in the right general direction. I don't remember clearly just how long we were out there, but I believe it was two days, possibly more. We had eaten the K rations our would-be liberators had given us and I remember, at one point, coming to a small house in the woods with a kitchen garden. The proprietors had heard something and panicked, leaving unfinished food on the table.

Another time, we sneaked by a farm and liberated a white Angora rabbit from a hutch, wrung its neck and, totally famished, tore off the skin and ate it raw. Several times we dug out rutabagas from the earth-covered piles where they were stored.

When we were finally caught, it was one of the most frightening moments of my life. Famished, thirsty, cold, and stiff, we were starting out one morning when we were taken completely by surprise by a patrol made up of young boys in uniform, armed with side daggers and an assortment of weapons, including one Schmeisser machine pistol. The problem was that they were as frightened as we were. We were obviously unarmed, but we must have looked pretty desperate to them. The boy with the Schmeisser was visibly trembling and his finger was on the trigger with the weapon pointed at my belly.

The Schmeisser has a rate-of-fire of about twelve hundred rounds per minute and, while it is hard to hold on target for a long burst, it can do stitches on you mighty fast. There was total silence, and I could sense the wheels turning in their little heads. I spoke as softly as I have ever spoken, and as slowly, hands in the air, *"Bitte, kanne wir sprechen mit ein unter Offizier?"* Lousy German, but slow and clear. The kid with the Schmeisser stopped trembling and yelled in a squeaky voice to one of his buddies to go get the *Feldwebel*. Within a very short time, the bad moment was over and we were once again guests of the Third Reich.

IV

AFTER THE WAR

12
Civilian
Doldrums

I don't remember just how we met, but Peter Auer was a young man with the same fishing hunger that I had and, furthermore, he had ideas. A Marine Corps veteran, he was a native San Franciscan who had a small back-alley apartment on Telegraph Hill, which he rented from his family for next to nothing. He was married, but not happily, and he wanted to get out of his store job with Roos Brothers, even though his job was at least in the fishing tackle department. He knew all the fly shops in town and had a wide acquaintance with sportsmen in the whole area through mutual interests and through his job. He thought that we could make a go of it tying trout flies for a living and selling them to the stores in the area, trying to build up our custom business over a period of time. The good money was, of course, in the custom work because the markups are high, and the price you could get from the stores was painfully low considering the time, skill, and effort involved in making flies of high quality.

I made the break with the City of Paris and, early that summer, with a small grubstake from Pauline, Peter Auer and I started our new partnership, Auer and Hemingway Flies. It was a crazy business which operated from his apartment. I had to leave periodically when his wife was out so he could have a rendezvous with his girlfriend. Going out meant going down the street to the Black Cat, a precursor of the many gay bars that now bedeck the area. My awareness of such things was not particularly well-developed at the time, and it was some time before I caught on to the nature of the establishment. A friend of Pete's ran the place and they served great, thick, roast beef sandwiches between slices of sourdough French bread for next to nothing if you had a beer as well. When the bar was crowded you might have to put up with a little good-natured pawing, but mostly these people sensed where your interests lay and left you alone if you weren't interested in doing what they were interested in doing. Amusingly, one of the people I ran into there was Freddy, the black corporal from the 780th MP Battalion who had been to Oxford. He was temporarily between jobs as a movie actor.

Pete and I went fishing often, far too often for the business to become successful, as it turned out. Once, we went up to Fall River, a beautiful spring-fed stream, which I desecrated with my spinning outfit. Another time, Pete, his girlfriend, and I took the bus up to St. Helena to fish a spot he knew in the upper Putah Creek Canyon called Hell's Half Acre. There was a pretty blonde girl on the bus who knew Pete and, first thing we knew, she was coming with us instead of going to spend the weekend in Little Switzerland, a resort on Clear Lake farther north, even though it was made eminently clear to her that we would all be camping out together. She turned out to be a free spirit and was good company, though she hadn't the slightest interest in fishing. Pete and I fished to our hearts' content, catching lively small-mouth bass in every pool, both spinning and fly fishing with streamers.

It didn't take long to find out where my blonde's interests lay. The location in the bake-oven-hot canyon called for frequent cooling swims, and it turned out, of course, that none of us had brought swimming suits. None were needed, and the nearest other humans were miles away, across one of the most desolate pieces of country I had ever seen. The situation with Puck was uncertain and, in any case, it would likely be several months before I saw her again, and then only if I were lucky. Anyway, you know how it is, kids will be kids.

The fly-tying business was certainly going better than we had expected, and a new wrinkle came along in the form of some new steelhead fly patterns that Peter Schwab developed and wrote about in one of the outdoor magazines. The new tie attracted a lot of attention in the West Coast fishing fraternity. It was essentially a bucktail, but was tied with a copper, brass, or silver wire body both for the flash it provided and for the evenly distributed extra weight, which helped get the flies down to the level where steelhead were then thought to prefer having their meals presented to them. Actually, late in the season when the water becomes very cold and the fish less active, chances are better when you can put a fly right in front of their noses. At any rate, those flies became a very hot item and, since they were difficult to tie well, and most people didn't know where to get the right wire, we did quite well selling them on special order for a dollar apiece, and we could each turn out about six to eight an hour. For us, this was big money. The only catch was that it was a flash in the pan and didn't last.

What finally made the fly-tying business lose its allure for both of us was an order we received through an orthodontist in Twin Falls, Dr. George Grover, a fanatic fly fisherman who practiced in San Francisco and had given us some special-order business. His brother owned a chain of drugstores scattered through the Sierras, and George prevailed on him to give us all his fly business. The price was more than fair, but the problem was that the order was so large and the diversity of flies so small (100 gross of only three patterns in two sizes) that we almost died of the utter boredom which set in. In addition, the time by which they had to be delivered was so short we found ourselves tying twenty hours a day without ceasing. Our backs and eyes were giving us fits, and our mental attitude deteriorated by the day. Friends would come in bringing cases of beer and would party all around us while we slaved away.

Puck was at last assigned to San Francisco and had a new roommate, Cappy Jones, to share an apartment up on Sacramento Street. I hardly had a chance to see her during this period. By the deadline for delivery of the flies, we were able to deliver only about three-quarters of the order, but we were paid for it, and we continued to operate but our hearts were no longer really in it. We found out what can happen when you try to earn your living doing something you truly enjoy for its own sake but have to compromise your values in doing it. Our total earnings from the giant order had been around eight to nine hundred dollars apiece, and we had taken two months to earn it. Meanwhile, we had lost a lot of the custom business, which was the most lucrative and interesting. I could see that the best way to be in the fly-tying business would have been to have others tying for you in a situation which would allow you have real quality control. Anyone doing so should have gone through something like we did just to learn materials and the true differences between a well-made fly and a piece of junk, just so he could then teach and supervise others.

Jack "Bumby" Hemingway, age four or five.

Bumby with Papa and mother Hadley.

Jack and Papa aboard the Pilar, *c. 1935.*

The Hemingway sons—Jack, Patrick, and Gregory (from left).

A handsome young boy.

Big brother Jack with Patrick (left) and Gregory (right).

A quiet moment alone.

Even in his youth, Jack enjoyed the solitude of the great outdoors.

Jack with a couple of good catches.

The Hemingway men
Patrick, Jack, Papa, and Greg (from left).

Jack looking dashing in his World War II army uniform.

Jack and his daughter Margaux fishing in Argentina.

Jack and Angela at the White House with President George Bush
accepting a bronze bust of Ernest Hemingway, July 1989.

Jack and Margaux biking in Sun Valley with Partridge.

Jack and Angela's wedding day
August 5, 1989—Sun Valley, Idaho, with Mariel, Muffet, and Margaux
at Borden Stevenson's home, (Adlai Stevenson's son).

Angela and Jack in Paris
October 1989
Start of our six-month honeymoon, where we visited Paris,
Germany, Venice, Spain, and England.

April 1989, Honeymoon, Key West, Florida
Ernest Hemingway House
If it seems strange to have two honeymoons, it's because we were
married twice, April 29 and August 5, 1989. Jack was afraid
I would change my mind if we waited until the August date.

Bonasa Breaks Ranch, our fishing and shooting retreat, Washington State.
Shooting pheasants with Partridge.

.   Bonasa Breaks cabin with Partridge, Basa,
Brittany (spaniel), and Gordon (setter).

Fishing in Norway on the Aa River, 1989. Jack's 45 lb. salmon, river record that year.

Fishing in Norway, 1989. Angela's first Atlantic salmon on the Aa River. 14 lbs.

Another catch. Snake River in Idaho, 1996.

Fishing in Iceland, 1997, at Laxa i Leirarsveit. This was the day the fish "followed" me around.

Jack and Angela fishing on Silver Creek in Idaho, 1998.
This was a creek Jack helped to preserve.

Angela with Basa after fishing on Silver Creek, 1998. (Courtesy of Steve Smith.)

Count Tolstoi (son of Leo Tolstoi), grandson Sacha, and Jack, Paris, 1995.

Jack and Angela in Iceland, 1999. (Photo by Bruce McNae.)

A typical day or evening with Jack tying flies.

Jack and Angela at Hemingway Bar at the Ritz, Paris, France, 1995.

Jack's 75th birthday celebration, 1998, Sun Valley, Idaho, held at Ernest Hemingway's former home, Ketchum, Idaho. Edwina Hemingway (her father Patrick, his wife, Carol), Jack, Angela, Gregory and his wife, Ida. (Photo by Martha Vanegas-Barrand.)

Sons of Ernest Hemingway, Patrick, Jack, and Gregory. (Photo by Martha Vanegas-Barrand.)

Jack with Sacha Tolstoi and fellow anglers.

Yvon Chouinard (owner of Patagonia), and Tom Brokaw, Russia, June 1996, on Kachkovka River.

Jack's 75th birthday celebration, 1998, Sun Valley, Idaho.
Jack's grandchildren, Langley and Dree. Held at Ernest
Hemingway's former home, Ketchum, Idaho.

Jack's 75th birthday celebration, 1998, Sun Valley, Idaho.

Jack's 75th birthday celebration, 1998, Sun Valley, Idaho.
Jack's grandchildren Langley and Dree and daughter Mariel. Held at
Ernest Hemingway's former home, Ketchum, Idaho.
(Photo by Martha Vanegas-Barrand.)

Ritz Hotel in Paris, France, 1999, celebrating Ernest Hemingway's
100th birthday. Reenactment of "liberating" the hotel after World War II
with Head Bartender Colin at the Hemingway Bar at the Ritz.

Home in Sun Valley with friends Albert Finney and Mickey and Karen Taylor.

Pictured are Caroline Kennedy, Jack, Angela, Patrick and Carol Hemingway. Recreation of the Nobel Prize winners' dinner, Saturday, April 29, 1962. This evening at the Kennedy Library on April 10, 1999, is celebrating Ernest Hemingway's centennial birthday. (Photo by Allan Goodrich, John F. Kennedy Library.)

Jack and Charlton Heston, judges at the Best of Bad Hemingway Competition in 1994, Los Angeles, California.

Jack with fellow judges Charlton Heston and Ray Bradbury.

A very happy fisherman.

Four happy fishermen, together in Iceland on Laxa i Kjos. Pictured are Orri Vigfusson, Uffe Ellemann-Jensen, Jack, and Bruce McNae.

Jack with a good cast.

Gray Ranch, 1996, in Arizona, with Averell Harriman Fisk (Averell Harriman's grandson), Drum Hadley, and man's best friends, Basa, Partridge, and Nickie.

*Pheasant shooting in
Montana, 1990.*

*Fishing in Iceland at
Laxa i Leirarsveit.*

Jack with Basa after fishing on Silver Creek, Idaho, 1998. (Photo courtesy of Steve Smith.)

Jack and Basa relaxing after a great day for birds.

Jack on another of his annual trips to Iceland.
Here he is at Laxa i Leirarsveit.

Jack once again in
Iceland, this time on
Laxa i Kjos.

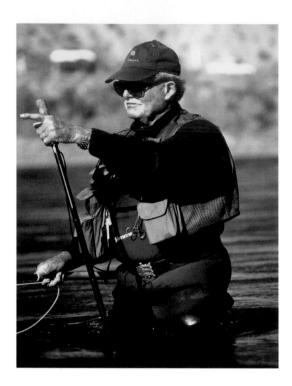

Jack looking right at home in the water.

London, England, 1994, at the apartment of Martha Gellhorn (third wife of Ernest). Jack had a lifelong friendship with her that lasted long after she divorced his father.

Fishing in Chile on the Argentine border at Tierra Del Fuego, 1996.

All dressed up for a pheasant shoot at Kelling Hall in Kelling Holt, Norfolk, England, 1999.

Kelling Hall in Kelling Holt, Norfolk, England. Shooting pheasant at Jim and Shirley Deterding's estate, 1999.

London, England, 1998. Party for His Royal Highness the Duke of Kent. (The Duke and Jack were having a bit of fun.)

Jack and Angela at the Hemingway Bar at the Hotel Ritz in Paris, France.

A good picture of Papa, Hemingway Bar in Paris.

*Jack and I fishing on Silver Creek, Idaho, 1998. Jack is giving
me one of his secret flies. (Photo courtesy of Steve Smith.)*

13
A Second Hitch

I t was now the fall of 1948 and so far I had met only dismal failure in everything I had set out to do since the end of the war. I had found the right girl, but I hadn't been able to find the right means to support her in the style to which I would have liked her to become accustomed. Further, I had already used up a lot of credit with my father, and I was sure that he, too, was disappointed in me. First for failing to complete my education, and then for not sticking to any of the various projects he had helped line up for me. I was determined now to make my own way without help and to achieve my primary goal: making a living in a satisfying way and being able to support a wife and family while so doing. Just about the only thing for which I could give myself any credit was that I continued to be a perennial optimist and so remained cheerful despite circumstances that seemed to forebode a gloomy future.

Geographically, the two parts of the world that stirred by imagination were the mountain West in the U.S.A., and Europe, especially France. Puck and I had pretty much eliminated the West because of the lack of opportunity for a person without capital resources. We both knew what it was like punching a time clock for a big employer and therein did not lie the answer. The logical course of action for me was to get back on active duty in the army.

My assignment came through almost immediately, to my surprise. I was to report to the S2 Section at Berlin Military Post, an innocuous sounding title at best. S2 meant intelligence, but I had no idea yet that the job I was getting into was one of the army's principal operations to try to get to the top of the heap in the intelligence game.

What I did find out very quickly was that the city was a hotbed of intelligence activity. The Berlin blockade had been going on for some time and the airlift was in full swing. The tempo of supply flights into the various Allied airports in Berlin was frantic. Even coal was being hauled in by cargo plane, both to keep people warm and to try to maintain what rudiments of an industrial effort the West Berliners had been able to resurrect from the wreckage of their city. I learned that Berlin is a very special place and that Berliners are as different from other Germans as New Yorkers are from the rest of us. They have a special toughness of character, a sense of independence, and a sense of humor which is often lacking elsewhere. When John Kennedy went to Berlin years later and said, "*Ích bin ein Berliner,*" it meant a great deal more to them than was apparent on the surface.

I had hoped that being stationed in Germany would afford me lots of opportunities to fish some of the fine trout streams there. Now, here I was in the only place in Germany where this was not possible casually, such as on an off-duty weekend. Because of the blockade, everyone coming in or going out of Berlin had to do so under written duty orders, and space on the flights going in and out was at a premium. I could usually wangle a couple of days of delay en route (military for time off), which I used to good purpose with my fly rod, but it took a special occasion to give me the freedom I wanted on the trout streams.

On one occasion, I was assigned to a movie company as a technical advisor for a part of their film which involved dropping an agent behind enemy lines in Germany toward the end of the war. I was assigned to them for a week in Munich. When I arrived, the director called me in and asked me about my own experience, and I explained that I understood that the methods used in occupied France were different than those used toward the end of the war, and that it was likely that something on the order of a Bristol Beaufighter would have been used for a night delivery. He said it didn't make any difference anyway because they had already decided to use a C-47, and wouldn't I like to join them all for drinks and dinner at the Fier Jahre Zeiten? I did and that evening met Eartha Kitt and Orson Welles, among others. They were quite a pair—a witch and a warlock. She was an enchanting witch, with her wit and hypnotic sensuality. He was a powerful warlock, whose mesmeric voice, you'd swear could "call up spirits from the vasty deep."

I was no longer needed as an advisor, so I spent the balance of my week attending the needs of a number of trout and grayling in the Ammer River above the Amersee and proved to my satisfaction that the bunyon bug, small version, was just as effective a deceiver of German salmonids as it was of the Western U.S. variety. I also discovered that the beer of Weilheim, the town where I was staying, in a small *Gasthoff,* was magnificent with a deep amber tint and a real kick, quite unlike the pale variety available to us in Berlin at the time. It was my first time off alone in a completely German community without the company of English or French-speaking friends. It felt strange but fascinating at the same time, and I think that I might very easily have acquired a facility in German had I been able to live there on that basis.

In the meantime, plans were being made for Puck's arrival in Europe in late June for our wedding. My mother and Paul had taken charge of the French end of things altogether. There was a fantastic amount of paperwork involved, especially so because of Puck's status as a widow which, in the French view of things, managed to complicate the issue unbelievably. Fortunately, Paul was a master of diplomacy and of the ways of French bureaucracy and managed to have everything organized for a late June wedding in Paris. Mamie was in charge of the guest list and the social amenities.

In Berlin, meanwhile, I had put in for married quarters and was assigned a nice two-story house within a couple of blocks of the officers' club, my office, and the Free University, which was then just getting on its feet. My financial status had been on the debit side by a considerable amount when I arrived in Germany. Now I had a fairly substantial credit surplus, and I'll explain how.

One of the first things I found out after my arrival was that there was, literally, no funding as such for the intelligence operations our section was conducting. Agents, just like other folks, don't function for you in the name of love, patriotism, or any other ideal. It helps if they have that sort of ideological motivation, but money of some kind is what makes the wheels turn. We were, in effect, forced to operate in the black market with the benign understanding of the Counter Intelligence Corps (CIC), one of whose responsibilities was to try to curtail black market activity among the armed forces.

We were issued additional supplies of foodstuffs, coffee, cocoa, sugar, tobacco, cigarettes, and whiskey, and expected to turn these into the cash we needed to operate. In many cases, of course, the people with whom we dealt preferred to receive the commodities directly and deal for themselves. Others preferred dollars or occupation marks. We had to be ready for anything. What we did have in plenty was the facility to establish safe houses at no cost and to maintain them with special funds. I don't believe I met one person during the period of the blockade and airlift who did not participate in the black market to some extent or other, and that includes the wives of both civilian and military personnel. The rumor around when Commanding General Lucius D. Clay and his wife left was that they had an entire freight car filled with the "spoils of war," not a small part of it in Meissen china.

I had just a small stake to start with, but since the mails were being used by everyone to order such items as one-pound bags of cocoa or coffee from mail-order houses which had gone into business purely for the purpose of filling the U.S. Army niche in the market, I started ordering those common items which were rare and valuable here. In the six months prior to Puck's arrival in Paris, I managed to pay off all my indebtedness and to have enough left over to pay for our honeymoon, and then some.

Two of my billet mates were in the quartermaster corps and their wedding present to me was two 100-pound sacks of coffee beans. When it came time for them to return to the States, both declined and volunteered to stay in Germany. I have little doubt that they laid the foundation for substantial personal fortunes during the immediate postwar years in Berlin.

14
Another Hitch . . . This One for Life

J une 25, 1949, was the wedding date. Two of my fellow officers in S2, Lieutenants Shankman and Kelly, came down with me to participate in the festivities. Because we were to be married first in the *mairie* (local town hall) of the Seventh Arrondissement in a civil ceremony and two days later in the American Church, there were festivities before the first ceremony and in the intervening days as well. Puck looked absolutely wonderful and had a beautiful tan acquired at home before her departure. Because Mamie knew Puck was tall, she had made a point of getting hold of her friend, Julia Child, to be the matron of honor. Julia is over six feet tall. She and her husband were both ex-OSSers, and Paul Child was not working in Paris for the Marshall Plan. Her sister Dort (for Dorothy) is six-five and Bob Shankman squired her around during the festivities. He was about five-feet-six, and when the two of them got out of her little MG TC and stood up, crowds would gather and stare in awe at the wonderful mismatch.

Both weddings took place as scheduled and the only problems were my mother's in trying to keep Puck and me apart during the two-day interim between the civil and the church ceremonies.

We received a number of congratulatory cables including the one from Papa and his fourth wife, Mary, in Havana where he was working hard on his new novel, *Across the River and into the Trees*.

The reception was held at Mamie and Paul's apartment, only a short walk around the block from the church. David Bruce, the U.S. ambassador and former chief of OSS, Europe, honored us with his presence, as did may of Mamie and Paul's old friends, some of whom I remembered and some not. But the hit of the reception was Alice B. Toklas. I remembered her as one of the two giant women gargoyles of my childhood. Now she had turned into a chattering little bird, who moved without cease and came through the reception line three times, pouring out an endless cacophony and sparkling conversation laced with questions she never gave either of us time to answer. Moreover, she brought a lovely gift of an antique silver chalice. It had not been that long since Gertrude Stein's death, but Alice B. seemed to be doing just fine.

There seemed to be no end to the flow of champagne. It turned out Mamie had wisely chosen Dick Meier, an old friend who bought champagne for a living, as one of the first invitees. But whether it was the champagne or just my delight in finally bringing my lovely bride to the altar, spirits were high and it seemed to be as fine a wedding as any man and woman could ever want. And since we still feel that magic together all these years later, it must have been a charmed affair.

We all drove out to Crécy in the early afternoon and, after a few photographs had been taken of us by the garden wall by Paul Child, Puck and I started off on our honeymoon in Paul and Mamie's late-model Pontiac sedan, alighting the first night at a tiny country inn on the west side of the Loing River just above an ancient stone bridge. The scenery and almost everything else was lost on us. The champagne and the Pernods we had at our table in the back garden beside the river did us in.

I think Puck first began to realize what she had gotten herself into when the rumor of possible fly fishing for Atlantic salmon reached us at our honeymoon hotel in Gavarnie, high in the western Pyrenees above Lourdes, where Paul had reserved a room for us. My immediate reaction was to decamp from the beautiful alpine valley, where the local trout seemed only interested in maggots and seldom exceeded six inches in length. We headed for Oloron-Sainte Marie, where the Gave d'Aspe and the Gave d'Ossau join to form the Gave d'Oloron, the only obstacle-free tributary of the Gave de Pau and the Adour River, and where our native informant claimed the salmon were running.

We found an inexpensive hotel in town on the river which then had a Michelin star. I set about making inquiries in the local tackle shop about a possible salmon guide. We were directed to a young man who was anyone's dream of a guide. He was a full *chef de cuisine* in Chamonix during the winter season and returned home to Oloron every year for the spring and summer to fish for salmon professionally. French salmon fishing at that time suffered from an ailment inflicted on it during the Napoleonic period when, in an effort to achieve some semblance of naval superiority, salmon netting rights were given out in perpetuity to those who would sign up for a lifelong naval career. These *inscrits maritimes* were limited in the amount of time they could extend their nets, but there were excesses and the salmon resources suffered greatly.

The Gave d'Oloron was one of the few rivers where there was still a viable run of salmon and, along with the Allier in the north, provided most of the domestic table salmon for French kitchens. The netting season closed before June, and the price of salmon rose sharply then in the marketplace, along with the sudden decrease in supply.

Enter our guide, Jean Terens, who, with his sixteen-foot-long Calcutta two-handed fly rod and giant antique brass reel with oiled silk fly line almost as thick in the mid-section as a lady's little finger, was a first-rate classic wet-fly fisherman and knew the river well enough to average two fish a day for the balance of the season. These smaller summer fish averaged around fifteen pounds, and the going price was then the equivalent of $3.50 a pound. That came to very big money then and, fortunately, Jean was the only one around who consistently did that well. The beauty of it was that the water was low and clear, and the salmon absolutely refused the lures constantly being presented to them by the spin fishermen. Flies presented near the surface were the ticket.

We had several wonderful picnic days with Jean and his wife and their four-year-old boy, who took a shine to Puck and kept kissing her in the ear, much to her consternation. Watching the two women trying to converse with everything from sign language to sand drawings was a sight, but the picnics were delicious. I never caught a salmon but enjoyed watching Jean land several on the giant rod. Puck and I went several times alone but were warned by Jean not to leave anything around on the shore while we were fishing. There was a local character called *l'américain* who would steal anything, including a fish, if you left it on the beach. He had gotten his name because he had once traveled to America and never ceased speaking of its marvels.

15
Some Hunting Sketches

The SGS (Secretary of the General Staff), a major whose skills as a staff officer were only matched by his abilities in the hunting field, took me under his wing to make a hunter out of me. Once, he even had Puck and me sitting in a *hochsitz*, a well-disguised tree stand, where we remained for several long hours, from dusk to dark, neither uttering a sound nor even smoking while waiting for wild boars to come out of the woods to a baited area below us along the edge of the woods. We heard the boars in the undergrowth beneath us, but they sensed something wrong or were made nervous by a change in the weather and refused to leave the shelter of the woods to approach the pile of corn cobs. However, the wait was not without its rewards, and we were fascinated by being able to witness one of nature's minor dramas as we watched a fox stalk a hare feeding in the open field, nearly succeeding in the capture.

On several occasions I was invited on organized *battues*, or drives, for wild boar, where large groups of the local peasants formed a line and used everything from old pans and spoons to horns and sticks to drive all the wild game in the area toward the line of hunters awaiting them.

The hunters were placed about twenty yards apart and could expect anything from roe deer and hares to wild boars to come exploding from the dense cover toward them. Wild boars are courageous and smart, so, when the drive was specifically for boars, we refrained from shooting at anything else and were often treated to the sight of red deer and roe deer halting in front of us, totally oblivious to our presence while they stared in the direction of the oncoming cacophony of the beaters.

I never had the good fortune to have a boar break out on my stand during one of those drives, but I heard them coming out nearby on several occasions and heard the shots and the hit by other guns and rushed over to witness the death of the savage beasts. Wild boars are one of the few big game animals which inspire no sympathy. They look like the very personification of evil, and their features are those used since earliest times to inspire fear and loathing, in art as in ancient tales of wickedness and lycanthropic transformations. In the art of the Middle Ages, the faces of evil, a wolf's mask, or that of a wild boar are virtually synonymous. It would be impossible to portray them as sweet innocents with Bambi-like eyes and long lashes; therefore, I actually enjoyed hunting them, and to top it all, they are a gastronomic delight when properly prepared. They were hunted year-round but still managed to keep up their numbers and were a plague to the small farmers whose row crops were often ruined by these *Wildschwein*, as they were called.

The most exciting hunt for wild boars I ever participated in was a truly international affair. The French SGS, a German *Jaegermeister* (professional hunter), and I managed to fake a drive when a local farmer called in with a depredation complaint in a wild part of the Black Forest not far from Freiburg near the village of St. Peter. The terrain was precipitous, and there was a long ridge, like an *arête*, with one side wooded along its length and the other a cornfield where the boars uprooted the young shoots. The *Jaeger* knew the place and he positioned the SGS and me inside the hundred-yard-wide strip of wood, with me above near the crest and my French friend halfway between me and the lower edge of the woods. He then proceeded by a long, roundabout route to the farm in a hollow just under the top of the ridge where, along with the farmer, he started shouting and making loud noises, barking like a dog, and then loosed his dachshund who joined in the noisy fray. The SGS and I kept the silence of the dead during the long wait and concentrated our attention on the spacings between the trees ahead of us. All the noise being made came from a kilometer away, but within a minute or two at most we could hear the approaching boars as the galloping sound of their cloven hooves and the stirring of the underbrush grew louder.

Suddenly, there they were, no farther than thirty yards in front of me and coming fast in single file with a rolling, stiff-legged gallop, four of them led by what seemed to me, in that indelible instant of excitement and fear, to be a monstrous big old tusker. I stood up directly in their path and aimed my rifle at the shoulder of the lead boar. Sighting me, they veered off to the right and kept on going. Altogether, I fired four times as quickly as I could work the bolt. To my knowledge, only one of the boars fell. The SGS got in his licks as they darted across in front of him.

We checked the ground and, with some difficulty, found the boar I had knocked down. It was one of the smaller ones but already weighed nearly two hundred pounds and had razor-sharp tusks burgeoning from its lower jaw, and was quite able to kill a man if wounded and cornered. There was blood spoor everywhere. The SGS had shot at all three that passed him and said all three were hit but not fatally. When the *Jaeger* arrived with his dog, we found another one, then followed the dog about seven or eight hundred paces to the third, which was dead. But the big one was still out there and after two or three kilometers, with the blood spoor varying from heavy to finally nothing, we gave up and went back to retrieve and clean the first three, all of them about the same size. The dog refused to come to the hunter's call, and the *Jaeger* said he thought it would stick to the trail until either it found the wounded boar or the scent disappeared. He felt certain the boar would be reported and that we would receive word before too long. As for me, I had seen more action in a short space of time than on all the previous drives put together.

The next day we found out the final outcome. The dog, one of the unbelievably courageous large dachshunds, had tracked the boar all the way out of the *Kreis* (county) and had cornered it and stayed with it until found by the *Jaeger* from the next *Kreis* who, quite properly under the local ground rules, claimed it for his own then returned the dog who had been seriously but not fatally wounded. I don't recall the exact weight of the big boar, but it was twice of the size of the others. The straight-line distance it had traveled, wounded with the dog on its trail, was over fifteen kilometers from where we had shot it.

The SGS had a part of the ham prepared for each of us, then we had a feast of civet made from the smaller boars and gave the rest away to the sergeants' mess. The previous year, the SGS had shot the postwar record boar for the Black Forest, a monster weighing in at over 300 kilos, or 660 pounds, and not an ounce of fat.

There was excellent bird shooting on the Rhine plain, and the French officers' hunting association had over thirty thousand hectares set aside for their exclusive hunting use. I took full advantage of the hunting there and was joined on several occasions by our friend, Woody, and another pilot, John Brons, a Midwesterner turned Floridian, whose wife, Penny, was the only woman I ever met who made it unnecessary to have a bird dog along. She had an extraordinary ability to hear pheasants hiding in thickets and would even go in and flush them for us if rewarded properly at the end of the day with her full quota of refreshment.

I had no hunting dog then, and it is a tribute to the vast amount of game available that we did as well as we did. Our family dog, a miniature poodle called Bumby, so-named in the hope that, hearing of it, Papa would allow me to grow out of that nickname, came with me once but bolted at the first shot and reappeared only hours later cowering under the car. Since, in addition to pheasant, there were plenty of grey partridge, woodcock, snipe, and waterfowl in the area, I very much wanted a shooting dog, but a tragic event put me off the idea for a long time thereafter.

Puck and I had driven up to Coblenz for a visit with John Stockton, the liaison officer with French II Corps, to do a bit of duck shooting. One evening John and I were to meet with one of the French hunting fraternity at the shooting grounds along a stretch of the Rhine where there was excellent duck flighting and where it was possible to shoot at night against the light of the full moon where there were ducks passing or coming in to alight on a slow stretch of the reed-flanked current. The French officer had a dog, a curly-coated pointer who retrieved well, and he had promised to bring it along. But when John and I arrived at the appointed place and time, our French friend hadn't shown up, and after a full hour wait, we decided to go down to the river's edge and station ourselves well apart in such a way that we could see the birds against the newly risen moon just above the horizon to the east.

From up above, we had heard wing beats most of the time we'd been waiting. We agreed that once we were both sure we were in position we could shoot. It was amazing. Every once in a while you could actually see one of the ducks outlined against the moon and you had to swing on it and pull the trigger ahead of where you imagined the duck would be on impact. I dry-fired a couple of times to get the feel of it, then shot and heard the bird hit the water out in front of me. I heard it thrashing about in the water and, assuming it was only wounded, I fired again at the spot on the water lit by the moon's shimmering glow where I could see some splashing. To my horror, I heard the pained yelping of a dog. Apparently, our French friend had arrived late and was just sneaking down the bank to join us when the shot was fired, and his dog broke for the water to retrieve the bird. I was standing in the reeds in water up to my knees and never heard a thing. I waded out in the shallow water with the Frenchman at my heels to find his dog, dead, and the duck floating right next to him. It cost me many a sleepless night and almost a month's pay to replace the dog which, unfortunately, had been the family pet as well as a hunting companion.

Among our German friends was a family called Gutterman, who owned a thread factory in the little town of Gutach where I sometimes fished the Elz River above the town. The water there was clean and trouty. Frau Gutterman's father was a Scotsman who had been personal physician to the Sultan of Zanzibar in times past and had died before the war. She spoke perfect English but was almost equaled by her internationalist husband, whose family operated thread factories in scattered places around the world. I wish I had been able to take him up on his invitation to be initiated in the rite of shooting *Auerhahn*, the capercailzie of Scotland, known for its size and the rarity of its plumage. The *Auerhahn* is supposedly the largest grouse in the world. The hunt is a matter of serious tradition in Germany and is followed by an initiation ceremony dating from medieval times.

I had an amazing experience while fishing a border stream on the way to the hunting property I had leased that season. I had paid one hundred dollars for the lease but was amply repaid by the sale of the game shot on the only drive I held there. The stream, named the Wutach, is the border between Germany and that part of Switzerland known as the Schaffhausen Enclave for much of its course. What happened there is, I'm certain, nothing more than a trick my mind played on me, but at the time it seemed absolutely real.

I had been fishing one not-very-attractive stretch of the stream, where the brush and woods had been cleared on both sides because of its function as a frontier. The stream, however, was productive, and I caught several fine trout in the two-pound range when my concentration wandered and I visualized this very place as a spot I had been in during my prisoner-of-war time. I clearly saw in my mind the narrow footway crossing above the weir and the attack dog the three of us had killed when he assaulted us as we tried to cross over. The stream had been in spate, and we were afraid to wade it because the current looked so deep and powerful, but now I saw that we could have made it across anywhere, no matter what the water level. I know that the vision was only a trick of the mind, but I've tried to explain it to myself by logic and reason and I simply can't. It was like a feeling I'd had as a child in Brittany wandering around the ruins of a Trappist monastery in which sheep were grazing. Within those ancient walls, open to the sky, I had a strong sense of having been there before, perhaps in a past life. Half-formed memories crowded into my mind, too vivid to dismiss. But the vision of events along the Wutach was totally distinct and clear and went considerably further than I am revealing here.

This brings me back to the matter of memory. Many years later, on returning to the sites of some of my wartime experiences, I discovered that certain events I'd have sworn were real had apparently been pure fantasy, and some of the things I thought might easily have been imaginary, were verified in complete detail by other witnesses. The only thing that appears certain in all this is the possibility of the existence of greater dimensions of the mind than those in which we are accustomed to thinking.

16
Papa's Son Becomes a Papa

A t the conclusion of our honeymoon, I took Puck with me back to Berlin to set up our house and start our new life together. Despite the lifting of the blockade during our stay, life in Berlin was a bit of a culture shock for her, but she adjusted quickly and was well accepted by my group of friends and associates. And apparently something else had taken root, and she soon showed signs of impending motherhood.

On the 5th day of May 1950, Puck gave birth to our first daughter, Joan Whittlesey Hemingway, at the American Hospital in Paris, where she had spent the previous month in a hotel alone awaiting the birth. She was so tall and regal-looking that the taxi driver who was called to fetch her to the hospital refused to believe that there was any impending childbirth. She scarcely showed at all except for that wonderful skin quality and ripeness of breast with which expectant mothers in good health are endowed. We both had been determined that our first child should not be born in Germany but in France, which I loved so much. There had been May day riots in Berlin, and I was obliged to stay throughout the high-risk period in which all Allied personnel were on full alert, but I left as soon as I could on the train through the Russian zone of occupation with a good connection to arrive in Paris early the next morning.

The morning of Muffet's birth—for that's what we started calling her—I got off the train at the *Gare de l'Est* and took the first taxi in line. I recognized the driver; I had spoken to him the last trip to Paris when making arrangements for her at the hotel, the hospital, and with the obstetrician, Dr. Ravina. At that time I had been in civilian clothes, and the driver conversed with me freely, but now that I was in my U.S. Army uniform, it didn't matter how clearly I spoke, he wasn't capable of understanding a word I said. There must have been a built-in mechanism within him that said, "He's American, therefore he can't speak French, therefore I can't understand him."

Puck looked great and so did the baby. For some reason, one's own babies look great while other people's always seem kind of shriveled up. Puck was breast-feeding her fine the first couple of days but then developed a staph infection and had to switch to formula. In those days in France, they still kept mothers in the hospital for a full ten days following childbirth, so Dr. Ravina told me to bring my wife a bottle of champagne (the French cure-all) and some nylon hose for her nurse and take off for a few days. I was doing more harm than good, he said, hanging around aimlessly.

With that news, Charley Ritz invited me to join him for a couple of days' fishing on one of the famous French chalk streams, the Risle, in Normandy, which flows through the same zone of solid chalk downs which runs across the south of England. A close friend of his had spent years acquiring bits and pieces of the river and at this time owned outright about five kilometers of the most productive and beautiful water. There was a lovely Norman country house with the typical outside beams, Tudor style. There was also a guest cottage with a thatched roof. The weather was cool and blustery and, so far, there had been no sign of any emergence of the famous mayfly which is known for bringing even the largest old brown trout out of hiding to feed on the surface. The large size and vast numbers of mayflies in the spring constitute a sufficiently filling meal to attract even the old hook-jawed males, who spend most of their time feeding on minnows and even others of their kind.

Each guest was assigned a specific beat, or stretch of water, for the morning fishing and then another in the afternoon. Along each beat there were little posts which marked the location of a live-fish basket into which you were expected to release your catch. Twice a day the keeper would come along and either release the fish or kill a few if some were needed for the kitchen at the manor house.

It was all terribly well organized, but what struck me most was how dressed up everyone was. I felt quite ridiculous and out of place in my old jeans, borrowed boots, and my old plaid shirt and sweater. These people all wore plus-four knickers or riding trousers and never took off their hacking jacket and tie, or the wool hats and caps, which have only recently become fashionable here in the States. Each also carried a red bandana fastened to his belt at one corner; its purpose was to wipe off any fish slime which might inadvertently get on the hands during the handling of fish. Wading was not permitted because it was felt it could damage the aquatic vegetation, so you knelt to keep your silhouette low and out of sight of the fish.

Well, I must say, despite all their chichi getup, most of those folks were damned fine fishermen, and the fish they were going after were as difficult as you could find anywhere, with a sprinkling of very large fish.

The Norman chalk streams, like their English counterparts, are rich in aquatic insect life, and they are clear and slow moving. Because of this, the fish get a good look at any fly you put over them, and they become finicky in the extreme so you have to know what you're doing to succeed in catching them regularly. It was a great treat for me and I especially appreciated Charley's guidance and the generosity with which he shared his special knowledge. He showed me some nymphing techniques for catching these trout when there was no apparent hatch of flies coming off the water. We did get a hatch of a smaller species of mayfly, and I did well on my own when that happened.

After the two days, I was ready to return to Paris and see my family. Robert Capa was in town, so he and Noel Howard, the actor whom

I had met on the movie advisory job, showed me around the hot spots, and I had a chance to see Magnum Photos' first working office and the system they had set up for selecting the best pictures from among the many thousands that the brothers Robert and Cornell Capa and the other photographers in their early troop were constantly shooting all over the world. Capa explained to me that taking good pictures wasn't the problem, but rather, selecting the great ones that told the story you were after constituted the real art of photojournalism. Although Capa's taste in clothes was suspect in my mind after Papa had entrusted him with outfitting me properly at Abercrombie & Fitch during my prep school days and I ended up in a bright green Harris tweed, he was without a doubt a true master photojournalist.

That turned out to be my last visit with Capa. The last time we'd seen each other before that was in Hollywood, where he was doing a stint as an assistant director, just after the war. He was being paid a ridiculously large stipend but wasn't allowed to do anything, so he spent the whole time at the racetrack trying to win back the money he'd lost to his producer, who forced him to play, then cheated openly at gin rummy.

Capa's wife had been killed in combat during the Spanish civil war, crushed between two loyalist tanks she was photographing when they ran together during an attack. Capa was later killed, himself, taking photos in combat during the French war in Indochina. I can't help but come to the conclusion that combat photographers deserve a great deal of respect, and they have mine.

17
Another Start
. . . and a Pact
with Papa

W e got used to the rain in Portland, and I fished a lot more than I should have. What clients I had were almost all people I had met on rivers. I discovered something I should have known before, and that was that I was a very negative cold-call salesman. I shrank from calling strangers on the telephone, or even calling on them in person, to try to talk to them about their finances. When you're new in a city and trying to get started in the investment business, calling on strangers is one of the things you simply have to do. I even tried to remedy this failing by taking a Dale Carnegie course, but it eventually became evident that I was not going to be able to earn much more than my guarantee, and that was obviously not enough for a family of four. I left Zilka with great regret and made a couple of half-hearted attempts in other fields but found myself deeply depressed and badly in need of two things: a boost in morale and a financial shot in the arm.

One of the projects in which I had become involved was a foundation started by a clever fellow Dartmouth alumnus who had me working for the group with high hopes and no remuneration. It looked at some point as if there might be some advantage in bringing the foundation to the attention of my friend, Joe Dryer, whose North Atlantic Kenaf Corporation was starting to get off the ground in Cuba with a special decorticator developed for them by Krupp. Joe was starting to grow Kenaf fiber, from which jute-like material could be woven to make bags for Cuba's sugar crop, once the Krupp machine had solved the problem of removing the worthless cortex from the usable fiber. It made sense for me to use this excuse to visit Cuba and see Papa for the first time in two years. I had the promise of a paying job with George Patten, an independent investment broker with a fine reputation, who had a small one-man operation and was interested in taking on a youngster to help him service his growing clientele. Nevertheless, I wanted badly to discuss the question of my future with Papa with complete candor and possibly to find a totally new and more rewarding direction. Although Puck was holding up well under the circumstances, her spirits were only kept from flagging by Muffet's obvious brightness in her first school at St. Helen's Hall, and little Margot's alertness and charm. To make matters worse, I had to borrow to pay for my airline ticket to Havana.

When I got to Havana, preceded by a cablegram, it was some time in March 1955. Mary was back from seeing her mother and making arrangements for her after her father's recent death, but Papa didn't look at all well and was obviously badly overweight. He did seem pleased, however, to hear about the trouble-free birth of his second grandchild and was especially glad about her name.

I couldn't get around to the object of my visit right away and shied away from it for several days, during which time I made contact with Joe Dryer and his brother, Peter, who was sharing digs with him in an apartment near the Malecón on the edge of old Havana. Their project sounded interesting, but there was no place in it for me, and the idea having to do with the foundation turned out not to have been appropriate. It had really just been an excuse for me to come down anyway.

Papa had recently been awarded the Nobel Prize, and he complained often about the greatly increased loss of privacy it entailed. "Privacy," he said, "is the most valuable thing a man can have and an absolute necessity for a man to be able to write. Now every son-of-a-bitch in the world thinks he has the right to steal it from me." I did not express aloud my own opinion that Mary's love of the limelight and entertaining did little to aid in meeting that need, despite the protective shell she erected around him to keep him from being disturbed unnecessarily. The trouble was that I felt strongly that I was one of those she was keeping out, and that feeling remained in full force as long as he was alive.

There was little doubt in my mind that Papa had undergone drastic changes from the man I had viewed all my life as my number one hero. He could still be as gentle and warm as ever, but it was more and more infrequent, and his mood generally seemed to me plaintive, occasionally truculent, often so with Mary, and with an underlying bitterness.

This, then, was the setting for our "man to man" discussion, as I came to think of it. We had all three had the usual midday preprandial martini, despite his supposedly having given them up, and I took this moment to ask for a private powwow.

"Papa, can I speak to you alone?"

"Of course, Schatz," he replied. "Let's go in the living room." I received what can only be described as a hard look from Mary who then said, "I think I'll go have a nap, lamb," and closed the door to her room none too gently.

Papa settled into his big armchair, and I sat down nervously on the couch opposite with only the big woven reed mat on the floor separating us.

"How are things really going?" He made it easy for me, but it still wasn't easy.

"I don't know why, Papa. I just can't seem to make a decent living. Not enough to support my family. Whatever I've tried just hasn't worked for me."

"You were a damned fine soldier."

"I probably never should have left the army. It's just that it was no life for a family, always unsettled, and it was actually getting so Puck would know when I was jumping the next day, even though I never told her. I was twitching in my sleep and she could tell."

"Goddamnit, Schatz, you're going to have to stick with one thing. If you keep switching jobs much longer, you're going to find yourself unemployable."

That hurt. I was thirty-three years old and already faced dismal failure.

"Papa, it isn't that I don't try. I know I should have finished school, but right after the war I just wasn't ready for school. I'd already been in real life, and school wasn't real any more. Anyway I didn't finish and now there just isn't that big a choice of jobs. The sales field is the only area I have any chance of making real money in but I just can't seem to cut it."

"Look, Bum, you're in a good place, a place you chose. You'll just have to stick with it. I'll help all I can with monies, but you're going to have to stay with one job in one business until you learn to make a living."

"I'd give anything not to need money help, but God knows I do need it." I broke down almost completely, "Sometimes I get down so bad I wonder if it's worth going on living . . ."

I believe this shook him for he cut in, "Schatz, listen to me. I know how bad it can seem. There have been times when I felt the same way. Christ, if you had any idea of the shit I live with all the time." He went on through a litany of problems, including Mary and his lawyer, which made mine pale into insignificance. Then he reminded me about what a mistake it had been for Grandfather to shoot himself as it had turned out that his financial worries would have solved themselves. At that point he elicited a promise from me I shall never forget. He said, "Schatz, the one thing you must promise me you will never do, and I will promise you the same, is that neither one of us will ever shoot himself, like Grandfather. Promise me and then I'll promise you."

So I promised. And then he promised.

That night there were guests for dinner, as was often the case, but Papa arranged for us to have a tiñosa (buzzards, or turkey vultures, which we jokingly referred to as *enemigos,* or enemies) shoot the following day. He had René get hold of a dead carcass to put on the roof of the Finca to attract our quarry within range. The tower Mary had had built since her tenure as chatelaine would provide an ideal platform on its parapeted roof for our shooing, and I, looking forward to another chance to be alone with Papa—truly alone this time since Mary's room would not abut on our meeting place as it had that afternoon in the living room.

The occasion of the *tiñosa* shoot is one of the most memorable moments of my lifelong relationship with my father. It was the single time in my life when Papa and I were alone together since my adulthood when no holds were barred and we both let down all our defenses. It started at about eleven in the morning when Papa and I climbed up the outside spiral iron staircase to the top of the tower above his new workroom. We used only one side-by-side shotgun, the Duke of Alba gun I think, and we had plenty of boxes of twelve-gauge shells.

Papa set forth the rules: "We'll just use the one gun. Each of us gets two shots. Then we trade off. The one not shooting is observer-fire controller—you know, like incomer on your right about two o'clock high . . . air force style."

As senior officer present, he got first go. One of the big black buzzards who had shifted their flight away from our hill when Papa and I arrived on the tower slanted down an air current towards the dead goat on the red tile roof below us. I called out, "Incomer, ten o'clock, range 75 yards. Fire at will."

Papa let the big ugly bird swoop within 20 yards, led him perfectly and crumpled him just over the edge of the roof and he crashed into the mango trees and hit the ground with a thump. Another one had dropped in from the right and I called, "Enemigo in range three o'clock low." But Papa had already fired his second barrel at him, and he crashed on the front terrace. He had a double and, pleased, yelled for René to bring up a pitcher of martinis and two glasses. Meanwhile the ripeness of the goat seemed to be having an hypnotic effect on the giant carrion eaters, bringing them swooping toward our hilltop from miles around. The shooting didn't put them off for long and before the martinis arrived Papa had called one for me, which I needed to pump both barrels into to collapse him.

They were no easy target. As any goose hunter can tell you, the flight of big birds is deceptive in the extreme, and a bird can appear to be going very slowly while actually traveling at high rates of speed, particularly when there's a strong wind. The fact that the *tiñosas* were mostly soaring made their airspeed that much more difficult to gauge accurately, and we had variable winds.

It was a never-to-be-forgotten shoot, and after a while we yelled down for René to bring up yet another pitcher. By the time we had expended all our shells, well over two hours had gone by, and we were drunk as coots. Mary kept coming out onto the patio beneath the tower calling for us to "stop this at once" and "come down and eat lunch right now," but we just kept on drinking and shooting and laughing and shouting after the third pitcher, which René had the good sense to accompany with some sandwiches.

Papa finally growled, "Cease fire." Then René's volunteers, youngsters from his family or friends from the town, started the big cleanup, which we likened to the graves registration unit going onto the battlefield after a big firefight, and both Papa and I directed them from our vantage point on the tower. I have forgotten how many of the big stink-ugly birds were picked up, but I hasten to explain that *tiñosas*, while protected at home, were not protected then in Cuba. And since we never made a habit of shooting them, the minor diminution in their numbers inflicted on that memorable occasion cannot have had any serious effect of the ecological balance. Furthermore, nobody had yet used the world "ecology" in public.

We climbed down the spiral staircase very carefully and headed into the living room.

"Let's watch *Casablanca*, Mister Bum."

"Wonderful, Papa. Can we see it okay with the light?"

"Sure. The bulb's strong, and René can rig up some blankets over the windows. Help me set up the projector."

We were in no shape to set up the projector properly, especially not to thread the film. René finished the job as we settled into the two big easy chairs with the screen set up in front of the couch and the projector behind us near the capehart record player.

"René, traiga una botella de tinto, haga el favor!"

"Sí, René y con dos vasos!" I chimed in too loudly, bringing Mary to her door behind the screen to the right, where she took one long glaring look at us, then went back into her room, slamming the door hard. She was furious and stayed that way until my departure.

I can't really blame her for being angry at the moment, but she needn't have stayed that way, mean, angry, and silent. Anyway the film came on. Papa shrugged, and the two of us were swept up in it as always, perhaps, more so because of all the alcohol.

It was a bit like going to a movie in a college town. Neither of us could keep quiet though we kept shushing each other.

"Isn't the Swede beautiful? I mean truly, really beautiful . . . beautiful."

"Yeah, Papa, beautiful. She's really, truly, truly beautiful."

"So beautiful, so, so beautiful."

This went on and we started crying and repeating over and over how beautiful she really was. We were overwhelmed by her beauty.

It was totally maudlin and wonderfully close and human all at once, and I'll always be grateful that it happened.

I never had another chance to be that close to him again. Much later, I wondered if, during that time, he had already foreseen the onset of his ruin. The signs were there for others to see, but I must confess I hadn't the wit to see it for myself. Either that, or I didn't want to.

18
A Bad Ending

I came in from the early morning's fishing having had my first glimmer of a take in the fast water just above the rapid at Wright Creek. A fish came short but refused to come again. Even so, the near miss bucked up my spirits, and I came back into camp full of hope and with a big appetite. Puck was down at the cabin when Frank came up to me and said, "Jack, I think it's bad news. You're supposed to call this number in Ketchum." I recognized the number. It was Papa's, at the house he'd bought overlooking the Big Wood River just outside town; the house he had bought from his friend Dan Topping's brother, Bob, which had never really become home because he hadn't yet been there for all the seasons of a year; the house where he had shot himself early that morning, as Mary told me when she answered the insistent ringing.

Frank Moore came to the rescue again, as he had done so many times on the river, by volunteering to fly us from Roseburg to Ketchum. We landed on the short strip just north of town by the dump (now a nine-hole golf course flanked by expensive homes), and half a mile north of the cemetery. The flight was over hot, black desert, the air rough, and Puck and the girls got sick. I was tense and miserable. We had called Puck's folks in Twin, and they had driven up to take Puck and the girls home with them until time for the funeral a few days later. Mary had checked into the hospital, where she was under sedation and the press were starting to home in like wasps at a barbecue. The phone never stopped ringing, and it was a madhouse only made bearable by the yeoman duty being performed by Papa's friends, the Arnolds, the Andersons, the Atkinsons, George Saviers, Duke McMullen, and George Brown, who had traveled west with Papa and Mary from the Mayo Clinic.

I was thoroughly briefed between phone calls and was shocked to learn how long the problem had been going on, but my priority was taking care of the details and coordinating the funeral arrangements with Patrick's arrival from east Africa. When Mary was able to face the onslaught again, most of the arrangements had been made, but she assigned me one of the worst jobs I have ever had to do. We had received a telegram from Marlene Dietrich saying that she was coming right away to attend the funeral. Since the day I had been too shy to approach her in Regensburg, I had met her and talked with her when Puck and I went backstage following a show in San Francisco. She had been kind and generous with her time with us. But Mary was furious at the idea that Marlene should even consider coming to the funeral, and she ordered me to telephone her immediately and tell her that we were having no outsiders because it was going to be a simple, family-only funeral. I was never more ashamed and, of course, I couched my call in more diplomatic terms, but I could sense the hurt at the other end of the line.

I slept in Papa's room until Puck and the family came back for the funeral. The night before Patrick's scheduled arrival, other family members and close friends were already in town and staying at the Christiania Motor Lodge. Mary was starting to regain her form but continued to be adamant in her insistence to the press that Papa had shot himself accidentally. I suppose the possibility that someone might conclude that Papa had willingly left a life in which she played so large a part was anathema to her. Before retiring that night we had a long talk in which she recounted the whole history of Papa's illness, how pathetic had been his last attempts at making love to her, and how difficult it had all been for her. We both had had quite a lot to drink, and I found myself being sympathetic to her position. She even thanked me for sending Papa the check and said she hadn't had a chance to show it to him so she hoped I would understand when it was returned endorsed by her. It would go a long way to help defray all the expenses that had piled up.

She told me that Alfred Rice, Papa's lawyer, would be arriving and that he would get us all together after the funeral to discuss the future. She also thanked me for taking over during her stay in the hospital, an exaggeration since Papa's friends had rallied to do all the legwork. I had only helped make the hard decisions, and some of those had been made for me. As it turned out, my role was completed and, like an actor killed off in an early scene, there was really no further need for me.

Patrick arrived and he, Greg, and I spent some time together before the funeral. The grey eminence of our lives made his lawyerly appearance and, once the funeral was over, convoked Mary and the three of us upstairs and laid the chill hand of our father's will upon us in a short summation to the effect that Papa had left everything to Mary and that no provisions of any kind had been made for anyone else. Weeks later we saw part of the holographic will published in *Life* magazine before having seen a copy ourselves. I never saw a copy until years later when I had my attorney get a copy made from the probate records.

19
And a New Beginning

All of a sudden it was 1970 and not only was it a gubernatorial election year but there were some hot environmental issues dividing opinion in our state. This was early on, and environmentalists had had few successes, particularly in those states whose orientation was more rural than urban. In Idaho, there were two issues that loomed large and in which the outcome meant much to me personally. The first was the possibility of a giant molybdenum mining operation in the White Cloud Mountains close to where we lived which would badly pollute a primary salmon and steelhead spawning stream as well as ruin a giant piece of completely pristine country used by thousands every year to find the magnificent solace only wilderness can give to those who approach it with respect.

The proposed mine was an issue which the incumbent governor, widely known as "Dumb Don," stood four-square behind, and the conventional wisdom was that he would win reelection and the mining issue would in no way hinder him. It was an issue, however, which could swing an election if enough of the general public could be made aware of what was really being stolen from them should the mine project go through as envisioned.

The second issue was not quite as immediate but was just as surely sinister in its implications. It involved the building of a giant impassable dam at a location called High Mountain Sheep on the lower end of what remained of the Hell's Canyon of the Snake River after previous dams in the upper and middle reaches had effectively blocked all upstream migration of salmon and steelhead to the historically important spawning streams above the canyon. Although a program had been initiated to transfer all the fish that still ran up the Middle Snake to a hatchery operation in the Salmon River drainage, it was no substitute for the real thing. The proposed dam would also have flooded an area which has since proved itself to be a valuable and irreplaceable national treasure.

The governor's challenger took the risky stand of supporting the protection of Idaho's natural resources, and with a lot of letter writing and speaking around the state, he and his supporters, who included me, managed to win over public support on these issues, as well as the election. I was, and am, a Republican, and I formed a Republicans-for-Andrus group which may or may not have been helpful. The new governor apparently thought so, and he appointed me to the most challenging, gratifying, and exciting job I have ever had; I became a member of the Idaho Fish & Wildlife Commission.

It was a six-year appointment, and it was filled with controversy from the very beginning. For a while it even looked dicey as to whether or not my appointment would be ratified by the state senate, which was heavily weighted with strongly rural elements who viewed environmentalists as the new evil in the world sent by the devil to deprive them of their God-given rights to do any damn thing they wanted to their own land. Somehow or other, the older and very valid concept of stewardship of the land had been lost along the way, yet I know that most Idahoans really feel a sense of stewardship when their dander isn't up. I was finally able to convince them I wasn't a Socialist or a Communist, and that I truly did believe in private property and, despite a delegation of disgruntled sportsmen from my own area whose chief honcho felt he had been overlooked for the commissioner's job, I was confirmed with only one dissenting vote.

The following six years was a period of education, exercising of opportunities, and a personal campaign to change some prevailing points of view about fisheries management in particular, where I could at least pretend a little theoretical expertise. A marvelous coincidence had created a situation which was extremely helpful to me in keeping a step ahead, so to speak. My best friend, a fly-fishing attorney *cum* wildlife photographer named Dan Callaghan, and Frank Moore, my friend from Steamboat on the North Umpqua, were both serving as fish and game commissioners in Oregon and kept me current on all the new developments there. Dan and I first met at Steamboat in 1962, the year after my father's death, when I arrived in camp from Mill Valley with a beautiful eleven-pound steelhead I caught along the way and brought to show to Frank Moore. Frank said he wanted me to meet somebody and suggested I bring the fish along to the guy's cabin.

It seemed this fellow had a bad case of flu and was lying in bed, miserable. We went down, and Frank introduced me to the pitiful figure of one Dan Callaghan, obviously suffering from the tortures of the damned, eyes and nose swollen. I shoved the steelhead in front of him, and a remarkable transformation took place. Within minutes he was up, clear-eyed, and ready to go fishing. It turned out, however, that nothing could be done about his nose. That's the way it always was, I found out later. We became fishing partners then and there, and we both learned from each other and shared all new knowledge, as friends will, and over the years we've fished so many places together we've lost count.

Dan and I had met a young biologist named Dick Vincent up in Montana. He was conducting some experiments in the effects of stocking hatchery trout on the populations of wild trout, and he was doing it in different water types but all in streams and rivers. His findings, we learned, were conclusive and indicated that areas where there was no stocking of adult hatchery trout had much better populations of wild trout. The survival rate for hatchery trout through the severe winters was negligible, but their very presence in streams where they were put caused abnormal conditions for the wild fish. Wild fish were driven out by the hatchery stock much the way Indians were driven out by settlers or the way farmers flee from developers.

The stocking of so-called catchable trout had become a way of life in Idaho, and a commissioner who was against it would appear to be a threat to jobs and careers built around stocking. Anyway, I was able to persuade my fellow commissioners that it was something that would bear looking into and that we should do something about it. Finally we did, and we did it without jeopardizing any of the hatchery jobs because we determined where their efforts could be most effective. The process was very intricate and much more complicated than it appears, and it took years, but during the course of my six-year term we were able to bring about some of the most forward-looking fisheries policies anywhere in the world, including the institution of vast areas of catch-and-release fishing in waters which otherwise could not withstand the heavy burden put upon them by the ever-increasing number of sport-hungry anglers. The amazing part was that home folks started accepting these new policies because our plans had included something for everybody.

For all the catch-and-release fisheries on first-rate streams lost to the meat fishermen, there were increased opportunities in reservoirs and lakes where the bulk of the hatchery fish were being put in as youngsters, and where the vast quantities of feed allowed them to grow into fat fare for the table. I felt that a new attitude toward sportsmanship was emerging, and a greater acceptance of sport for its own sake was taking hold, to the point that *macho* no longer meant a long string of dead fish. I personally encourage the policy that one should always believe any fisherman who tells you about the huge number of giant fish he has caught and released, no matter what a dedicated liar you know him to be. Otherwise, he will feel constrained to kill what fish he catches to prove his superior skill.

They were a wonderful six years and by the time they came to an end—when I refused the new governor's suggestion that I accept reappointment—I had seen great changes take place and the begin-

nings of even greater changes to come. I suppose I made a few enemies, but most of the people I came in contact with were men and
women with whom I felt a strong bond. My fellow commissioners,
who came from every walk of life, all of whom arrived on the scene
with their own deeply entrenched points of view, did what they felt
was best for the resources with which we had been entrusted and for
the people whose careers and futures were our responsibility for a
short period of time. The professionals in the department proved
their dedication time and again for relatively low pay and a lot of public scorn. They are the real heroes of the ongoing fight to preserve our
natural heritage for generations to come.

The Federation of Fly Fishermen was organized in the late sixties to represent the interests of fly fishermen, first in America, and
then around the world. I attended the first of its conclaves with Dan
Callaghan in Jackson Hole, Wyoming, and, believe it or not, we took
our wives along. It was a wonderful experience because it was close to
outstanding fishing and because we were able to meet some of the
greats of fly fishing. While there, we were also able to help influence
the choice of Sun Valley as a site for one of the next annual conclaves.
In view of the fame of Silver Creek and the resort itself, it wasn't so
difficult a feat.

The first conclave at Sun Valley was a special treat for me for two
reasons. I had a chance to renew my friendship with Roderick Haig-
Brown, whom I first met on his own stretch of the Campbell River in
British Columbia in 1955. There had had generously turned into reality the wonders I had read about so avidly in his fine books. No finer
writer about nature's wonders, as viewed by a fisherman, ever lived.
Rod and his loving wife, Ann, joined us for the conclave and for a few
days thereafter when he found one of the tributaries of Silver Creek
an evocative reminder of his beloved Frome in Wiltshire, the English
chalk stream where he'd learned to fish as a boy.

One evening we had a picnic there. After we'd all had more than a
few nips of the stuff that killed Dr. McWalsey, one of my friends, Jim
Davies, crept to a place in the willows just above the spot where Rod
was making a few farewell casts in the fading light. He sneakily threw

several of the abundant meadow muffins (or cattle droppings) into the water near the bushes about a minute apart, convincing Rod there was a gigantic trout feeding in the dark shadows above him. We dared not disabuse him, and I hope he always carried with him the memory of that big gulper in the meadow.

Some of my most exciting fishing adventures I owe to another friend I met at a Sun Valley conclave, Ernie Schwiebert. Ernie is as good a fishing author as there is, and his works had guided me well long before I met him. Because of him I had my first chance to fish in Chile, where I have returned year after year to turn late winter into early fall. Ernie took me first just before Christmas and my appetite was permanently whetted for the lovely country near Lago Ranco, where Adrian Dufflocq runs a great lodge for visiting fly fishermen.

It was also through Ernie that Ed Rice made an Alaskan dream trip possible for me, to Kulik and later to Enchanted Lake. I was supposed to be substituting as Ernie's photographer, since Dan Callaghan couldn't make it because of prior business. Poor Ernie! When he needed me to take photos of the enormous rainbows he was hooking and playing with the casual skill of a true master, I was so busy with my own fish that I refused to move from the hot spot I had found where I was taking the biggest rainbows I had ever seen. Result? No pictures, save a few of the gang and of the scenery; not the stuff a writer needs to illustrate the pages of his stories.

A conclave friendship led to a memorable test of western steelheaders against the masters of the Atlantic salmon on the famed Grand Cascapedia as guests of Nathaniel Reed, then assistant secretary of the Interior for Fish, Wildlife, and Parks. What a lineup it was: Reed, Grant, and Schwiebert *versus* Moore, Callaghan, and Hemingway. The home team won, but it was close. Ernie lost a great fish and felt worse about it than I would have thought it warranted. He explained that he needed that fish for the hungry maws of those outdoors magazines which insist on perpetual success and not the reality of oft-confronted failure, the stuff of learning. But such failures couldn't hold down a man of Ernie's caliber for long; he was the man who taught me that "Anything worth doing at all is worth doing to excess!"

I owe my brother Pat for the great George River of Ungava and the continuing friendships with Lou and Tom Black, and that little Italian comedian who needs two ordinary men to balance the other end of the canoe, Dick Lumenello, known to his friends as "Captain Salmon." The pals one makes in the course of a lifetime of fishing are irreplaceable. Though I prefer to fish and hunt alone, a large part of the wealth I have is in the friends who shared the camps and the evening fellowship and never ceased to plan the ultimate trip.

I still have many untold tales of fishing and hunting, which I will spare you. I'm reserving them for those among my kindred spirits who, like me, dream the closed season long of the shooting of swift birds in flight, and of the dogs, all good, some great, who point and fetch; and for those as well who, like me, dream of unfished streams yet to explore and of those small past triumphs we all so magnify in our winter thoughts.

TWO

A SPORTSMAN'S LIFE

I

SOME WORDS ABOUT FLY FISHING

1
Seasons of the Angler

The spring of my fishing life began in the West, at a dude ranch in the valley of the Clark's Fork of the Yellowstone. It was my sixth year, and my father had the wit and wisdom to let me build up a desire to fish on my own. In fact, allowed me only to watch him for the greater part of that summer before finally permitting me to try with some of his old, back-up equipment.

A pond with some lovely little eastern brook trout and a back eddy of the Clark's Fork near the cabin became my haunts for the last few weeks of our stay. Though I used a fly rod and line, I threaded morning-caught grasshoppers on old, worn wet flies my father had discarded. I learned that the back eddy would sink the baited fly if I let if float naturally until the vortex sucked it down. This was almost invariably followed by a hesitation of the line and an overstrong strike. Sometimes such a strike resulted in a small golden-hued cutthroat trout being snatched from the water and landing at a point behind me. There I would pounce on it and put it in one of the Hardy Bros. woven grass bags that, in those days, my father used for creels. The pond, on the other hand, proved frustrating and the green-backed brookies with their white-edged pectorals haunted my winter dreams.

My second summer at the ranch, I converted from grasshoppers to wet flies, the method my father used. It was basic wet-fly technique, casting down and across with silk lines and tapered gut leaders nine feet long with two or more flies premounted on droppers in addition to the tippet fly. It served me well, and I was soon catching more and slightly larger fish than I had with the hoppers. I also became more mobile, riding my horse farther and farther afield to explore and fish lakes, ponds, and streams throughout the area. In those first few years of fishing at the ranch, my objective was to catch lots of trout. Whatever fish Papa didn't want for breakfast were welcomed at the ranch kitchen.

A book from my stepfather set the stage for expanding my fishing sphere. *Trout* by Ray Bergman captured my imagination, introducing me to the vast number of places to fish and techniques to master and stimulating a voracious hunger for all of the literature of fly fishing. First the American authors and then the British inspired new dreams of fishing.

This springtime of my fishing life continued into my late teens. Being sent to prep school back East in the Hudson Highlands did not interfere with my progress for I managed to develop a certain skill in upstream low water worming in the little brooks that ran through the Black Rock Forest. It was there in the few stretches of those tiny streams adequate to the purpose that I discovered the possibilities of upstream nymphing (without the travesty of an indicator). The number of fish caught continued to have some importance, but my father's early admonition never to waste any fish or game established my limits. The concept of catch-and-release had not yet spread beyond a few experimenters in Michigan, where the Hazzard plan was first instituted on some waters by Trout Unlimited, and the Paradise in Belfont, Pennsylvania. I had not yet heard of this idea and was much too busy learning and honing my skills to worry about anything more than finding new fishing grounds and more and bigger fish.

When I was sixteen, my mother and stepfather, Paul Mowrer, gave me a used Pontiac, which I was permitted to drive by myself from Chicago to the Crossed Sabers dude ranch west of Cody, Wyoming, where they were spending part of the summer. Having the car at the ranch enabled me to broaden my fishing horizons well beyond the nearby waters of the Shoshone River and its tributaries, and Yellowstone National Park and the surrounding area became my next nirvana. A fly fisherman also vacationing at the Crossed Sabers helped me along with some Bivisible dry flies and a few pointers on line handling during the drift and retrieve. He was just one of many fishermen over the years who helped to point me in the right direction. He encouraged me to try the dries on the big water of the main Shoshone, where I had my first few successes, but the clincher came when I drove into Yellowstone and had my first session of dry-fly fishing on the Madison.

The stretch I chose has seldom ever produced well for me since, but that day it was to provide a magic moment. I chose fast water, the type I was familiar with in the freestone Shoshone, but with the dark bottom lent by the volcanic rocks and, of course, verdant weed beds wherever the current slackened along the sides of the run. Although I detected no apparent rises, I had read George LaBranche's *The Dry Fly and Fast Water*, and, trying to follow his dictates, fished the current methodically, false-casting between drifts to dry my fly. In the shallow water at the head of the run, my fly disappeared into a hollow in the current created by what then seemed to me to be the biggest trout I had ever seen fishing. My reaction was slow because of my surprise, and consequently, I did not strike too fast. The fish was on. It turned out not to be any bigger than the cutthroat trout my mother and Paul and I had caught on wet flies along the shores of Yellowstone Lake and on the upper Yellowstone River, but what a difference in its strength and my excitement. At eighteen inches, it was my first brown trout over fourteen, and though he was an ugly hookjawed male, he looked beautiful to me with his spots Ming red in the afternoon sun.

The dry fly became an obsession after that first brown on the Madison, and I think that I caught the "big fish" bug then as well. That marked the late spring of my fly fisher's life.

The following year, I was introduced to Silver Creek in Idaho. It turned out that my father's accounts of the creek in his letters to me at school were up to the mark. It truly did resemble my dream of an English chalk stream, which I had constructed from reading and rereading Halford's *Dry Fly Fishing*. The problem was that my skills were not up to the challenges it presented.

My first try was with a young guide, Clayton Stuart, who years later became mayor of Sun Valley. Stu was one of a fine crew of local fly fishermen recruited by head guide Taylor Williams. They knew their locale well but were limited by what we would now view as inadequate tackle and a limited knowledge of aquatic entomology. This was true of most trout fishermen of that time.

On our first foray, I remember creeping up to a point just below a U-bend where an old fence post in the middle of the stream had gathered weed that hung below in the current. There were multiple rises both above and below the post, and Stu assured me that some of those rises were made by three- to five-pound rainbows. Although Stu tried, he could not assure my success, since I was determined to fish only dry flies. The patterns he recommended to me were the Woodruff (insect green wool body, grizzly hackle tip tail, brown hackle tied full, and grizzly hackle tip spent wings) on a #12 or #14 hook and the then ubiquitous ginger quill on the same size hooks. I believe he also mentioned the Renegade as a possibility, which I rejected out of hand though I probably shouldn't have as it does a fair job of giving an impression of an egg-laying caddis. Try as I would, I could not fool the fish. The flies I was using certainly didn't look much like what seemed to be floating down the stream, though the ginger quill wasn't that far off the mark except that it was at least two or three times too large. Apparently, there were times when these flies produced, but not then and not for me. I still see Stu now and again, and he recalls that despite my lack of success, I was, even then, an accomplished caster.

This was due in part to another angler who played an important role in helping me develop my skills. Leander McCormick, author of *Fishing Around the World*, spent part of a weekend afternoon, the summer at Crossed Sabers helping with my casting. He taught me something that was to prove invaluable over the years—steeple casting. This entails throwing the back cast as close as possible to straight up before the forward stroke. A high back cast is the hallmark of all good casters.

Looking back, there were some positive aspects about the tackle limitations. For one thing the false casting to dry the fly would, if done properly and well out of the fish's sight periphery, rest the fist to some extent. The need to keep gut leaders properly dampened and to stop fishing altogether for periods of ten minutes to half an hour to wipe off, sun dry, and regrease the fine silk lines gave the angler a chance to sit and observe what was going on in and on the water and to appreciate the world around him. The finest leaders available then were 4X gut and were not as strong as 8X is today. This necessitated a much better presentation to avoid drag and very careful handling of any fish hooked. Needless to say, few very large fish were landed, especially in weed-infested streams such as Silver Creek. When they were, it was the result of luck and a level of skill seldom achieved by today's anglers.

The last summer before World War II, I returned to Yellowstone for a six-week idyll with several of my prep school classmates. Over the six weeks, we all improved our level of sophistication. We bought a fabulous little book, *Waters of Yellowstone* by Howard Back, in a West Yellowstone tackle shop and followed many of its pointers. (The book has since been updated by Charles Brooks with photos by my friend Dan Callaghan.) We had brought with us our own fly-tying equipment as well as a supply of eastern dry-fly patterns we had used our allowances to buy from the Darbees in Livingston Manor, New York. Prior to our departure, Paul Stroud, a well-known fly tyer in Arlington Heights, Illinois, had helped me learn new tying skills and had given me a supply of a then new material—nylon. Paul had dyed it brown with silver nitrate, and it suited the Yellowstone streams perfectly. It was much stronger than gut, though somewhat unreliable in those days and prone to surprise breaks when cold, nicked, or badly knotted. I remember a particularly frustrating day at the Widow's Preserve (now a public pond), where we were hooking enormous brook trout that broke free time after time even with our damselflies tied onto the butt of the leader!

Later that summer, my classmates and I moved on to temporary jobs at the Hines Lumber Mill in central Oregon and had our first experience with summer steelhead on the North Umpqua. Again, we relied on a book, devouring the chapter devoted to steelhead in Ray Bergman's *Trout*. Nevertheless, the experience had its disappointments. I raised a fish to the fly but it almost immediately broke off, and one of my companions had his prized Granger Aristocrat fly rod confiscated by a state trooper who found he was fishing without a proper license. The river, however, captured all of our imaginations with its beauty, its power, and the magnificent fish we knew it harbored.

During the war that followed that last carefree summer, I managed some occasional fly fishing. Once I had become an officer, I took advantage of my new privileges by bringing my basic fly tackle with me wherever I was sent, much to the amusement of my military fellows. I even carried it during a parachute mission into occupied France, where I had several opportunities to ply my craft. One of these turned out to be hair-raising when a German patrol passed me while I was midstream.

After the war, I attended the University of Montana, where my continued education included fly fishing between classes in a river running through the campus. While there, I learned about positive drag with dry flies, that is, specially designed dry flies cast crosscurrent and allowed to swim while dragging along the surface, leaving a small wake. This technique was used locally with hard-bodied imitations of giant stoneflies with stiff horsehair wings during the famous Salmon fly hatch. Later it proved effective with smaller damselfly patterns on Silver Creek and in Germany while fishing for grayling and brown trout on the Eder River and the lower Ammer in Bavaria.

Between Montana and my return to the army and Europe, I spent several years tying flies for a living in San Francisco and working for a fishing line company, Ashaway Line Company, in their home office in Rhode Island. I demonstrated casting at sportsman's shows and later traveled the West Coast selling their new over-the-rod spinning reel. This reel led to the great fishing revolution of the twentieth century.

Had it not been for the introduction of the fixed spool reel to the U.S. after World War II, it is quite possible that interest and participation in sport fishing generally, and trout fishing particularly, would never have exploded. What spinning tackle did was make an instant expert out of every novice in the country who had never before been able to cast a bait-casting reel without getting a backlash, or cast a fly without catching bushes and trees, or drift a bait through a run without losing it. Spinning made all of these skills easy to possess. I must admit, even I was enticed early on. It was great fun to be able to cast light-weight lures tremendous distances and reach fish that had never been fished effectively.

In much the same way, many of today's anglers have been seduced by the relatively easy success that can be achieved with deep-drifted wet flies and nymphs beneath an indicator. Guides have promoted this method since it can guarantee satisfied customers, and, then, tips for the guides. However, as with spinning, success with this method comes at the expense of the fishery and of other anglers. Methods that circumvent the inherent difficulties in fly fishing defeat all that is best about the sport. Later, when I realized the damage spinning was doing to all of our great fisheries across the country, I rued the day I participated in its introduction.

After I left active duty in the Army, I settled my family in Portland, Oregon, close to the scene of my first successes with steelhead on a fly, the Kalama River in southwest Washington, and, of course, many other fine steelhead rivers. Then, Merrill Lynch sent me to training in New York followed by an assignment in Havana. A bad case of hepatitis and the subsequent arrival of Fidel Castro led to my transfer to San Francisco. There, I was within weekend reach of good fishing and close to reasonable winter steelhead fly fishing. The North Umpqua became the target of extended long weekends and of vacations not taken in Idaho.

It was about this time I met the man who was to become my closest and best fishing companion, Dan Callaghan. A recently married young attorney with the same sort of fiendish devotion to steelhead fly fishing that I was developing, Dan joined me on innumerable fishing expeditions all over the country and overseas as well. His photographic skills and organizational ability were vital to the formation of one of the strongest member clubs of the Federation of Fly Fishers, the North Umpqua Steamboaters. The federation was one of two separate but similarly intentioned groups formed to protect and enhance our cold water fisheries. Trout Unlimited, the other group, had existed for some time and was national in scope. It aimed its efforts at saving resources, while the newcomer federation worked to convert the heathens to fly fishing. These important activities were gaining momentum in the early sixties.

My fishing in the early sixties was limited to vacations and extended weekends due to family and business responsibilities. I have to admit my failure to be a world beater in business was due in no small part to the fact that the world of fly fishing was infinitely more important to me than such mundane matters as economic survival.

After a permanent move to Idaho and the Big Wood River valley, I built a home along the river five miles out of town, being careful to keep it well away from the floodplain. The next years I spent in learning all I could about two rivers, the Big and Little Wood. Of course, this was interspersed with annual expeditions to the Yellowstone area with Dan Callaghan.

Dan and I were privy to current developments in the research of Swisher and Richards, authors of *Selective Trout*, a new book that became a significant factor in awakening interest in fly fishing. *Selective Trout* was the first work to popularly present trout stream insects and how best to emulate them with a fly since Ernie Schwiebert's *Matching the Hatch*, came out. Schwiebert's book was too early to gain as wide an audience. Dan and I were similarly privy to current developments in research being done in Montana by Dick Vincent, a fisheries biologist. His work finally gave scientific credence to what serious trout fishermen already knew. Wild trout were superior to hatchery-reared trout in their ability to survive in the wild with the glaring exception that, because of their territoriality, the larger mature fish had difficulty surviving the pervasive schooling tactics of hatchery trout dumped into their environment. Both Dan and I as well as another pal, Frank Moore, were appointed to our respective state fish and game commissions and were able to influence the gradual institution of wild fish programs in those areas where they were appropriate, permitting the hatcheries to concentrate their efforts on supplying urban fishing areas, reservoirs, and the growing anadromous fish programs.

I feel I achieved my true maturity on the Little Wood. I spent, according to my family, an inordinate amount of time there. It was one of the first streams in our part of the state to receive fry plants of brown trout, and I was like a mother hen, keeping track of their development. I had my first eighteen incher and first twenty-four incher caught in the river mounted, and after that I stopped any killing, though several trophies of over thirty inches have fallen to my dry hoppers over the years. Unfortunately, despite a three-mile fly-only, catch-and-release area, the quality of the fishing has not held up. Local fish hogs regularly poach the area, and trophy fish are scarce due to heavy bait fishing throughout the drainage. Nevertheless, the trout population is self-sustaining, and both wild rainbows and browns comprise the quarry. The possibility of a whopper still exists for the careful, thoughtful, skilled fly fisherman. Spending time on a stream, not just fishing but also sitting and observing, gave me a true appreciation of a stream's complex ecology. The seemingly barren lava badlands along the Little Wood were teeming with wildlife. All that was required to make this discovery was time spent being quiet and still and always nonthreatening.

My fall expeditions ranged farther afield, to the area around Lewiston, Idaho, to fish the great steelhead producing tributaries of the Snake River, where it leaves the state to wend its way through the eastern Washington desert to the great Columbia. Part of the time I spent hunting chukar and Hungarian partridge. British Columbia drew us for the same reasons, with ruffed grouse replacing partridge, but giant steelhead still the prime objective. Over the years, we had gradually come to fish for these noble fish with floating lines almost all of the time and more and more with dry flies fished in the same manner as I had learned as a student in Montana. A few tricks, such as a loop between the reel and the rod hand to help give sufficient slack on a tight line for the fly to be sucked into the fish's jaw, improved our hooking success immeasurably. There is always something new to learn.

An improvement in my finances enabled me to devote some serious efforts in the pursuit of Atlantic salmon, an unfortunately expensive sport. My steelhead skills proved to be quite adequate, but the salmon fishing led to some new techniques that proved valuable in their turn for steelheading. Most steelheaders scoff at the long, two-handed fly rods used by most European salmon fishermen, because they can catch salmon with their shorter, single-handed rods. However, they are missing the point. Once the two-handed casting is mastered, it is infinitely less tiring over a long day's fishing, covers much more water efficiently, can be used effectively where there is no room for a back cast, and, not by any means least, nothing is lost in the enjoyment of the fight.

Now, at seventy, in the mid-autumn of my fishing life, I still look forward to great new experiences, though I tend to look back as well, I realize what enormous changes I have witnessed and, to a considerable extent, have participated in. The explosion in fly fishing of the past decade and a half has probably created as many problems as it was supposed to solve. The greatest of these have been commercialization by the fly-fishing industry of what has always been a national birthright and the ignorance of the new generation of fly fishers of both the etiquette and values that characterized their predecessors.

2
Fly Fishing
Manners

W e were enjoying the greatest steelhead season in the Snake
River system since records were first kept of the number
of fish over the dams. We were also experiencing the
greatest number of steelhead fly fishermen ever to assemble in the
general area of the Clearwater, Snake, Grande Ronde, and Salmon
rivers. There was a time when this would have delighted me. That so
many of the good runs should be occupied by fly angers would have
been a joy. That time has long passed. No longer are the odds with
me that a fly fisherman met on the stream will possess at least a fun-
damental understanding of streamside etiquette and a modicum of
manners. What was particularly disturbing during this season was that
a substantial proportion of the fly rod wielders were guides from other
areas. They were on businessmen's holidays. Nothing wrong with
that had they set a good example. Instead, they were pool hogs.
Scarcely the sort of behavior one would expect from those who intro-
duce beginners to our sport.

On one occasion, after finding most of my favorite runs already in
use by one or more anglers, I parked off the road near a long broad run

on the Snake River. I put on my waders and laced up my boots and, as I started to put my rod together, a four-wheel drive vehicle pulled in right beside mine. The driver, a youngster in his early twenties, got out and, waders already on, started for the tailgate of his car to fetch his already set-up rod. When I asked him rather pointedly, "Are you actually planning to fish this run?"

He replied, "Of course," as he started for the best part of the run. "In that case I'll go somewhere else," I said. "You don't have to do that. There's plenty of room for two." "Only if you fish for companionship," I replied somewhat ungraciously. I left him with the pool all to himself and a puzzled look on his face. He hadn't a clue, and therein lies the problem.

When we "old-timers" first became involved with the fledgling Federation of Fly Fishermen in the mid to late 1960s, most of us already had years of fly-fishing experience under our belts. We had suffered through the spinning gear revolution, which followed World War II and populated our rivers, lakes, and streams with an explosion of newcomers. We hoped that we would be able to start a meaningful move to convert many of these newcomers to the ancient art of the fly. The reasons were many, but certainly among the most important, were the gentler aspects of the sport and that it lent itself to such conservation measures as catch-and-release. While it formed no formal part of our logic, there was an unspoken feeling among us that fly fishermen were somehow a superior breed and more likely than other anglers to be gentlemen. Initially this attitude created some serious difficulties in our relations with other groups and opened us to the valid criticism that we were "elitists." Nevertheless, the federation made enormous strides in the years that followed and, along with the less method-oriented Trout Unlimited, was instrumental in changing attitudes about the value of our freshwater fishing resources. What these efforts also accomplished was totally unanticipated: an explosion in fly fishing, augmented by the booming economics of the Reagan era and the rise of the yuppie.

Also born of this era was the proliferation of the fly-fishing industry. The positive aspects were many—marvelous technological innovations in tackle, and rebirth of fly-fishing literature, new learning tools such as video, and the ubiquitous fly-fishing school. The tackle industry suddenly recognized the importance of the fly-fishing sector, and fly fisherman mailing lists grew five to ten times their size almost overnight. Specialty magazines were born and thrived. Fly tying became not just a serious hobby but, in many cases, a profitable enterprise spawning fly-tying conglomerates based in low labor-cost countries. The best created a self-policed system for awarding royalties to the innovative American tyers whose patterns were changing much of fly fishing and being reproduced en masse in South America, India, Sri Lanka, and East Africa. Old fishing lodges were refurbished, and new ones were created by the hundreds in heretofore unlikely locations. Entire communities previously devoted to logging suddenly spewed forth fly-fishing guides as their principal product. While some states, such as Idaho, sought to control guide numbers by limiting outfitter licenses, others viewed the trend as an income producer. Anyone willing to pay for a guide license became a guide. Even limiting the number of outfitters in any particular area failed to solve the problem as the outfitters could employ an unlimited number of guides. Outfitters, however, by having to post bonds, did impose a measure of responsibility on their guides.

Perhaps the single biggest development of the new age of fly fishing was the research done in Montana on the Madison River and O'Dell Creek by Richard Vincent in the late sixties and early seventies. While there was a growing interest in special regulations such as catch-and-release, fly-only, and single-hook-artificial-only, the solidly entrenched state fisheries agencies were loathe to cede any ground to plans that would inevitably lead to a diminution of their role in cold water fisheries. They had the support of a constituency nurtured by years of easy handouts. These were becoming increasingly expensive in view of higher feed costs and the poor rate of return to the creel in all but heavily fished urban waters. Vincent's research, done in stages over a number of years, proved beyond a doubt the following:

- Hatchery catchables that survived the fishing season had a poor chance of surviving a severe winter in the wild.

- The cost of providing hatchery fish was substantially greater than fees from fishing licenses.
- In those sections of river where catchables were introduced, the populations of larger wild trout were almost entirely eliminated.
- This was caused by the social behavior of the catchable hatchery trout, whose schooling patterns—learned in the confines of crowded concrete rearing ponds—totally disregarded the territorial behavior of the larger wild fish. The wild fish were used to defending their favored lies against the attempted forays of a few competitors but were unable to do so against the continuous crowding of the congenital idiots from the concrete pens.

These conclusions and a growing interest in fishing for wild fish in streams and rivers eventually led fish-and-game agencies to modify their views and, finally, to advocate wild trout management in those places where it was deemed appropriate.

Research on such endangered late-maturing species as the West Slope Cutthroat led to the adoption by Idaho of catch-and-release regulations in much of their habitat and a consequent resurgence in populations of this wild, native trout. Later moves toward catch-and-release were in response to public pressure exerted by fly fishermen. The hatchery bureaucracy was able to perform yeoman service in stocking fingerlings in reservoirs and lakes where nature could grow them to suitable size. The bureaucracy also assumed a leading role in the new steelhead and salmon recovery programs that were then just coming on-line. The byword of this time of change was "quality." Strangely, the word became an adjective and suddenly everyone was seeking a "quality experience."

For years it appeared that nirvana was fast approaching. Each new area designated for special regulations brought joy to all fly fishermen and especially to those of us who had struggled for years to help bring all this about. Unfortunately, we hadn't counted on the herd instinct of the new fly fishermen. None of them wanted to fish anywhere but where there were special regulations. Within a ten-year span, such former paradises as the railroad ranch stretch of Henry's Fork of the

Snake and the Sun Valley Ranch stretch of Silver Creek became over-crowded hells.

The plus side was that above and below these stretches one could fish in unregulated waters in more or less complete solitude with only an occasional immobile bait fisherman to add flair to the landscape. Unfortunately, the guides soon brought clients to even these places as their hunger for new secret fishing spots grew unabated. Waters fished only by a few cognoscenti and locals sported guided all-day float traffic. The new generation of guides considered these fisheries their private domain, owed to them so they could make a living. A guide today who doesn't spend his winters in the tropics or the antipodes hasn't got it all together. The far corners of the world are currently being invaded by a horde as devastating to the art of contemplative angling as the barbarians to Rome or the sodbusters to the old West. Fortunes are being spent in the feverish pursuit of Atlantic salmon throughout their range, and the pursuit of steelhead has created crowded fly-fishing conditions throughout their range, with the possible exception of a few fly in locations and the newly opened areas of Kamchatka.

While hatchery stocks of steelhead seem to be holding their own in many areas, there are already signs that drastic measures must be taken to rejuvenate the area. Furthermore, the success of some salmon programs in British Columbia has imperiled wild steelhead races. Commercial fisherman are taking huge salmon quotas in non-selective fisheries at the mouths of such key rivers as the Dean and Skeena. The ratio of steelhead to salmon is now so small that those segments of the steelhead runs entering the river during the salmon-netting season are being virtually wiped out. This has diminished the early fly fishing available in many Skeena tributaries and in the Dean River. It has also concentrated the best fishing into the latter part of the season when the vagaries of equinoxial weather and possible early freeze-up can add obstacles in addition to already crowded conditions.

The search for the grail of large, relatively easy fish in uncrowded waters has become the new fetish of our sport, and few of us can plead "not guilty." When the promised rewards of a costly and lengthy journey fail to materialize, it can be a serious blow not only to our pocketbooks but to our egos. Many newcomers to the sport don't realize that something very important has disappeared from fly fishing. Strangely, that something, which I would describe as a combination of tranquility, gentleness, quiet, modesty, solitude, appreciation, consideration, and contemplation can still be found in a few backwaters that have been passed by.

Rare indeed is the angler who acquired his skills or his ethics entirely on his own. Most of us old-timers learned by example. We watched and emulated veteran fishermen and benefited from those who generously gave of their precious time astream to help us. While the angling literature of the past also guided our progress, most of it was sufficiently vague to require our experimenting on our own and consequently evolving our own techniques to solve the myriad problems a stream and its trout can pose.

Problems presented by crowding due to steelhead and salmon runs on waters close to urban areas were solved by practical working rules adapted to the majority method of angling. Where wet-fly fishing was the accepted norm, for example, it rapidly became understood that a rotation system with no one breaking into the middle of the run was the rule. Anyone seeking to break into the pattern anywhere but at the top was severely chastised by all present. Under more normal, less crowded conditions on public waters, a strict code of ethics prevailed. It was unheard of to enter any pool or reach of water being fished by another angler unless invited. Conversely, it was considered extremely poor form to hog a pool by staying indefinitely in one spot. If you found an angler fishing one of your favored spots, it was unthinkable to position yourself obviously while awaiting his departure. The proper procedure was either to go elsewhere, leaving him to enjoy his fishing undisturbed or to hide in such a manner as to remain totally undetected. This, by the way, was one of the best ways to learn, whether by detecting errors in the angler's approach or by noting something innovative and successful.

In relatively featureless waters such as long freestone flows without obvious riffle pool sequence or on meadow waters, the protocol was to ascertain whether an angler was fishing up or downstream and only to fish the water behind him and at a distance sufficiently removed that he could in no way ever feel that he was being hurried. The newcomer was to work at the same or slower pace than the angler with precedence.

To tell the truth, some of the finest stretches of stream I've ever fished were discovered as a result of the old, popular, obvious spots being already occupied. In years with goodly numbers of summer steelhead showing in the sparkling pools of the North Umpqua, Dan Callaghan and I fished the river together, alternating who would fish the principal runs while the other concentrated on water above and below. These sections were nameless and outwardly featureless, but often provided exciting surprises. Several of these runs have since acquired name status and have proved reliable even in years when fish have been scarce. Unfortunately, it is becoming more and more difficult to find waters to fish without the company of others. Such stratagems as avoiding the major hatches like the green drake, brown drake, salmon fly, willow fly, and Tricos can prove helpful. For instance, if a particular hatch attracts all the anglers for its emergence at 9:00 A.M. every morning, these fellows tend to leave when it is over at 11:30. The rest of the day can be quite pleasant with much of the stream to oneself. Opening day circuses and the major, large fly hatches, such as the salmon fly in the West, should be avoided at all costs unless you do indeed fish for the company of other fishermen. My preference is for "dog day" fishing, when no one wants to be astream and the fish are not interested in anything. Catching any fish then is a true achievement, and solitude is possible.

A certain portion of the South Fork of the Boise River here in Idaho remained the almost exclusive province of a small group of serious fly fishermen during the fifties and sixties. Their secret was some professionally prepared signs, which they posted, proclaiming the area to be thick with dangerous rattlesnakes. Today's fly fisherman is too competitive to be put off so easily. The rattlesnakes have long since been crowded out of that canyon.

These stratagems are only escapes from the real problems of commercialization, the new fly fishers' general ignorance of the manners and morals of fly fishing, and the elevation of technical knowledge and result-oriented success over the appreciation of the real values of our sport.

At one time, I took pride in knowing the Latin, or scientific name of every fish and every insect with which I was ever likely to come into contact. To take some of the wind out of the sails of those new experts who know everything and nothing about fly fishing for trout, who are totally and expensively equipped, and who have been inappropriately educated by hero-figure guides and fly-fishing school gurus, I have joined the "little grey fucker" school of fly fishing, size and color being adjustable. I continue to encourage honesty and lament when the question "Where did you catch him?" receives a response such as "in the mouth" or some fictitious location.

My friend Adrian Dufflocq, who sees many anglers fish at his Cumilahue Lodge in Chile, rates them according to their "slime factor." This is an exponential number indicating the extent to which an angler will lie about the results of his fishing in order to appear to be a better, or at least a more successful, fisherman than he really is. I remember a crowded August on the North Umpqua when the water skeleton was low and no fish were being caught—no fish, that is, except for those one particular angler reported having caught and released on each of six otherwise fishless days. Six turned out to be his slime factor. I sacrificed one shameful day to spying on the poor fellow with my ten-power field glasses and nary a fish did he touch. However, at kiss-and-tell time over iced Bombay gin, he reported that six fish had again been released. I decided thereafter to believe all fish reports. I'm convinced that a doubted tale teller may kill fish he would otherwise have released because he thinks he will not be believed without the cold *corpus delecti*.

Some four hundred years ago on the ninth of August, 1593, the patron saint of fly fishermen, Izaac Walton, was born into what was essentially a pastoral society. Until the heavy water demands of the past decade caused damaging abstractions of groundwater from the chalk downs of Devon, Hampshire, and Wiltshire, trout fishing survived in Walton's bailiwick, almost in the shadow of London, despite the Industrial Revolution. While the fly-fishing explosion had an impact in England, it was mostly in reservoir fishing, which became available to the general public on a daily ticket basis at fairly reasonable prices, but with fly-fishing restrictions. Stream fishing remained, as it had for generations, the purview of the landed and wealthy. Riparian rights include the water, its fish, and the right to fish. Good manners tend to be characteristic of the British. Fishing there is still a pleasure, if you can afford it.

Americans have been the legatees of a wonderful tradition of hunting and fishing available to one and all. Public hunting is, sadly, already becoming increasingly expensive except in the national forests and the holdings of the Bureau of Land Management. As for fishing, recent court decisions have guaranteed public access to navigable rivers, but the restriction to remain below the high watermark has eliminated the nonboating fisherman in many instances. Pressure is building geometrically on public waters countrywide. It is not inconceivable that fish-and-game agencies might be forced to limit access in premium areas by using drawings as is done for special game management units. It would require thorough planning in order to give weekend access to locals and make the time slots of sufficient length to be of value to vacationers. In a survey regarding the Nature Conservancy waters on Silver Creek in Idaho, a surprising number of anglers felt that since the increasing numbers of fishermen didn't adversely affect the fishing results, any attempt to limit numbers would be an imposition. My own position is that results are not what's at stake but enjoying the angling experience. Since that poll was taken, there are indications that angler numbers are stressing to the fish.

What is badly needed is a strong educational program that can give a different slant to the attitudes and expectations of so many of today's fly fishermen. A behavioral coda needs to be established and taught with the same vehemence as catch-and-release and given a high priority by organizations that promote fly fishing—from the clubs to the businesses. Furthermore, the competitiveness that is taking over fly fishing must give way to a greater appreciation for the quieter aspects of the sport. The "in your face" angler so often encountered these days—who when confronted with his trespasses typically retorts, "What do ya think? You own the fucking stream?" —must somehow be shamed into modifying his behavior.

A whole generation of fishermen has missed an integral part of its education. It should be the objective of every old-timer to try to do his or her bit in teaching these values. We can start by replacing the standard "How'd you do?" with "Enjoying your fishing?" We can keep the gains we've made and learn to share our enjoyment of the sport.

Eventually, I came to realize that I had demonstrated an ungenerous spirit when I left that young fellow on the Snake to fish the run alone. My remark, though meant to illuminate, may well have reinforced a bad habit. I should have stayed and given a little of myself. Only by analyzing our own errors and correcting them can we all set the right example and help to lead others into the New Quiet Revolution—the one where tranquility, gentleness, quiet, modesty, solitude, appreciation, consideration, and contemplation comprise the standard of perfection.

II

SOME MEMORABLE ANGLERS

3
Charles
Ritz

When Charley Ritz suggested to me in early May 1950 that I should leave my wife and brand new baby daughter in the American hospital in Paris to recover undisturbed, as the doctor had already suggested, and join him for a couple of days of fishing on the Risle River in Normandy, I didn't take long to say "yes." So with a fairly clear conscience I joined Charley at the Gare St.-Lazare for the train to Évreux. Charley had already played an important part in my fishing life. A longtime friend of my father's, he had helped me obtain employment with the Ashaway Line Company in 1948, and now he was introducing me to the world of European trout fishing. He briefed me thoroughly on the train, and we were soon at our destination. We were met by Edouard Vernes' driver, who took us to the large thatched farmstead Edouard and his wife, Michou, had converted to a fishing headquarters on the Risle. Edouard had spent many years acquiring bits and pieces of this prime Norman chalk stream, and by making trades, had managed to put together close to six kilometers of both banks of the finest stretch of the lower river before it became polluted. Fortunately, the Vernes enjoyed sharing their bounty with friends and enthusiasts and took enormous pride in the quality of their fishing. The Risle was the first place I saw numbered live baskets scattered along the river for placing caught trout. There they survived until picked up by the keeper if needed for the table or released back into the river if not. This was as close to catch-and-release as I ever encountered in France. The Vernes were perfect hosts and great traditionalists. One was expected to dress properly to fish, and although nymphing was permitted, it was discouraged whenever the flies were up.

It must be said that when the French go about emulating the British, they outdo themselves. On the Risle, there were no ghillies, but the keepers did a superb job of weed and bank control, and the beat and rod assignments were totally under the personal control of Edouard Vernes himself. Charley took me in hand and put me in a good area with the advice that if no surface flies appeared and no rises were seen I should not hesitate to put on a small black and silver wet, which he favored when things were slow. As soon as he had checked out my casting abilities and left me to my own devices, I reverted to my George LaBranche methods and started fishing the water with a dry fly in what seemed to me to be the natural feeding lanes where currents joined or where they sped up between weed beds. The weather was cold and blustery, and I saw no obvious rises though some very occasional small mayflies were visible at times for a few instants before being blown away and taking wing. Two small browns fell to my efforts that afternoon and were promptly returned to the water as they were well below the thirty-centimeter (twelve-inch) limit Vernes imposed.

The next day the weather was the same except that we were on a better stretch for larger fish and it was a bit warmer. None of the big ephemera mayflies appeared as it was still a week early, but there was a bit more activity on the surface and we did see a few rising fish. Most were "oncers" and were not seen to rise again in the same place. A few were occasional risers on station, and both Charley and I managed to hook and land several fish in the fourteen-inch range. They were in good condition, though not yet fat, and we put them in the keeping baskets. We had to get back to Paris on the afternoon train, and it wasn't until twenty-one years later that I had another chance to fish the Risle. By then Charley's mother had died, and he was running the hotel. He had made many innovations and, but for a shortage of capital, would have made many more. Despite these responsibilities, he was eager for our second trip together to fish the Risle.

After some casting sessions at the Bois de Boulogne, where my photographer companion, Bill Rousey took some fine shots of Charley casting a long, beautifully controlled line with seemingly effortless ease for a man in his late seventies, Charley called Michou, now a widow, to arrange for our fishing the Risle. Charley, Rousey, and I drove a rental car to Normandy and engaged rooms at a local inn within a few kilometers of the fishing. It was midsummer, and we were presented with a totally different scene from my first visit when the leaves had been only just budding. This time it was hot and muggy, and in a short briefing, the keeper indicated that we would catch nothing as the trout were totally off the feed. The preceding day some angers who were reputed to be highly skilled had come away with nothing and left in disgust.

To start Rousey took many pictures, and I spent a good deal of time studying the water with the field glasses I always carry on the stream. I began to detect the very faintest of rise forms, rises almost imperceptible to the naked eye. Due to the glare and the density of the weed beds, it was difficult to see the fish themselves, and because I could not see the fly on the water, I presumed—correctly it turned out—that we were dealing with minute spinners. As is often the case, American patterns work fine when dealing with foreign trout. I put a tan-bodied hen wing spinner on a 6X tippet and a long leader. I was fishing an eight-foot Winston bamboo rod for a four line. It was just the ticket for these finicky fish that had never seen truly small artificials before. Many of the tiny rise forms were made by large fish, but with the abundant weed growth, landing them was extremely difficult and only a very few reached the net. It was, however, very satisfying fishing and as challenging as anyone could ask for. The keeper came along during this exercise and couldn't believe his eyes when I showed him the tiny flies I was using to hook the fish. I think the reason the previous anglers had not tried anything that small was their unwillingness to use extremely fine terminal tackle. Apparently, they relied on very heavy leader tippets, and fish, when hooked, were horsed out and skidded along on top of the weeds. Their success was limited to those times when conditions permitted such tactics.

On that visit in the seventies, the Vernes' water was not as extensive as it had been, and the keeper did not do the thorough job of weed and bank control that characterized the stretch when Edouard was still alive. A recent visit to the area in the mid-nineties was disillusioning in the extreme. A rash of commercial fish-rearing ponds had abstracted the water from the river, and when it was returned, its temperature had soared so high it could no longer support trout. Now that only the very upper reaches of the Risle are still viable for trout fishery, I appreciate more and more having had the opportunity to enjoy its many charms when the many accomplished angling friends of the great Charles Ritz and Edouard Vernes regarded it as the queen of the Normandy chalk streams.

4
Chez
Tolstoi

In 1949, Charles Ritz advised me where to find the best fly-fishing tackle in Paris. In those days, it was in a store near the Gare St.-Lazare. The chief clerk was the famous Preskaviec, whose name had been given to numerous fly patterns and even to one especially effective weighted spinner. There I bought a lovely little Pezon Michel fly rod for my bride-to-be. It turned out not to be just what she had always wanted. It did, however, turn out to be just what I had always wanted.

During a visit in Ritz's latter years, he told me the best new spot in Paris was a store called Au Coin de Peche. I love good tackle shops, and aside from the unavoidable overspending, they are a great source of pleasure because there is always something new to discover and the people in the good ones know how to speak the angler's language. Au Coin de Peche was one of the good ones. The shop looked small and cluttered, but there were cases of the most beautiful dry flies I had ever seen. I found classics by Mme. De Chamberet including the Serie Gallica and a whole collection of flies by Aime Devaux. The Devaux patterns were not named but were all identified by number

173

and included many representing caddis flies. I had just become something of a caddis enthusiast, and these all looked as if they could be killers back in the western U.S. I indulged myself like a kid in a toy store. Finally, there came the moment of reckoning: two new fly rods, a supply of leaders and tippet material, and a lifetime supply of French dry flies.

The clerk wisely never interrupted my gatherings. He could obviously spot a self-seller when he saw one. As he finally toted up my debt, I realized I didn't have anywhere near the cash needed to cover the transaction. I did, however, have an American Express card. I uttered the then not yet classic query, "Do you take American Express?" The answer in perfect but accented English, "Yes, with the greatest pleasure," completely relieved my anxiety. As he processed my card the clerk innocently inquired, "Are you by any chance related to the author Hemingway?"

I replied I was his eldest son.

"Glad to meet you, Hemingway. My name is Tolstoi, and my grandfather also was a writer."

A friendship that lasts to this day was born. While his lifetime interest has been deep sea fishing, Count Sacha Tolstoi is no slouch as a fly fisherman. We have fished together on Norway's Laerdal, in my backyard in Idaho, Washington, and British Columbia, and in his bailiwick in Normandy and the Jura. Sacha is a man's man who served as an officer in the French foreign legion during the Algerian war, loves to gamble, and loves to play. Overgambling probably led to his opening a fishing tackle operation. It turned out to be a winner and soon had a reputation as the best. He was editor and publisher of a magazine for the French Big Game Fishing Club, and at various times served as its president, while living in a Paris apartment. A couple of years ago, he sold the shop, which almost immediately went under without his personal touch. This enabled him to realize a lifelong dream—moving to a mill house on a Norman chalk stream. Located on the Andelle, a lovely midsized river flowing west and south into the Seine from the north, Sacha's mill house lies in the upper reaches of the river, where it is still quite small. The springs that give birth to the Andelle are especially cold, and consequently, it will never suffer from the problems of the Risle, even in its lower reaches.

On the negative side, the hatches tend to start much later than they do in other Norman streams. My first fishing visit there was in early June and the big mayfly, Ephemera Danica, had not yet made its appearance. The fishing, nevertheless, was both delightful and fascinating. The trout were extraordinarily difficult. Their rises were hard to spot, occurring as often as not in small indentations of the riverbanks or in the reverse currents of the whirlpools caused by obstructions in the main current. The morning risers were smallish for the most part but hard to see as they were picking off the nymphs of very small mayflies just prior to their emergence or the partially emerged duns themselves. I was able to deceive a few of these morning risers using some of our American crippled dun patterns by Rene Harrop, but the few morning trout of any appreciable size that came to my fly so surprised me that I invariably tightened too fast.

At the other end of the day, the evening risers in difficult positions were a tremendous challenge. Many of them were good fish and totally intolerant of any sloppiness, inaccuracy, negative drag, or other failing in my presentation, which would invariably put them down for a long enough time that, with the light rapidly failing, I was better off trying to find another undisturbed fish. The evening fish were for the most part sipping spinners, which permitted them to be much more deliberate in their take since there was no chance of the spinners trying to escape. Fortunately, mayfly spinners all resemble each other to a considerable degree so it is relatively easy to find a pattern that works. Also trout taking spinners seem to be more relaxed, and this is true the world over. If I could manage to get a reasonably close spinner pattern properly presented, there was a good chance of getting a fish on. The caveat was that the strike had to be as deliberate as the take of the fly by the fish. During my first visit, I had very little success but enjoyed every minute. There were wonderful walks in the Norman countryside along the trail system of walking paths that have recently proliferated in France.

Sacha had under lease about a kilometer and a half on one side of the stream and a little less than that on the other, as well as the part on his own property. He was in the process of reaching an agreement with another owner downstream, who had a chateau sometimes used as a site for filmmaking and was higher on the snob scale since he was a prince. The aspects of the agreement under negotiation during my visit were the degree to which stream and bank improvements could be made and who would pay the farmers for any lost grazing for their cattle or sheep. Strangely, there was an ostrich farm along the river, and the giant birds made an odd but imposing-looking audience for the fishing.

While Sacha still travels the world over in pursuit of big game fish, I have a strong sense that he derives his greatest satisfactions from his home waters and most especially from his little Andelle, where, like Charley Fox in his day on Pennsylvania's Letort, he is busy every spring and summer discovering new surprises.

5
Dermot Wilson

D ermot Wilson and I became friends through the good graces of two people. One was Charles Ritz and the other was Jim Barnett, an old friend who did me the kindness of putting me up for membership in the Flyfishers' Club in London. Jim had spent years in England as an advertising executive and one of his confreres had been Dermot Wilson. Dermot suffered from one of advertising's occupational diseases and had the wisdom to transfer his full energies to pursuits less stressful and more satisfying to his soul. He started a small mail-order fishing tackle business in the old mill at Nether Wallop in Wiltshire, close to three of the finest chalk streams in all of England. Furthermore, Wallop Brook ran through the mill and into the mill pond right out the front door of the mill house and contained some of Britain's largest rainbow trout. It couldn't have been a finer setting for a man who loved fly fishing and needed to be closer to country streams than to city life.

Through Jim, I contacted Dermot and arranged to fish the water he had leased on both the Test and the Itchen not far from his Nether Wallop mill. His practice at the time was to have his fishing clients put up at the Sheriff House in Stockbridge on Test, a delightful little inn in a charming town. Dermot had served honorably in His Majesty's Armed Forces before entering the advertising field and had that fine way of expressing himself common among British officers. He ran his show efficiently and put me in the hands of a ghillie named Len Bishop for my first day on the Test. I had read about the river since my early teens and knew it must be on the itinerary of any serious angler who has an interest in the traditions of fly fishing. Len Bishop gave me the royal treatment, which included calling me "Your Lordship." On one occasion, he asked me if I would care for a well-chilled pint. When I allowed as how I would, he produced with a flourish that would have done justice to a royal major domo a bottle out of a live box hidden in the stream. Because of his last name, many of Bishop's clients referred to him as "Your Grace."

While I had a delightful time fishing such hallowed waters, the Test is much changed from the days of Frederick Halford, the grand muckimuck of dry-fly fishing. Because of the demands for large fish and the limited time available to the new generation of British businessmen, there is a tendency to supply the required large fish from fast-growing strains of rainbow trout produced in hatcheries rather than growing nearly wild browns in side channels called stews, as had been done previously. Prior to World War II, the browns' feed was supplemented in the stews, but they at least learned to make an honest living before being released into the river proper. Today's large rainbows have been fed fish pellets, and for many of them the best approximation of natural food is a fly suggesting the appearance of a pellet. While there are some holdover browns and rainbows that acquire a modest veneer of sophistication and wildness and can give some serious sport, the Test is not the great river it once was.

However, the Test is still one of the truly beautiful rivers of the world and is cared for and manicured in a manner unthinkable in the Americas.

I soon discovered that Dermot's true love was the Itchen. In surface appearance, it is not much different from the Test, its neighbor to the west. Its many adherents include a number of the graduates of

Winchester, whose campus adjoins one of its lower reaches. Dermot had some of its finest beats leased, and one of his favorites consisted of a small tributary, which he kept for his pleasure and that of his close friends even after his retirement and the sale of his Nether Wallop mill to the American tackle and outfitting firm of Orvis.

The Itchen was an entirely different proposition than the Test. I particularly remember a late April visit in the mid 1970s. I had arranged for a driver to take my wife and twelve-year-old daughter to see both Stonehenge and Salisbury Cathedral so as to give myself a full unencumbered day on the river. The weather was perfect for fishing. There was a light intermittent drizzle, and various species of flies continued to hatch during the course of the whole day. Best of all, the damp and lack of wind kept them afloat on the water's surface much longer than on sunny windy days. The trout, all of them wild, were confidently and actively feeding for at least half of every hour all day long. I have seldom had such an ideal day of dry-fly fishing. Dermot had told me to expect most of the fish to be in the twelve- to fourteen-inch range. Although he said there were some much larger fish, he implied that these were mainly uncatchable. He had no way of knowing how ideal the conditions were to be for our outing.

The great event was the early appearance of the Iron Blues in great numbers. This fly really excites fish in a way the earlier olives do not. Wild trout of unusually large proportions and recovered from early spring spawning came readily to well-presented imitations of the Iron Blue duns. I say well-presented because, on the numerous occasions when I flubbed my presentation, the fish were "put down" and refused to return to the fly. Fortunately, it was one of those magical days when so many of the stream's large trout were ready and willing that I could merely switch my attention to another equally large fish in another location. These trout were lovely and were excellent fighters. I shall be ever grateful to Dermot for the experience.

In his latter years, Dermot took advantage of the generosity of one of his fine fishing friends, H.G. Wellington, who invited him to fish O'Dell Spring Creek in Montana. Dermot found himself in seventh heaven as O'Dell has as fine spring-creek fishing as can be found anywhere. Fishing on Wellington's water is especially good as the fishing pressure is kept at a minimum. The trout are big, and because they are relatively undisturbed, the large browns are often found foraging in broad daylight rather than keeping hidden until night as is their habit in more disturbed places. They are by no means easy, but they are possible, and Dermot became the longest-staying guest ever to visit.

It was not long after his last visit to O'Dell that Dermot's health failed seriously, and after several years of illness, he left us with a fine legacy that includes a notable book on dry fly fishing, the conversion of many of his fellow Britons to catch-and-release fishing, and lasting valuable contributions to the conservation of the aquatic environment in his native land. My fellow Americans and I who were first introduced to trout fishing in England through the graces of Dermot Wilson will be forever in his debt.

III

SOME SEDUCTIVE STREAMS

6
The Loue

I owe a visit to one of France's greatest trout rivers to Sacha Tolstoi. After a pleasant but ill-fated visit to Ireland in May of 1995 and after introducing me to his beloved Andelle, Sacha made reservations for us to fish one of the premier stretches of the Loue. The river was in the part of eastern France known as Franche-Comte, not far from the spectacular fortified city of Besançon. The drive in Sacha's BMW station wagon was along the toll roads until we reached Besançon, where we left the high-speed routes and found our way through the maze of the city onto a twisting climbing road. It led out of the limestone canyon, where most of the city is located, and up onto one of the plateaus, which soon gave way to hills and forests. Sacha had made reservations for us at La Piquette, an inn with several kilometers of the best fishing on the middle reach of the Loue. The inn's owner, Marc Gatez, has the good fortune to be married to a wonderful cook, who runs her own delightful inn about a half hour's drive from Marc's operation. We arrived at her inn the evening before we were due at La Piquette and were settled for the night in a comfortable

181

little cottage, where we cleaned up before, what Sacha promised would be, a never-to-be-forgotten dinner.

He was close to the mark. The entrée, which we both had was a dish of scrambled eggs generously flavored with fresh thinly sliced black truffles. The trouble with truffles is there are seldom enough of them to really tell and all too often they aren't fresh and, believe me, that makes a difference. Sacha popped for a couple of great bottles, and the rest of the meal is lost in a pleasant daze.

The next morning we departed early, following the pretty little trout stream on which the quaint inn and its retired old flour mill are perched. We descended from the wooded heights to the plateau, through which the canyon of the Loue winds its way from its giant spring source to its juncture with its mother river, the Doubs. Let me explain this seeming anomaly. In its upper reaches, the Doubs passes through an area where nearly a third of its flow disappears into some sinks in the limestone only to reappear as the giant spring where the Loue emerges in near full force. This spring was some thirty kilometers upstream of where we were heading.

To reach La Piquette, we turned off the paved departmental road onto a dirt road that soon deteriorated into a track which pitched steeply along the side of the canyon through thick mostly deciduous woods. Then the road went down to the meadow bordering the river, where a substantial stone farmhouse surrounded by outbuildings was our destination.

La Piquette is a fisherman's dream come true. The guest rooms are large and comfortable, kept clean as a whistle by the farm women who do the cooking along with Marc. The rooms overlook the meadow and the river beyond, and although the bathrooms are down the hall, they are numerous enough that no one is held up. The food is not on the same plane as that of Marc's wife's inn, but it is wonderful in its own rustic way and infinitely better-suited to the appetites of hungry fishermen. His wine selection is local but the guests, at least when I was there, seem to compete in bringing a generous supply of rare and even great vintages.

Marc keeps an ample selection of the flies that work best on the river. These can make your final reckoning grow substantially if you're as much of a sucker for new fly patterns as I am. On his recommendation, I loaded up on two patterns in particular, the Peute and a CDC version of the big mayfly, *Ephemera Guttulata*. At the time the Peute was working well for the grayling, and the mayflies were effective for the trout on overcast mornings and in the evening.

The spring had been disastrous, with all the valleys in eastern France flooded and the runoff late. Although originating from underground, the Loue was nonetheless affected, and its flows were only just reaching fishable levels when we arrived. However, plenty of flies were about, and the daytime fishing for grayling promised to be excellent, although the trout were still somewhat inactive especially on the surface. The Loue is a river rich in nutrients, as are all limestone streams, and is capable of producing very large trout. The largest tend to migrate to the lower end of the river and are for the most part piscivorous (fish-eating), only rarely feeding on surface insects and then only when there is a proliferation of the large mayflies common to the area.

We Americans have a tendency to believe that we are better at what we like to do than people from other countries. Although our trout bums have recently become fly-fishing guides with enormous egos, the true enthusiasts in Europe and the United Kingdom are surely on a par with our best. This was certainly true of the four Frenchmen sharing the fishing with Sacha and me on this occasion. These fellows were marvelous companions with a thorough understanding of the river and its insect and fish life. They came here annually from their homes in Auvergne, the mountainous and trout-rich central part of France. The best fly tyer of the group, was a surgeon. Two of the group were businessmen, and the fourth, a charmer who was scarcely five-foot-three and had a tough time with deep wading, was a landlord or *rentier*.

They teamed up to lease a stretch of trout water in their own bailiwick but also fished the always difficult public waters. I fished with them and can avow that their skills and knowledge would match most of our big reputation anglers. Not the least pleasing thing about them, aside from the wonderful selection of wines they brought with them and generously shared, was their deep and abiding appreciation for the values of our sport. They truly loved the valley and its beautiful wildness and had learned to live with, and appreciate, the vagaries of the local folk who, as is so often the case in trout country, thought fly fishermen crazy. Who else would pay to fish and then return their fish unharmed to the water?

The fishing was not spectacular, but the grayling provided sport most of the time, though they were far from easy. Grayling are fun to fish. They are demanding of a good presentation, and the fly pattern has to please them. They feed actively and are less subject to the morose moods of the larger trout. In short, they are an ideal fish to save the day when the trouting is slow. I had a wonderful time with them and took pride in catching many when the others had the good sense to take a nap prior to the serious business of the *coup du soir*, or the evening rise in our parlance.

Fishing the evening rise presented severe problems at La Piquette. Possibly the most serious was that supper was taken before it, and to perform decently, it was necessary to hold back on the prandial aperitifs and accompanying wines. I found this difficult as I was tired from staying on the river all day. As a result, I can only relate my friends' accounts of what went on. According to them, they had occasional success with some of the larger trout on the big mayfly, but their greatest excitement came when it was almost completely dark and they fished the banks to slurpers feeding on big caddis flies. It sounded to me a lot like fishing at night in the Midwest for the big browns feeding on the giant Hexagenia spinners. While several big fish were hooked none were landed which, in my view, must have made the experience all the more memorable.

I never even hooked a big trout in the Loue, although I saw them and I tried for them. I can promise you that I will go back there one day when conditions are better, but no matter what happens, I will be delighted with the experience. La Piquette is that sort of place.

7
North
Umpqua

In August, 1941, when my prep school pals and I left the North Umpqua, we had mixed feelings about the river. One of our number had his tackle confiscated by the state police game warden for not having bought the proper fishing license. Still, I already sensed the river would play a continuing role in my own future.

The war denied me another visit there until 1948, when I returned with a legitimate excuse. The job Charley Ritz had helped me obtain with a subsidiary of the Ashaway Line Company, Ashaway Inc., offered as its only redeeming benefits paid travel all over the West Coast and access to all of Ashaway's latest fly line developments at no cost. I took full advantage of the situation, and as soon as I could get through the obligatory calls on the big jobbers in the Los Angeles and San Francisco areas, I headed for the promised land of the Northwest.

Since my route was through Oregon, it seemed not only logical, but absolutely obligatory, to make a detour from Roseburg up to Steamboat, where I had fished the river before. The new highway was already on the drawing boards and now went as far as Glide, but the old road, only somewhat improved, was still the only way up the valley from Glide. Unlike today's river-hugging highway, it wound its way up the steep sides of the valley high above the river, yielding just the occasional tantalizing glimpse of its legendary summer steelhead waters.

Only in the last half mile, as the old road angled steeply down toward the level of the river itself, could the famous pools of the camp water be seen in their entirety. But a new intrusion had been added. Overlooking the boat pool was a small shack where you could get coffee or a burger and a beer. It was staffed by Clarence Gordon, who owned the lodge on the opposite side of the river. The lodge proper was originally reached by boat, but since the late thirties, one could drive there by crossing the Mott Bridge.

Clarence Gordon's Steamboat Lodge, made famous in Bergman's classic *Trout*, was a marvel of a log cabin fishing camp. Gordon's kindness and generosity to me on that trip were unforgettable. At the time, there were no fly fishing-only regulations on the river and, consequently, I had gone into the upper boat pool with my spinning gear, using a silver devon as a lure. I hooked and landed a steelhead that turned out to be the first of the season, and Clarence asked me to bring it to the camp and offered me his hospitality. The fish was served to the guests at dinner that night, and the rest of my visit he spent weaning me away from my dastardly methods. Clarence offered me a couple of hours of fishing the next morning in the camp water, and one of the guests promised to show me the lower water, which I had only glimpsed from the road on the way in. Clarence loaned me some flies and appropriate leaders.

I slept fitfully that night with half-dreams of everything I had read in Ray Bergman's chapter on steelhead and the North Umpqua. Although I caught no steelhead the following day, it was far from a disappointment but served, rather, to whet my appetite for this magnificent river. Clarence guided me through the camp water and took a fish himself before my delighted and envious eyes in the upper Mott pool. Later that same day a charming man whose name I no longer recall took me along the south side trail and showed me all the water down as far as Williams Creek. I had a go at Takahashi riffle, named after Zane Grey's camp cook and located at the head of the Ledges pool. I hooked an active fish who after two frenetic jumps parted company from me with my fly in his mouth. I can see those jumps to this day.

During cocktail hour in camp that evening, a surprise guest showed up dressed to the teeth. His name was Vic O'Byrne. A smallish man, Vic possessed great presence. I had heard much about him up on the Kalama River in Washington, where he had built a reputation using two-handed rods for spey casting. A World War I pensioner who had damaged lungs from being gassed in the war, he'd come to the American West for his health and for the fishing and just barely managed to exist on a pittance. He had left the Kalama valley and moved down to Oregon's Umpqua, where he built himself a small cabin a couple of miles up the Cougar Trail from Clarence Gordon's camp.

Considered a hermit, O'Byrne rarely socialized, though he did like his drink. This he proved in no uncertain fashion on this particular occasion. He had a pleasant brogue and held forth volubly and with passion on many a subject, but primarily on fishing for steelhead. I didn't hear until years later that he didn't make it back to his cabin that night but drowned in the river he loved and was only found days later fully dressed as he had been for the cocktail party. His health had been failing badly, it seems, and whether his drowning was intentional or accidental will never be known. All that survives of his existence on the river is the pool named for him in front of the moss-covered remains of his cabin. The Oregon rain is not easy on the works of man.

When next I was able to return to the Umpqua, it was after a stint in the army, serving in Europe and at Fort Bragg, North Carolina. After I left the army and settled down in Portland to start civilian life as a stockbroker, I was able once again to do some serious fishing. Initially, the lure of the nearby rivers like my old friend the Kalama, only an hour away from the office, held me close.

Eventually, I was able to wander farther afield and to visit Steamboat once again. Frank Moore and his wife Jeannie, were now the owners of the new Steamboat Inn, which combined with the lure of the river kept bringing me back. Clarence Gordon had sold his camp to the forest service and the little hamburger spot across the river, which at first served as the nucleus for the inn. When the new road had been built to ease access to the forests for the burgeoning timber industry and for construction of the new hydroelectric project, the fly fishing became almost impossible because of the nearly fulltime muddying of the river from the construction. Clarence had become more and more dependent on the sale of beer and burgers to the workers on the new road and the hydro project. With his fly fishing clientele gone, he finally gave up his camp and the stand. Frank and Jean took over the cabins on the roadside at a fortuitously chosen site overlooking a falls and aptly named Maple Ridge. Once the construction had finally ceased, Steamboat Inn soon became the annual summer headquarters for the fly fishermen who flocked back to the river. Under Frank's able leadership a group of dedicated fly fishers was formed and called itself "The Steamboaters" after the term used to describe the early gold miners on the river.

While the steelhead runs had held up reasonably well during the years of poor fly-fishing conditions, the river nevertheless suffered from a multiplicity of problems. Still far and away the best summer steelhead river in the continental United States, it was beginning to feel a great increase in bait and lure fishing pressure due to the spin fishing explosion. But this wasn't the worst of its troubles. The new road and the network of logging roads up the various tributaries, particularly Steamboat Creek, had basically made the river's most important spawning grounds and summer holding pools readily available to the many poachers in the area. The least damaging poachers fished for steelhead in havens where the fish crowded together resting until the time when their eggs and milt would ripen for their early spring spawning. To the poachers, the situation was a bit like the proverbial fish in a barrel. The worst of the poachers used dynamite and would kill a whole pool full of steelhead. They would then gather all they could carry away and leave the rest to rot. It should be understood that steelhead, particularly the summer runs, are seldom truly numerous the way salmon can be. The total destruction of a couple hundred in their holding pools is truly a major disaster.

A further problem posed by the proliferation of logging roads, and the subsequent clearcut logging of very steep slopes, was the resultant debris left in the small tributary creek bottoms, which made them in-accessible for spawning. Moreover, the denuded slopes washed silt into the beds, making any spawning that did take place virtually fruit-less and creating an environment where, because of the stripped bank cover, the water temperatures became intolerable, even deadly, to any young progeny that might have been able to survive.

These were the challenges facing the Steamboaters, that intrepid group of fly-fishing enthusiasts who loved this river as no other. One of their solutions involved enlisting the services of a dynamic young advertising executive, one of their group, named Hal Riney to make a film that would clearly demonstrate these problems and generate public support for major changes in forest management in the Umpqua drainage by both the Bureau of Land Management and the United States Forest Service. The film, named *Pass Creek* after the tributary depicted, was shown to sportsman's groups all over the country and caused a wave of revulsion at the sloppy management of these public resources. The outcry finally caused the two agencies to radically change their ways.

The Steamboaters then undertook a public relations campaign that included the conversion of then-Governor Tom McCall to steel-head fly fishing. The grinning photograph of the governor holding his first fly-caught summer steelhead that hangs on the wall of the inn tells the story. McCall soon appointed a Steamboater to the state fish and wildlife commission and at least one member has served on the commission ever since. These men have successfully protected the upper river by implementing fly fishing-only and no-kill regulations for wild steelhead. The Steamboaters continue to this day to fight an ongoing, but so far successful, battle against attempted encroach-ments on the river and surrounding area.

After a couple of years in Havana as a stockbroker during the last gasp of pre-Castro Cuba, I moved back to the U.S. and settled in San Francisco. From there I was able, once again, to spend time at Steamboat every summer. My daughters Muffet and Margot loved it. There were wonderful trails through the giant Douglas firs bordering the river and berries to be picked along the abandoned logging cuts.

On one of these expeditions, I persuaded my family to indulge me on the way up the river by permitting me to stop and fish one of my favorite pools. As luck would have it, I took a fish almost immediately. It was a beauty weighing nearly eleven pounds on the Steamboat scales. After we had settled into our cabin, Frank Moore took me aside and told me, "Jack, I've got a friend I want you to meet. The poor bastard is down in cabin one and sick as hell with the flu. Maybe we could go down there with your fish and cheer him up?" I agreed and down we went with the fish on some kraft wrapping paper.

We knocked on the door and heard a grumbling, "Come in." Introductions were made and the pale young fellow lying in bed rolled over on his side as we uncovered the fish and held it close for him to see. The result was nothing short of miraculous. He jumped out of bed and said, "I'll meet you at the dining room in a couple of minutes. I've got something I want to show you." This was my first meeting with Dan Callaghan who, despite the incident that follows, remains one of my best friends and finest fishing companions.

Callaghan and I met in the dining room and had coffee at the gigantic table hewn from a split Douglas fir trunk. The sight of the steelhead waved before his eyes had caused a sort of epiphany and a truly instantaneous recovery from whatever ailed him. He said, "Jack, there's a really *big* steelhead in one of the pools way upstream, and I want you to have a try at him. I know exactly where he lies, and I'll get you in to him." I thanked him for his generosity and thought to myself that this fellow was that rarest of fishermen, the one who will actually give away his secrets out of the goodness of his heart.

On the way up the river, he revealed that his secret spot was at Copeland Creek, close to the top of the steelhead water. He carefully showed me the pool, bade me start casting from a point about halfway down, and pointed out to me where I might start expecting the fish to come to the fly. This was a number of drifts below where I was to start casting. Once he saw that I was covering the water properly, he headed up to the top of the pool, where, on only his third cast, he gave a giant yell and was fast into a large fish. After a fine fight, the fish was beached and turned out to be a magnificent fourteen pounder, probably the largest fish of that season. My stretch drew a blank. To this day, Dan assures me that the big fish was where he put me and that the fish must have only just moved upstream into the slot above the rock. I believed him then, but after all these years, I'm beginning to wonder.

Frank Moore and Jeannie have retired but still live on the river. The inn was bought by Jim Van Loan and his wife Sharon. They have made many improvements, and it is now, although still rustic, much more sophisticated. Indeed, its cuisine has a reputation that reaches far outside the fishing fraternity. The river has survived many a crisis including the advent of whitewater kayaking through many of the best holding pools and the consequent disruption of the fishing. Peace and a compromise have been reached in this regard.

The latest controversy lies within the ranks of the fly fishermen themselves. It has to do with the increasing use of weighted flies drifted beneath an indicator, which is in effect a small bobber. Unfortunately, the method smacks quite a bit of bait fishing and is anathema to the traditional fly fishers who feel so many fish are hooked and released by this method that the stress on the fish is excessive. It most certainly adversely affects the sport available to the traditionalists. I personally feel it should be allowed when the winter steelhead are in the river and not during the summer and fall. All in all, the North Umpqua is still quite the most beautiful steelhead river anywhere and there is still sport to be had for anyone willing to put out the effort and use a little imagination. Long live this great river!

8
Irish Rivers

It turned out to be one of the busiest and most hectic summers I ever spent. I'm certain it seemed so to Angela. After closing up the cabin, we headed back to Sun Valley to get organized for the big trip. It started with visits to friends in San Francisco and then on to Pebble Beach, where we were rained out of the tennis we had expected to play but where the partying was so intense that it took several days to recover. I thought our plan was brilliant. We were to take the commuter to L.A. International and then fly New Zealand Airlines to London Heathrow, where friends had arranged for us to stay at the Royal Automobile Club on Pall Mall for our five-day stay in London. After that, we would begin the interesting part of the trip and finally head for Ireland via Aer Lingus.

It turned out to be one of the hottest springtimes in recent memory in the United Kingdom and our normally cozy interior room at the automobile club was instead a steamy oven. The dress code of the club required ties and jacket while in the public rooms and made for unbelievable discomfort, but, typically, the British members hewed to it religiously. As it happened, the celebrations for the fiftieth anniversary

193

of VE Day took place while we were on our Dublin flight. It was a relief to leave sweltering London for the friendly informality of Eire.

Our first few days in Ireland were spent in Victorian splendor at the Shelbourne Hotel on St. Vincent's Green in a magnificent suite arranged for us by friend John Baker. He also arranged our initial route across the north to the west, where we would get to the serious business of fishing. My very first taste of Irish fishing was most pleasant. It was not, however, what I had planned on, namely fly fishing for salmon.

I had come across two delightful and useful books by Peter O'Reilly devoted to the fishing of Irish rivers and loughs respectively and, as it turned out, the last inn we enjoyed before arriving at our first salmon-fishing destination was located on a high hill overlooking Lough Arrow, which O'Reilly recommended highly. Lough Arrow is about eight miles long and a mile across with many islets and a lot of wind, and a boatman guide is recommended. An inquiry at the desk revealed that a day permit could easily be acquired at a tavern a few miles away to fish a much smaller lough, where fishing was better done wading and casting from shore. Since I don't care much for boat fishing and avoid it whenever possible, I chose to go to the small lough.

It was windy on the lough, though it was sunk in a depression between high rolling hills. There was one other angler, an old-timer fly fishing in the shallows at one corner of the triangle-shaped lake. Angela and I parked along the track that skirted one side with the wind blowing into our shore. Angela opted for reading in the car, and I donned waders, rigged up the three-piece Winston for a five line, and put on a slow-sinking line and a ten-foot leader tipped with a rough olive nymph. The fish—lively, fat brownies ranging from thirteen to sixteen inches—had been stocked at some previous time, as indicated by their stunted fins, but had adapted handsomely to their new surroundings. My fly was apparently just what they'd been waiting for, and I soon had four beauties to take back to our inn, where the cook did them full justice in a *beurre blanc* sauce.

Sligo was the nearest town of any size, and we decided to go try to find some of the Donegal tweeds that come from a bit farther north. It was a pleasant little city and we were soon directed to Sons haberdashery where a most personable gentleman soon had us trying on various items while he provided fascinating stories. These tales enabled me finally to understand the full meaning of the terms "blarney" and "the gift of gab." We ended up buying much more than we had planned, albeit happily.

Our first serious objective was Peter Mantle's delightful salmon-fishing lodge called Delphi, sited between two small loughs feeding the short and precipitous Bundarragha River right in the middle of the famed west country. We stayed in a great manor house that Peter had fully restored. The rooms were spacious and comfortable, and the food outstanding. The principal topic of conversation at the long table centered around the salmon that run the little river into and through the lakes. The two chief runs are the springers, which run the river starting in February and continue into late April and early May, and the summer run of grilse, more numerous but small, although great sport on very light tackle. The springers, which should have been present both in the river and the lakes in goodly numbers during our stay, were still out at sea.

Since mid March, all of Ireland had been suffering from what passes in the Emerald Isle for a drought. The west coast rivers, which are for the most part spate streams and only rise sufficiently to support runs of fish after the periods of serious rain, nearly went dry, and rivers in the west and southwest had some of the worst fishing in recent history. It was not propitious for our visit. We soon learned one either fished the river, which at this level of water had really only one pool holding fish in its mile and a half length, or settled for fishing one of the two loughs. Peter gave me a thorough briefing of all the river's pools and how they would fish if the water came up.

I spent the first afternoon on the river, and the next day I was assigned a boatman on the lower lough. The routine, for those unfamiliar with it, was to row to the upwind end of the lough and then drift downwind with the boat sideways to the drift. The angler casts downwind and brings in line with a sink-and-draw retrieve timed to allow for the speed of the drift. Each drift down the lough was along a different parallel line, and one soon learned from the boatman's comments where the "hot spots" were likely to be. The local belief is that the best conditions are a combination of wind and rain. Wind was the only condition prevailing that day and all our casting, and that of the other boat on the lough, was to no avail. I did, however, take note of a fair-sized fish that showed several times quite close to the shore and within reach of a long cast from a wading fisherman. I determined to have a go at this fish on my own terms very early the following morning.

I chose the three-piece 8½-foot Winston for a number five line, a twelve-foot leader with an eight-pound tippet, and a #14 double-hooked Stoat fly and sneaked down the hall, out through the tackle room to avoid disturbing Peter's sleeping dog. I trudged the quarter mile to the spot along the shore near where the fish had shown. There wasn't the slightest hint of any breeze, and the sun had not yet climbed above the rugged little mountains to the east. Theoretically, these were the worst possible conditions. Still, I cast and retrieved with the hope that any brand new day engenders and the fly was stopped by something solid and initially unmoving. The fish started a power run climaxed by a heart-stopping jump. I finally beached him some ten minutes later after a long and somewhat tedious end game on the little rod. It was a lovely, well-conditioned fish that had been out of the salt for close to a month and, while still silvery, was starting to show a bit of color.

That ten-pounder proved to be the only salmon I was to catch during our stay in Ireland. It brought great cheer to our fellow guests and, following Delphi tradition, put me at the head of the long dining table for several days until the only other salmon of the week was landed by a lovely neophyte. Her reign lasted until our departure.

Peter Mantle generously made arrangements for us at two other fishing sites, one at Northport House, a short, two-hour drive to the north. We were warmly received there and provided for in a more formal atmosphere than at Delphi, but the cuisine shone and the fishing prospects looked better despite the drought. Two young men were celebrating the evening of our arrival, and the reason, a lovely bright eleven-pounder caught that afternoon in the lake, enlivened everyone's spirits and hopes for the next day.

The Northport River was larger and longer than the Bundarragha but, like its southerly neighbor, had scarcely any flow. Though its seven-mile length provided a number of likely pools, the lack of current through the holding water made the outlook on the lake far more propitious, and we chose to spend our only full day there. The lake was much larger than the ones at Delphi, and the hotel did not control all of the fishing on it. Because of problems with poaching, there was no fishing whatsoever allowed from shore or by wading. The water, as it was everywhere I visited in Ireland, had somewhat of a tea tint to it, definitely more pronounced in the streams and rivers than in the lakes.

Peter Kennedy, our ghillie, was a worthy representative of his kind. He charmed us through what would otherwise have been a rather desultory day of fishing, and I will be forever grateful to him for showing me a relatively foolproof method of fastening a dropper fly on a long leader, one that truly holds the dropper fly well away from the main leader. There were no fish or even pulls that day, and as the fishing was fully booked for the next few days, we headed south in the rental car and on the way saw a good bit of country. The great drainage projects in the Shannon Valley had brought a lot of new land into agricultural production but, sadly, had lowered water tables everywhere resulting in the ruin of a good many fine trout streams. The Shannon itself, a gigantic watershed flowing through many great lakes is for much of its length a slow-flowing canal-like waterway cruised by holiday craft of every description, but it still has runs of salmon swimming through it. These runs are, however, merely a remnant of their former greatness.

Peter Mantle had called ahead to the Greens to advise them of our arrival in the valley of the Blackwater, a sharp contrast to the wild and rugged west coast. The Green's house in its lush richly forested surroundings receives guests during the summer months. It was delightful and had quite an array of visitors though very few were fishermen. Mrs. Green did have under lease several very fine beats on the Blackwater that Angela and I hoped would change our luck. The river was lovely, but the water level was at historical lows with very few fish. Every day we hoped for rain, but it never came in sufficient quantity to bring in fresh, bright fish from the sea. The day before our departure, there were finally some good strong showers that stirred things up a bit, and I actually saw a bright fish jump in a junction pool. The next day might have given us some success after the fish had settled into new lies, but our departure could not be changed.

We spent our last few days as houseguests of Desmond Guiness at Leixlip Castle just outside Dublin. The castle is on the site of what had once been a waterfall where Viking conquerors had noted the salmon leaping and given it its name. There are still salmon in the Liffey, but they have to be helped past the hydroelectric dam now occupying the site of the original falls, and none make it back down unless they are caught above and released below, a very unlikely prospect. We loved Ireland as anyone with an open heart must, but I will want a bit of persuading to go back for the salmon angling alone. Should I have another opportunity to spend a month, I would want good meteorological forecasts for miserable weather, and I would plan to explore the trout-fishing prospects as thoroughly as the salmon, using Peter O'Reilly's books as my guide, of course.

9
Icelandic
Rivers

I t isn't often you get a chance to redeem yourself salmon fishing on the same fishing grounds and in the same season. But I had such an opportunity in Iceland in 1997. My wife Angela and I, together with friends, were Frankie Wolfson's guests on the Laxa i Leirarsveit in southwest Iceland during the last few days of June and the first days of July. Angela had a magnificent week, but the rest of us just squeaked through. During our first full day on the river, she drew the home pool just below the first falls. In two hours, she hooked three fish and landed one, while her successor on the pool drooled at the prospect of fishing what was obviously the hot spot. He assumed Angela a near neophyte who could not have fished the pool thoroughly or well. When Angela moved down to the next run, one of the guides spotting fish from above in the home pool observed an unusual phenomenon, which he later reported. As the new home pool angler moved into position, all the salmon visible in the pool dropped down and moved into lies in front of and below Angela in the next pool. She proceeded to hook three more in quick succession and landed two. No other salmon were caught that evening. Pheromones or black magic?

Just as in most other Atlantic salmon venues in 1997, it was not a great year in Iceland, and the early season was particularly poor although the group following ours on the Leirarsveit had an excellent week. After Angela and the rest of our group left for home, I joined Orri Vigfussen, chairman of the North Atlantic Salmon Fund, on the Big Laxa (Laxa i Adaldal) for a couple of fishless days. I did have two incredible days of trout fishing on the upper river near Lake Myvatn, where several of the trout were larger than my best salmon. The experience saved me from the deep depression that sometimes overcomes fly fishers when the fishing is lousy.

Just before returning home, I had a chance to briefly survey an interesting river an hour east of Reykjavík for a couple of hours. The Ranga is a fascinating springfed river, which in the past was known only for its fine sea trout fishing. A dearth of gravel and a bottom composed mostly of rocks, fine volcanic sands, and silt made for unsuccessful salmon spawning. The river runs through country famous for Icelandic pony studs and takes the usual gamut of a wide estuary serving several rivers, then has a series of low falls and a section of long, slow, deep pools before heading into rougher lava country with its consequent canyons, rapids, and falls. Its main west branch is entirely springfed and colder than most Icelandic rivers.

An experimental management system inaugurated by Throstur Ellidason has brought salmon to the Ranga. Using farm salmon stock and a very location-specific imprinting program for his smolts, he has created a successful fishery for salmon where none existed before. Under the watchful eye of the Icelandic Institute of Fisheries, Ellidason has conducted experiments in tagging smolts imprinted in a multiplicity of locations on the river and used the results to spread the fish more evenly throughout the system than had heretofore been thought possible. The program of smolt releases, which was initiated in 1989, has had great initial success. Suffice it to say that by the end of the 1997 season, the total catch on the Ranga exceeded that of any of Iceland's wild salmon rivers. It is clear, however, that this sort of management is only appropriate in rivers, such as the Ranga, where no important strains of wild salmon have preexisted. There is also some concern that the inevitable wanderings of a small portion of the returning farm-stock fish will eventually end up polluting wild stocks in other rivers.

After my return home, I received a call from my friend David Goodman. An Icelandic river owners association had contacted him about finding a writer to come to Iceland to fish a medley of their rivers. The tour would include rivers that had changed management practices and had new accommodations, which they hoped might kindle a rebirth of interest in Icelandic salmon fishing in general and the association's rivers in particular. David immediately thought of me, much to the consternation of some of his other writer friends. Angela, still full of the generous spirit imbued by her successful trip, gave her seal of approval, and I was soon on my way back to Iceland.

By now it was the latter part of July. After the early drought, which lowered river levels drastically, the weather was finally about to turn downright nasty; just what was needed. My host, Thorstein Thorsteinsson, picked me up at Orri's house in Reykjavík and outlined the plan of attack. It wasn't possible to give equal time to each of the four rivers selected in the six days available, so I was scheduled first for an evening's fishing and the following morning on the Grimsá. I was to share Gerald Richardson's rod, as his son had been unable to join him as planned. The Grimsá is already justly famous with Americans due to the efforts of Ernie Schwiebert and the fierce loyalty of Gardner Grant. No year would be complete for Grant without plying the Grimsá with his favorite hitched tube flies. Due to the luck of the draw that evening, I was unable to see more than the lowest beat, including the falls pool in sight of the comfortable Schwiebert-designed lodge. The following morning, I spent only a few hours on the next stretch up, which included a lovely piece of water reminiscent of the camp water on the North Umpqua but in miniature. In the evening the rain had not yet started, but I had four pulls from fish that I failed to hook on microtubes, and in the morning, had two fish on a hitched minitube, only one of which I managed to land.

Thorstein arranged my transport from Grimsá to Laxi i Kjos, where I was grateful to stay in place for three and a half days, although I was not looking forward to it as enthusiastically as I might. I had been told by our driver, the month before, as we crossed the mouth of the river on our way to Leirarsveit that Laxa i Kjos had gone down the drain and was no longer worth fishing. This proved to be an unfounded verdict as several changes in policy were having a beneficial effect on the fishing. On most Icelandic rivers that cater to visiting fly fishermen, the season reserved for fly fishing starts in late June and continues through August. This had not been the case on Laxa i Kjos. Until 1997 indiscriminate fishing had been permitted all season long. Another factor that has contributed to the river's success and has been important for all of Iceland's salmon rivers, was the complete buyout of all farmers' "in river" nets. Completed in 1997, this was a cooperative effort between the state, the farmer owners of the rivers, and those leasing the fisheries from the farmer/river owners. It came about through their united efforts with Orri Vigfussen leading the way.

The river's new manager, Asgeir (pronounced Oscar) Heidar gave me a marvelous overview of the whole river. The variety of fishing water on the Laxa i Kjos is quite remarkable. The bottom stretch of approximately a mile and a half is quite wide and flows through a shallow lava rock canyon with one serious waterfall and a series of fast rapids with wandering channels of traveling and resting water scattered throughout. Under Asgeir's management, which started at the end of the 1996 season, the lowest one-third of a mile is closed to all fishing. It had been determined that the early season worm fishing in the sea pool and the next series of shallows and runnels badly frighten many entering fish and delay their arrival into the main body of the river. The local worm fishing also exacted a heavy toll on larger fish arriving early in the season.

Next above this lower stretch of big river comes a long, broad meadow full of serpentine meanders with countless stretches of fine holding water once one learns the special techniques required to take fish there. At the bottom end of the meadows stretch is a junction pool where a small tributary, the Bugda, enters the south-flowing Kjos from the east. The Bugda is one of the beats that is fished in rotation, and I found it exciting with a wealth of fish, many of them on the large side. (In most Icelandic rivers this means over 9 Icelandic pounds or 9.9 U.S. pounds.)

The meadows are called an open beat, and anyone may fish them at any time if they are unhappy with their allotted water. There is plenty of room for a full complement of rods to fish this open beat without interfering with each other. It fishes best when the wind is up, which it is more often than not and making a riffle on the placid meanders. The recommended technique is no secret and involves long leaders, small dark doubles cast a bit above the holding water on the undercut bankside of the river and drifting into the lies, whereupon the fly is retrieved in foot-long pulls as fast as can be managed. The takes are incredibly solid and yield sound hookups. I write this after having failed to heed Asgeir's advice as my wrist was hurting and I couldn't retrieve fast enough to suit him. I only learned the true efficacy of the technique later on another river when my wrist had healed sufficiently to enable such a speedy retrieve.

Above the meadows the river changes character completely as it descends through increasingly rugged country. Because the water was very low, much of these gravelly pool, riffle pool sequences were too shallow to hold fish with the exception of a few corner pools in hard strata. Farther up were two separate canyon stretches requiring some degree of agility to negotiate but with fabulous pools and resting water. The top canyon had an impassable waterfall where, Asgeir informed me, many of the early running big fish accumulated until the weather cooled. In the fall, they would drop back down into the important spawning areas. The lower canyon also has a major waterfall, but the salmon are able to negotiate it successfully.

In my three plus days on Laxa i Kjos, I caught sixteen salmon and lost many more, one of which I will never forget. I hooked him on a small hitched tube fly in the streamy water just below a heavy chute on the side of a major rapid in the big part of the lower river. I saw his broad head come up to engulf the fly and, for once, was able to restrain the impulse to tighten up. I managed to let go the loop I always try to release when a fish takes directly below me on a straight line.

As usual the self-tightening of the line on a well-hooked fish seemed like a small miracle, and the fish took a power run down and across the river followed by a magnificent leap. Blessed is the sound of an old-fashioned Hardy click-type reel. At this juncture, my line was pointing downstream, and the fish jumped at the foot of the chute and was now headed up the heavy rapid at a breakneck pace. He finally stopped in a deep pocket, and I started regaining line until I could bring direct side strain against him and pulled his head off balance. This set him off downstream again where he settled into a lie in the center of the river about two hundred yards above the big waterfall.

He remained immovable in this lie for fully fifteen minutes before broaching for the first time. Then I could lead him shoreward for a little but with heavy head shakings. Every five yards gained toward the shore lost me twenty yards downstream until I started to worry seriously about his going over the falls. By now the fish was tired but too heavy for me to horse. I finally lost him when the tiny size 14 treble pulled out of its hold when he was about ten yards above the falls and about twenty-five feet out. I was applying the maximum pressure I could to try to turn his head toward me to lead him into a little beaching area.

My frustrated shout of grief was heard above the roar of the falls by an angler on the next beat down! I had seen the fish clearly and he was a deep-bodied, heavy shouldered cock fish, about half-bright and seemed over forty inches—a solid twenty-five pounder, rare for this part of Iceland but not as rare, it seems, as I had been led to believe.

The last day on Laxa i Kjos was accompanied by the advent of the long-awaited storm. It had rained hard all the previous night, and the fierce south wind continued unabated, bringing periodic fresh squalls. This storm continued throughout most of the remainder of my stay in Iceland. For a farewell, Asgeir took me to a stretch of the river that had been too low but now was at a good fishing level. The water was a bit off-color, and he suggested putting on a brass tube fly with a great split wing of green and yellow bucktail. It was unpleasant to cast, but the discomfort was quickly forgotten when the first cast brought a bright ten-pounder to the fly. Just as I landed it, a car appeared and a television crew that had come out for an interview arrived on the scene. The beautiful interviewer immediately ordered me to wait a few minutes while they set up. Then she said, "Now catch a fish." Three casts later I complied, and the whole incident was captured on tape to accompany the interview! Needless to say, I was loath to leave this delightful river. Asgeir tells me they will be building a fine new lodge this winter to be ready for next season's occupancy. Each room will have its own toilet and shower and a fine view of the lower falls. Given a year of good ocean conditions, the fishing should be superior.

Next on my itinerary was the Langa, which shares the same estuary as the Grimsá. The river at that time had three camps with the two upper ones under the same management. (It now has only two both under the management of Ingvi Jonssonn.) I was taken to the middle camp where a contingent of Brits was enjoying a good week. The camp manager was up north fishing with Orri Vigfussen on the Big Laxa, so I was put in the hands of his son, an experienced guide and angler. I only had late afternoon and evening fishing and a couple of hours the next morning.

I was taken up past the upper camp and, in our four-wheel-drive vehicle, we negotiated the canyon and a series of falls before heading up over a high col known as "over the mountain." There, we found a series of lovely meadow pools, where I was told there were still very few fish. The exact number was known because of an electronic counter at the fish pass above the falls. There were apparently about 125 fish scattered throughout the upper reaches in "the mountain."

We perched the jeep a couple of hundred feet above a series of slow middling-deep pools with a neck of faster water between the two longest. The heavy wind prevailing in the valley was absent here, and the neck seemed a good place to try the little hitched tube in the crystal clear water. My guide thought the water might be too cold for a surface fly but said to give it a try anyway since I had such great confidence in it. It paid off beautifully, and two fine fish were brought to shore and released. They had been in the river for a good spell and were already quite colored but still in fair condition. It was an auspicious start, and we headed back to camp where madame cook regaled us with a real meat and potatoes meal.

The next morning, the wind was blowing fiercely and I decided to cut the fishing short to get a few pictures of the Brits in action. The wind gusts were so strong I couldn't hold the camera steady. I had a good look at the valley, but the wind and rain made it difficult to see anything, and I really had very little feel for what sort of river the Langa was. Since that first visit, I have been back for a full week and enjoyed first-rate fishing. They built a fine new lodge, but the middle lodge, where I met the Brits, is still there. I have also heard that they are trying to encourage catch-and-release fishing by offering anglers one pound of smoked salmon for every four pounds of salmon released in a guide's presence. I can only hope this idea catches on. I noted that in all the rivers, the guides left it up to the angler whether he wished to keep or release fish, which is a step in the right direction. I hope to have a fairer go at the Langa some time in the future.

My last stop was a two-hour drive farther north and west to the Laxa i Dolum. My young guide from Langa took me as far as the old jeep would go, which was halfway up the last pass over a small mountain range. There the car would go no farther, despite my guide's entreaties. Fortunately, his cellular phone was functioning, and we contacted both a garage and the Laxa i Dolum lodge. The garage rescued him, and the young man who was to be my guide on the Dolum was sent from the lodge to rescue me on the road. Heimir Bardason proved both charming and knowledgeable. Thanks to him, the short bit of fishing on this river was a great success and a fitting end to a week of wonderful adventures.

After Heimir deposited my luggage at the comfortable lodge, which had been built by Pepsicola and blessed with larger than usual bedrooms with adjoining bathrooms, he then took charge of the fishing. As a rule, one guide is assigned two anglers, and Peter Stoop and I shared Heimir's services. Since we were both competent and experienced anglers, Heimir was able to place us in widely separated beats.

My first pool was at the very top of the fishery. A small narrow canyon with a deep pool below an impassable falls was followed by a boulder-strewn tailout. The upstream wind was fierce and gusty, but the skies had cleared and the water level, which had been at record lows, had returned to almost normal. Heimir stayed with me long enough to check my skill level and witness the taking of a fine eight-pounder on the hitched tube from the tailout. While he left me to my own devices, I had a delightful time moving several more fish but failing to hook them. I climbed the cliff to overlook the deep holding pool below the falls. Every time the wind subsided, I could see enormous fish, many in the upper teens and low twenties, finning and moving about the mixed currents of the pool. I tried to swim the little tube over them, but most of the time the wind would billow my line so badly that the fly was dragged across the surface at breakneck speed. This did elicit responses alright, but it was impossible to slow the fly enough for a successful take. It was a learning experience, however, to be able to see the way these fish responded to the fast-moving surface fly.

From the very top, we moved down to the lower end of the upper beat, trying various pools and fighting the wind until we came to one particular pool. It was difficult to read because it was relatively slow flowing, and it was nearly impossible with the heavily wind-riffled surface to tell where the deeper holding lies were. As a matter of fact, if we hadn't already known which way the river was flowing, it would have been hard to tell for sure. There were white caps on the water, and they were headed upstream. Heimir located us perfectly, and as it happened, I turned out to have drawn the better of the two lies. Peter was located upstream about thirty yards just above a thirty degree curve. With the wind blowing a solid thirty knots right up the valley, his location looked the more likely.

My part of the pool had a few boulders, and under Heimir's guidance, I was positioned well above these with instructions to cast down and across and to perform the high-speed retrieve after a few feet of drift. The fly was a version of the Laxa Blue with a black wing on a number 12 double. Trying to straighten out the fifteen-foot leader was tough, but the white-capped surface made for some pretty sloppy presentation. I followed my instructions to the letter, and despite not really believing, gave it my best effort. The first take jolted my arm in a way salmon takes seldom do. It was the first of four such takes in the next hour and a half in the very same spot. It was an easy place to land a fish with a nice shallow gravel shore on which to beach them. When landed after a strong fight, the fish turned out to be above fifteen pounds (Heimir said sixteen). I chose to release all my fish as I was leaving the next morning.

All four fish from this pool were about the same size, which surprised me. I had always been under the impression that Icelandic salmon were generally small with the exception of a couple of the northern rivers like the Laxa i Adaldal. Heimir, who has guided on many different rivers over a number of years and is well-informed, assured me that the reputation for small fish came about because of the earliest efforts to augment the natural stocks of many of the rivers in the southwest, which were then the most accessible streams. The stock came from the little river that flows through Reykjavík and, while very hardy, is a small race. The more remote rivers were the least affected by the introduction of the smaller strain. Laxi i Dolum, for example, yields considerable numbers of fish in the teens and the occasional twenty-plus-pounder.

I decided it was fitting to end my six days of fishing that evening even though I could still have fished the following day. Both Peter and I had had great fishing, although his part of the pool seemed to have held mostly smaller fish. I had landed twenty-six salmon, many of them larger than any I had caught in Iceland so far. I spent the next morning being shown the whole valley and taking pictures. Laxi i Dolum showed the same general diversity of water types that the other rivers had provided. I heard later on from Peter that he and Ralph Peters, a neighbor of my brother Pat's in Montana, had a marvelous week after I left. Peter matched my total of twenty-six fish for his week and was absolutely ecstatic about it. He'd never experienced anything like it in his native Scotland.

Here in a nutshell is my personal opinion about salmon fishing in Iceland today and of just being there in general. The landscapes are spectacular. There are essentially no trees, but everything else more than makes up for this. The rivers, even the largest, are small enough to be personable and fishable by any level of casting skill. Although expensive, it is doubtless the best place to have a good chance to catch a lot of salmon outside of the Kola Peninsula and the Ponoi River in particular. The people are marvelous—attractive and friendly. They like Americans, and best, they are almost invariably English speakers. If the Iceland-based North Atlantic Salmon Fund continues its efforts to buy out open seas salmon-netting fisheries, and other organizations, like the Atlantic Salmon Federation and Atlantic Salmon Trust, continue to influence the governments to save Atlantic salmon, sport fishing for salmon in Iceland will improve astronomically over time. Right now, as research and river conservation are ongoing, Iceland is a great place to fish for salmon in appreciable numbers and with all the creature comforts. The food at the lodges I visited was consistently great. At least one of the young chefs was a graduate of CIA (Culinary Institute of America). Iceland will always play a role in my salmon fishing plans as long as I remain physically able to cast a line and wade its rivers.

IV

TRAVELS WITH DAN

10
1944
Revisited

The tan rental Peugeot 504 shivered as we wound along the tight curves of the stone parapeted road leading to our rendezvous with Raymond Rocher. I had first heard of this paragon of the fly rod seven years earlier in 1970 while fishing in England with Dermot Wilson on the Itchen and the Test. I had since then read and reread Rocher's first book on fly fishing, *Les Confidences d'un Pecheur á la Mouche*. After friends of mine, Jim Barnett and his wife Harriet, had followed Rocher's well-documented trail through the Cévennes region of the southeastern Massif Central, the mountainous region of central France that gives birth to many of its principal rivers, my friend Dan Callaghan and I decided to contact Rocher and combine some fishing with a quest into the past.

Raymond Rocher enjoys an enormous reputation on rivers flowing through the chalk downs of Hampshire. He is viewed as a magician who deceives enormous fish with his precise nymphing technique. He was the translator of Frank Sawyer's book on nymph fishing for the French fishing magazine, *Plaisirs de la Peche á la Mouche*. As Dan and I were soon to find out, he is not only a versatile fly fisherman but also, as we came to describe him, the "fastest rod in the West." A man of great nervous energy, Rocher justifies his confirmed bachelorhood by using his every free moment from his duties as an English professor at the venerable Lycée of Tournon to fly fish. He fishes not only his own region but the rest of Europe as well. Across the Rhône River from Tournon are his digs in his beloved Tain L'Hermitage whose vineyards have blessed us with great wines since the days of the Romans.

Our rendezvous was at a tiny country inn run by his friend Pierrot at the juncture of two small streams. There they flowed into a small reservoir that fed a penstock for one segment of a power project. Rocher fervently believed the project had ruined a series of the finest wild trout streams in all of France. He greeted us with enthusiasm, and we were soon tasting the local country vintage, which perfectly suited the pan full of crisply browned trout, fried in a mixture of butter and oil, which Pierrot's wife set before us. The fish was accompanied by cottage-fried potatoes and a salad of curly endive and dandelion greens with pieces of browned fat bacon called "lardoons" mixed with the vinegar and oil dressing. The cold April night and our full stomachs led to a sound night's sleep in the deep feather beds and we dreamed of the day ahead.

Dan was determined to take pictures of this super angler fishing his "home" waters. It proved one of the toughest photographic challenges of his career, so rapid was Rocher's pace up the stream. His technique was characterized by quick exploratory casts up and between boulders to trout only visible to him. They were feeding, with barely perceptible rings, on the winter chironomids that constituted the principal diet of these slender mountain brownies. The stream was tiny in the bed of a large river, its normal flow having been permanently abstracted by another hydropower project farther upstream. It was really just the skeleton of a river, but its thin flows still held trout that were in every sense challenging to deceive and marvels in the pan.

Catch-and-release fishing is only just now becoming known in France, where the culinary rewards of fishing are still highly regarded. Fish are hard to come by since the law of diminishing returns comes into full play, and the few remaining trout become geometrically more difficult to catch. Let me assure you this is not all bad. Once a stream has the reputation of being "fished out," an angler can pretty much have it all to himself and then discover its most closely guarded secrets in relaxed solitude.

Relaxation did not, it seemed, constitute an integral part of Raymond Rocher's approach to fishing. So rapid was his thorough coverage of the waters, Dan was not able to stabilize his Hasselblad on its tripod quickly enough to capture his darting progress up the narrow gorge. Dan had to switch instead to one of the two Nikons hanging from his neck. When Dan takes on a photo project, this great fisherman totally sacrifices his fishing to concentrate completely on his subject. On this trip, he daily carried the two Nikons, one with black-and-white film, the other with color transparency film. On his back, in a green backpack, he carried the Hasselblad and the balance of his Nikon paraphernalia. Strong though he is, this constitutes a mighty load and photographing the fitting figure of Rocher required near superhuman effort as Dan tried to position himself on the steep, rocky sides of the gorge. He assures me that he did indeed capture Rocher in action, but the only prints I ever saw showed a blur in hip boots. The "fastest rod in the West" had earned his new moniker.

Rocher assured me that there was a sprinkling of fair-sized mayflies on the water this time of year. I have forgotten their name, but they had bluish grey wings and pinkish brown bodies with the segmentation remarkably obvious. My attempts at a much slower pace with a fly of this description were met with haughty disdain by these remarkably sophisticated little brownies. Only later, when there was some concentrated feeding on chironomids in the short stretch where the two streams flowed as one into the little reservoir, did I obtain some measure of success using the tiny snowfly imitations made for me by Rene Harrop in sizes 20, 22, and 24. The trout took them with complete abandon, and most were landed without any problem. Rocher expressed considerable surprise at this as he had previously been convinced that flies smaller than #18 were impractical and incapable of hooking or holding fish adequately. His #18 chirono-mids were tied on necked hooks but with very small hackles fore and aft and obviously intended to represent the mating or clustered insects. When I offered to leave a few of the Harrop creations with him, he did not refuse.

The following day we drove for about fifteen kilometers up the winding road that followed the gorge of the river where we had fished. Along the way, Rocher pointed out the terrible pollution of the lovely wild valleys. The ancient villages, which had always thrown their garbage down ravines from the sides of the mountain roads with no more damaging effect than some rust heaps and mild enrichment of the drainages below, had kept up the practice despite the advent of new, nonbiodegradable materials. The occasionally violent floods that occur with some regularity in these regions served to spread what used to be no more than compost heaps, but now contained an enormous amount of plastic of every color and hue, all the way down each of these formerly pristine valleys, festooning the trees and shrubs with a sickening array of garish colors.

When we came to a larger town perched further along this crest, Rocher pointed out the multihued scum from garbages and laundries and the effluent of houses emitted directly into these tiny trout streams. That the streams managed to cleanse themselves in their rapid dash down the mountainsides seemed a miracle, but the burden was increasing every year. This area is one of the least densely populated in all of France. A budding awareness of the environment may stave off some of these destructive practices. That, anyway, is the hope.

Raymond Rocher had to leave us at this time to return to his teaching as we had caught him at the tail end of his spring holidays. He had given us several useful tips regarding the next part of our venture: retracing the route that Robert Louis Stevenson had followed in his epic *Journeys With a Donkey Through the Cévennes*. Essentially, our route took us from the picturesque valley of the upper Loire across oak-covered hills to the parallel flow of the upper Allier, then south and up into the headlands where these rivers were born. It is wild and desolate country and uncharacteristic of how one imagines the French countryside. Gone are the geometrically perfect pastures and fields of the north, replaced instead by scrabble rock pastures and ancient stone villages piled on top of one another on the steep sides of hills wherever the flow of springs made settlement possible. Many of these tiny hamlets are either deserted or are being rebuilt by young people who wish to return to the soil. They have tried to relearn the old skills of stone masonry and subsistence farming along with crafts they hope will make cash for them.

In the highest of these central highlands, we could see a panorama of the ancient volcanic cones of the Massif Central, and we overlooked mountain meadow and pine woodlands splashed with patches of lingering snow. To the south we could see waves of long dark ridges that seemed to go on forever. These east-west ridges mark the Cévennes, and they are the beginning of the south, where the harsh highlands of Auvergne give way to a softer but still wild country. The people of the south were also different. They were noticeably warmer, more outgoing and welcoming like the climate, and for those who have tried to learn proper Parisian French, exceedingly difficult to understand. The land was still precipitous and poor, but it was a land where the snow doesn't linger late and where the limestone plateaus called Causses become verdant. In the spring and summer, wildflowers and herbs abound especially the wild thyme that flavors lamb and mutton—the basic meat of the region.

The Causses are cut by deep and spectacular canyons in which flow some of the most tantalizing rivers and streams in all of France. Most of them have spring sources rising from the limestone in rich clarity and would be classified as spring creeks were it not for the heavy mountain freshets and floods that can turn them into raging mountain torrents. As a result, they seldom acquire the dense weed growth of the lowland chalk and limestone streams of Normandy and Champagne. They do, however, provide a varied food base for their trout populations, which benefit from the rich insect hatches as well as the other elements of their food chain.

Dan and I followed the route the sickly Stevenson had taken on his truculent little donkey one hundred years before, camping out for the most part with his bedroll, staying barely ahead of the fast approaching winter. As we traveled, we read and reread the pertinent passages of his moving account of the turbulent events that had made this area the scene of a bloody religious rebellion and an even bloodier repression in the first decade of the eighteenth century. The first town we encountered to have played a key role in the Camisards' insurrection was Pont Du Montvert on the upper Tarn River. Local Protestants assassinated the Abbe in charge of enforcing the dictates of the recently revoked Edict of Nantes, which guaranteed Protestants the right to practice their religion without interference.

This delightful little town clustered along the river provided us with two treats. The first was the sight from the old stone bridge of some fairly good-sized brown trout fanning their fins in the boulder-strewn stream, a sight we found not uncommon throughout the region. The second was a tiny restaurant tucked away in a back alley with a sign indicating that wild game was its specialty. We climbed the narrow stone steps to a dining room where we were seated at a table next to two dark-haired beauties. The game, incidentally, which for lunch turned out to be *lapin de garrenne*, the equivalent of our cottontail, cooked in a rich red wine civet sauce. Both Dan and I remembered the meal as having been delicious but, frankly, the sidelong glances from the girls were distracting, particularly after the wine. Acting purely as interpreter and not at all in my own interest, of course, I asked the girls if they would care to join us for coffee and after luncheon brandies. They turned out to be working girls taking a spring vacation with their boyfriends who were joining them later. So much for that ploy. Still, Dan found the lighting in the old stone dining room with its small windows and the slanting sunbeams fascinating and had me get the girls to pose for him. He retains a record of these events, which I hope he will let me see some day.

Our next stop was a bit farther down the Tarn valley in Florac. The road down the river passed medieval châteaux, some in ruins and others that had either been kept up or been rejuvenated in recent times. There were chestnuts in bloom on the slopes for most of our sojourn along the river. Florac was on Stevenson's route, but our interest was an account in Raymond Rocher's book detailing a day of April fishing near the mouth of the Tarnon, which runs through the town before emptying into the Tarn.

We found a place where we could get to the river just upstream of the town. The water was crystalline despite a light drizzle that had been with us most of the way down the valley. We rigged up and waded in carefully but were unable to avoid sending some waves across the smooth surface. The stream being wide and shallow in that place, I took the far side and we worked our way upstream, fishing the water in the long pool before us with long fine leaders and tiny dry flies. Nothing happened, and we decided to sit and simply watch. I always carry small field glasses to scan the water for those quiet rises or surface disturbances so hard to see with less than perfect aging eyes. With the aid of the 7X40 glasses, I finally spotted a faint dimple just below a trailing willow branch toward the head of the flat on my side of the stream. I signaled Dan to hold up so I could make a cautious midstream approach to a point below and to the right of the rise location. Seeing no obvious flies on the water, but with the knowledge that a fly closely resembling our own *baetis*, though larger, was common these waters this early in the season, I put on a small olive emerger. After successfully dropping it just by the trailing willow strand, I was rewarded by a visible bulge under the fly but no take. I waited a few moments and tried again, this time catching my fly on the willow resulting in a V-wake that frightened fish and ended the adventure.

We saw no more fish there and headed back into the hills and along Stevenson's route.

The names we encountered during this last part of his route were moving as they commemorated many of the massacres and killings that had taken place in these parts in the name of God and of religious fervor. Our next objective, after leaving St. Jean Du Gard, where Stevenson's journey ended, was to return to the area where I had parachuted in during the summer of 1944. It was to be a more difficult task than I could have imagined.

The difficulties Dan and I encountered in 1977 trying to find and reconstruct my misadventures of 1944 were to be expected, I suppose. So much had changed since those days. Our first course of action was to drive through the country following the same sort of Michelin maps I had used much of the time during the war. The changes we found were the result of dam building and hydroelectric projects similar to those that had afflicted the region farther to the northeast, where Rocher's favorite streams had been severely dewatered. The stretch of the Orb where I had been able to catch some lovely fish after the Germans had left our operational area was now completely underwater. Nevertheless, I was able to recognize quite a lot of the country, although it was vague at best after thirty-three years.

I wanted to find some of the people I had known and worked with during the war. Le Bousquet d'Orb, where so much had happened that summer in 1944, was still an ugly place, essentially the French equivalent of an Appalachian company coal-mining town. But it did have a touch of what makes even the ugliest parts of France charming, and of course, the Orb river, which is a trout stream in its upper reaches, runs through it. I decided to set up base over the mountain in Lodeve, about twenty-five kilometers away. Lodeve, unlike Le Bousquet, was an attractive little town with a fine old twelfth-century cathedral and a pleasant little hotel with good inexpensive food and a selection of local wines. The baths at the Croix Blanche were down the hall from our rooms. They were the kind you have to fold yourself in half to fit into and were equipped with a hand-held showerhead. But we were comfortable and ready to tackle our investigation into the past.

After many questions to many people, we finally found a lead. The local armorer who had a shop where he repaired guns and knives as well as sold them, was supposed to have been a participant in the Resistance. We found the shop, a dark cubbyhole of a place, and the old armorer, who listened to my story with more than a little suspicion. Eventually, he suggested that I might find out more by going to the Restaurant Du Nord in Le Bousquet, where the chef was reputed to have been important in the Resistance.

The restaurant, which was a part of the Hotel Du Nord, was not yet open when we arrived at about ten the next morning. Nevertheless, we knocked at the door and after a long wait heard the unfastening of the latch and saw a wisp of a dark-haired woman still in her badly mussed pink cotton bathrobe. I explained that I was an American who had parachuted into the area during World War II and was trying to locate members of the Resistance I had worked with. Her reaction to my unfinished explanation was a cry of excitement and a rush up the dark stairwell, all the while yelling, "It's him. It's the American. I'll get René. Come down René . . . Tout d'suite. Viens!"

Several minutes later a disheveled figure with silver hair in a brush haircut came down the steps wearing a stained white chef's jacket. He rushed up to me, took a long look, threw his arms around me, and then burst into tears. It seemed he had seen me on a TV broadcast from Paris, where I was being interviewed about my father and had wondered if I would ever actually reappear in this part of the world. It was the beginning of what turned out to be three days and late nights of revelry. All the surviving old-time Resistance people from the whole area came into the restaurant, where René kept us all filled with spirits and food. There are very few bad meals to be had in France. It was, however, an unfortunate fact that while René Ribaud had been a brave and resourceful resistance leader, this did not qualify him to be a good chef. It was certainly the worst food I had ever tasted in France, but the good will, the cheer and the quantity of the spirits almost made up for this.

I was referred to as the crazy American who had parachuted with the fishing tackle, Dan was welcomed like a brother, and we drank numerous toasts to Jimmy Russell, who I then erroneously believed to have been killed in late 1944. After visits to the sites of all my adventures during the war, Dan and I took our leave from the old-timers of the Resistance and started once again to follow our natural bent as fly fishermen in a country with many streams to explore.

We inadvertently poached a pretty stretch of the Orb below the new dam, where it ran through the little village of Avène. We noted that the villagers all looked very much like one another, and several feeble-minded members of the clan were in evidence. We also noticed that there were some lovely rising fish right on the edge of town and more or less out of sight of the road. Dan photographed while I fished the ubiquitous chironomid midges with some success. It was then that we spotted a small sign shaped like a target. A check of the regulations later at a tackle shop revealed that these target signs indicated a closed-to-fishing stretch within town limits. This explained our great success at spotting trout in Pont de Mont Vert. Visible fish were nonexistent in those stretches open to fishing between the villages. French brown trout are no stupider than ours and seem to know when it is safe to show themselves.

Dan and I did not make a truly valuable fishing contact in the area until we met Dr. Jean Ster in Lamalou-les-Bains, the town where René, Jim Russell, and I had driven in our wild ride to make contact with the Maquis de la Montagne Noir outside Mazamet in 1944.

Sacha Tolstoi had advised us to check in with Ster and had dropped him a note warning of our arrival. We were impressed with the magnificence of his clinic, which specialized in the remedial treatment of industrial accident victims and made use of the therapeutic hot mineral springs. Jean warmly received us and invited us to dinner at his home, where we met his son François.

I was fascinated to hear from Jean the story of his night in the summer of 1944 when Jim Russell and I had parachuted in near Le Bousquet. Apparently, he had ridden his bicycle all the way from Lamalou—where he was a new young doctor as well as the new father of the baby François—to Bedarieux, the largest town in the district and only a few kilometers down the valley from Le Bousquet. The only functioning bakery in the area, was in Bedarieux, and Jean traveled eighty kilometers round-trip to fetch a few loaves of bread. While peddling back late at night he saw a German light-armored column heading up the valley, where it was to join in a fierce firefight with the local Maquis even as we were parachuting into the hills only a few miles away.

Jean invited us to join him the next day at his weekend house on a small spring-fed stream near the hamlet of Fondamente, just a few short kilometers from our old hideout headquarters during the Resistance. The brick and stone house was large and pleasantly situated in a lovely grove of trees. The stream looked trouty, but we were told it was badly overfished as well as polluted by the town's effluent although it did support a trout hatchery in its top reaches near the headwaters spring. We were invited to spend the night, and in front of an oak log fire and while enjoying a leg of lamb perfectly roasted on a fifteenth-century wind-up mechanical spit, we were told of the plans for the following day.

Dan and I were to meet Jean and son François for lunch at a little hotel restaurant on the banks of the Vis River between the famous Cirque de Navacelle and the large town of Ganges, where the Vis runs into the Hérault. During the morning, we were to visit the Couvertoirade, a magnificent ruin in the process of being renovated, where the Knights Templar had headquartered after their return from the crusades and until their dissolution in the early fourteenth century. Jean Ster was determined that we should come to know more than just the partial history of the region, which we had gleaned from our reading of Stevenson's little book. We were frankly fascinated by the ruins but not nearly so much as by the drive down the steep canyon wall to the boulder strewn-valley of the upper Vis.

Our fishing instincts forced us to stop and stare at the beautiful waters at every point where they became visible from the road. They were absolutely crystalline upstream from the ruins of an old château (since become a fabulous hotel called the Château de Madiere) and the little hamlet where we were headed for our rendezvous. Each part of the stream that we could see held deep green pools with just enough lime in the water to keep them slightly opaque. These were interspersed with shallow-appearing runs punctuated by holding rocks and gravel bars. We were to find that they were not shallow at all but often deeper than our wader tops.

We arrived at our appointment on time and enjoyed a memorable lunch of *ecrevisses* (fresh water crayfish) *a l'armoricaine,* local dried sausage, local blue cheese (Bleu D'Auvergne), limited vegetables, and a simple salad accompanied by an assortment of local wines of much better than expected quality. We then drove to the fishing hut, where we all took a much needed nap while awaiting the hoped for evening rise.

Over a period spanning many years the Vis has assumed the role of my dream river. It has all one could possibly ask for in one short piece of water. It was beautiful beyond imagining; it runs through a limestone canyon with real castles and châteaux rising above its banks; its waters are of extreme clarity yet rich in lime and as a consequence produce profuse hatches of most of the insects that make fly fishing such a rich experience. This then was the little fiefdom, which Dr. Jean Ster had put together within a few hours' drive from his renowned clinic in Lamalou les Bains.

The bottomland surrounding Jean Ster's fishing digs was farmed for him by a man who also served as river keeper. The fresh vegetables and legumes grown there were sent to his clinics' commissary in Lamalou. It was altogether a beautiful operation. On the occasion of my first visit with Dan Callaghan, the only facility was the rustic fishing hut stocked with such necessities as wine and fishing paraphernalia. There was an old, unused house of considerable size that had once been a principal residence. Its upper story was a giant loft heated by ducts form the many fireplaces below. These had been used to dry the long silkworm strands that were the main product of valley in the seventeenth and eighteenth centuries. At that time, of course, the most profuse plantings in the valley had been mulberry bushes upon which the silkworm larvae fed prior to their cocoons being gathered for pulling and drying in the hot sheds. Now chestnut trees were everywhere. Almost three kilometers of the river were within Ster's domain. The river farther up was in the ownership of a private fishing club and was heavily patrolled but usually overfished as the members killed all fish caught. The water below belonged to various small holders including the little hotel restaurant where we lunched so well.

Ster's fishing stretch had, overlooking it a spectacular white limestone château with crenelated turrets. It had been renovated a few years before by a successful merchant from Montpellier who had married a young trophy wife. The wife thought of herself as a chatelaine and insisted on the purchase of the château which had been built by Louis XIV to house a mistress he kept for visits to that part of France. It had become a near ruin through disuse and neglect until the merchant refashioned the interior into livable space on a grand scale. As it turned out, the wife's interest in being a chatelaine faded fast before the realities of living in a stone castle on the heights above a canyon where the winter and spring winds whistle ceaselessly and it is a two-hour drive to serious shopping. As a result, the castle was available for purchase. The land on which it stood comprised some two hundred hectares, most of which were near vertical. All of this I learned much later on a second visit, but that first evening in the flats, above a long deep pool, was a never-to-be-forgotten experience. It fixed the Vis forever in my subconscious as a river against which all other must be judged and, more often than not, found wanting.

As I fished that night, I was watched intently by a critical guest who was none other than Jean Paul Pequegnot, the renowned author of several books on fishing in eastern France and now known in our country as the author of *French Fishing Flies*, the book that started the CDC craze in the United States. On this occasion I felt a little of what gunslingers must have felt in the old days when called out. I can only say that I did manage to cast without making a complete fool of myself and to hook and land several fair fish under Pequegnot's watchful eye. He did not fish during my visit so that I could not exact a performance from him.

The next morning Dan and I had the river to ourselves as our host and his guest had to return to their respective lives. Dan and I each went our own fishing way as is our wont much of the time. I spent more time exploring than fishing and developed a longing to be able to return on a regular basis to the area, so diverse and beautiful were the various reaches of this magnificent river. Unfortunately, our schedule took us back north, and it was several years before I was able to visit the Vis once again.

The occasion was a business trip to France that found me with a spare couple of weeks, the first of which I spent at Pierre Barthes's tennis facility at the Cap-d-Agde, thanks to an introduction from my son-in-law, Jean Denoyer. After a week of being put through my paces on the courts, I was ready to look around the old haunts and gave Jean and François Ster a call. As usual they put out the welcome mat, and I was invited to meet them on the river.

Jean had fixed up the silk drying house with complete guest facilities as well as comfortable quarters for himself. After two days of delightful, though difficult fishing, I found myself thinking more and more of the possibility of buying a property in the area and quizzed Jean on the subject. He seemed to feel that the castle up the hill at the base of the cliff might be available for a high five figures (in dollars), if he were to act in my behalf. Since I did not have such a sum at my disposal, but might have put it together with time and the possible help of friends, I put off into the future any further action. Although there was no fishing with the property, Jean assured me that I would be able to have limited access to his fishing, and there was considerable evidence that there was some interesting shooting in the area as I had seen some red-legged partridge (similar in appearance to our chukar but smaller) while exploring along the river.

By my next visit, about a year later, I had all but determined to try to buy the château property through Jean. I visited a friend in the Luberon, and he kindly loaned me his old Citroen Deux Cheveaux. It could barely get up to fifty miles an hour and had to gear down for any and all hills. It was fun to drive, however, and used almost no gas. I had mentioned the château to my daughter Margot and her husband, Bernard. They decided to come down and have a look. The Sters were not there at the time, but it was arranged with the keeper for me to have the keys. What I hadn't bargained for was that Margot would arrive in her big and pricey 918 Porsche. Nor had I realized the extent of her fame in Europe. Before the afternoon was over, everyone in the area knew that a rich American movie star was going to buy the château and the word got to the owner, who did what anyone would under the circumstances. He tripled the price, and there went my dream.

Later, I filmed a portion of a pilot for a TV series, which never was sold, on the river with Ster's permission. The director insisted on the fishing taking place in the prettiest stretch but not where there were fish, and I suffered the consequent frustration and disappointment as our time was limited by a stringent shooting schedule.

My last visit was very late in the fall while on my honeymoon with Angela. It was past fishing season, and the cold winds were already blowing down the canyon. Jean Ster had bought the old château and had wisely left it as it was. Angela and I stayed at the Château de Madiere, which was delightful and had wonderful food. We used it as a base for long walks and for me to show her the country where I had operated during the war. The Vis valley was just turning into fall colors, and Angela found it difficult not to gather every fallen chestnut to bring home to the States. I finally convinced her this would not be economically sound. We also came, finally, to the conclusion that living in France was an economic impossibility for us. A booming European economy had changed the country's living patterns. Small towns off the beaten track now had heavy traffic of trucks trying to avoid the high-speed toll roads. Many of the towns in the region had acquired substantial Arab populations, and there was much friction with the locals. In our absence, security problems would become serious. Burglaries, break-ins, and vandalism were becoming commonplace. We would require a full-time caretaker, which was well beyond our means. Still, whenever I think of an ideal setting, the Vis comes inevitably to mind. Jean Ster passed away recently, but his son François now has the property. Happily, it is still in his good hands, and the wild zebra striped browns of that part of the Cévennes called the Causses continue to challenge the most sophisticated of fly fishers.

V

IN THE FIELD: BIRDS, DOGS, AND GUNS

11
Guns and Shooting

G uns and various kinds of shooting were always a natural part of my life and my brothers' as boys with Papa. I was the oldest and, due to the divorce, my time with him was limited for the most part to summers, usually in Key West. Key West in the summer was not paradise in those days. There was no air-conditioning. It didn't yet exist. For a light-complexioned little boy who lived most of the year in France with his mother, the heat, the damp, and the ever present prickly heat, chiggers, and mosquitoes were a constant torment—none of which seemed to bother my younger darker-complexioned siblings. Even the few dogs we had were miserable, mangey, tick-ridden, flea-bitten mutts, requiring high maintenance on our part to make their lives bearable. Under these conditions and the constant need for morning quiet to protect Papa from disturbance during his writing time, it wasn't surprising that any distractions—a day of fishing or going up on the Keys to accompany Papa shore bird or dove shooting—were high points.

During these Key West summers, I could hardly wait for the annual car trip to Wyoming, where the climate would be fresh and clean, and I could stop itching and peeling from constant sunburn. It was on these trips that I learned to handle and shoot Papa's .22-caliber Colt Woodsman semiautomatic pistol. When we got "out West," prairie dogs and other forms of ground squirrels and gophers along the road made fine targets. They did, however, require my going out to find them and verify a kill as they usually dipped down into their holes at the crack of the shot.

I think that, on the whole, I had more serious practice in proper sighting with a very unusual weapon. I don't know where, but Papa had acquired a legitimate Swiss crossbow with a supply of very serious bolts. It was obviously a proper hunting weapon and intended for killing chamoix in the Alps. I don't know its vintage, but the bow was steel and the bow string was almost a quarter inch in diameter. It had a special cocking lever and leaf sights and was unbelievably accurate at the short ranges we shot in the backyard in Key West. Papa had a complimentary subscription to *Fortune* and would tear out the portraits of the successful business executives and thumbtack them to the door of the pump house. He would offer a nickel for a hit in the head and a dime for either eye. It was possible to make a quarter on a target with the three shots allowed. This doesn't sound like much incentive today, but a dime bought you a movie matinee ticket in those days and a nickel got you an ice-cream cone. The pump house door took a licking, but fortunately the metal crossbow bolt tips were threaded so we could twist them out.

During two winters spent in Key West, I was able to go along with Papa to shoot a wide variety of shore birds, all of which he tended to lump together as snipe although he well knew the difference. There were some true snipe, but what we mostly went after were greater and lesser yellowlegs, his favorites to eat, as well as plover, sandpipers, and the occasional curlew.

In those days, the overseas highway was not yet completed and the Keys were pure wilderness. In a half-hour drive, you could find complete solitude, and a short walk through the scrub would put you on sandy strips alongside flats exposed at low tide and teeming with birds. Papa was expert at spotting the most desirable species from a distance. They would often flush out of range from our approach, but we would hunker down and he would start whistling them back. This was successful more often than not, and a pass by the birds within shotgun range usually resulted in a few for the table.

Unlike my brothers, who were introduced to shotgunning at a very early age, I did not get seriously involved with wing shooting until I was sixteen. Papa had moved out of the Key West house and into the Finca outside Havana, and we were now members of the Club de Cazadores del Cerro about halfway between Finca Vigia in the little village of San Francisco de Paula and Havana. In those days, the principal attraction was the Tira al Pichon, the live pigeon shoot. Every Saturday club members and their guests gathered for some very serious competition. It was definitely a betting game, and Papa loved betting, especially on sports. While I became fairly proficient, I was not a natural, and Papa's technique, which he had acquired as a youth shooting ducks on the Mississippi flyway with market hunters, seemed totally unnatural to me. He kept his feet widely separated and bent low at the waist, cradling his gun like a baby. I must say it worked for him. His favorite shotgun was a 12-gauge model 12 Winchester pump. With it, he could get off his second shot as fast as most shooters with a double gun.

The gun I shot most of the time was a 12-gauge double with Damascus barrels and double triggers that Papa called the "Duke of Alba." He had "liberated" it from the Duke's residence during the Spanish civil war. It was well balanced but quite light and kicked like hell so I had to concentrate on keeping my weight forward and mounting it solidly so as not to end up with a sore cheek and shoulder. More often than not, if I was hurried, I failed and eventually ended up flinching with every shot from the anticipated pain. I think that if Papa had started me with a 20-gauge, I might not have built up the early aversion to shotgunning, which stayed with me until well after World War II. However, I must say that what Papa instilled in me as a young boy and on through my teenage years was a true and healthy respect for firearms and for the damage they could do. He absolutely insisted on gun safety.

I shall be ever grateful for having been introduced early to many different kinds of weapons including even the Thompson submachine gun as it served me well when I went into the service during World War II. It was not, however, until my mid-forties that I found my true love of shotgunning and that was because I came to appreciate shooting over gun dogs.

12
Snipe near Cotorro

In 1945 Uncle Sam in his wisdom gave me sixty days of leave for my rehabilitation after six months as a wounded prisoner of war in Germany. My father was living in Cuba on a permanent basis, and my mother and stepfather were not at their home in Lake Bluff, Illinois. My stepfather, Paul, was already on his way to Paris to start up a Paris edition of the *New York Post,* but Mother and I could get together in New York for a couple of days before she joined him. After a somewhat tearful visit with my mother, during which she was a bit nonplussed at some quite offensive speech habits I had acquired during the six months of womanless company, she left for Paris and I, somewhat jubilantly, left for Havana. This was despite news that the girl of my prison camp dreams had found a new love. Fortunately, resilience is one of the positive qualities of a twenty-one year old. The hurt may be bad, but the recovery is quick, which leads me to believe that the current academic opinion that my father was permanently scarred by his rejection by Agnes Von Kurowski is nothing more than bull manure. He was pissed off certainly, but permanently scarred, no.

After the initial shock of meeting my new stepmother to be in her birthday suit, I settled down to some serious nightlife and occupied my days with reading, long walks, and some exploring of the local countryside. I looked for sporting possibilities that might have been overlooked by my father and his friends. Since gasoline was still a bit hard to come by and there wasn't always a car available for my use, I used the local bus system, which consisted of old Ford buses driven for the most part by certifiable crazies. Invariably, the horn was used in lieu of the brake pedal and no turn signals of any kind were ever given. On the other hand bus travel was extraordinarily cheap and, as I had found out during the war, you can get used to damned near anything.

My expeditions into the hinterlands initially were to faraway towns like Santa Catalina de Guines, where a beautiful spring river with waving weed beds and deep pools flowed between steep banks and wound through the sugar cane fields that covered the greater part of the arable land outside the town. The most attractive parts of the stream were near the town itself where there were some flow control structures with flumes. Since they looked trouty, I concentrated on them with my fly rod and some trout flies and bugs, mostly too small I now realize. Still, I persisted to little avail for the small-mouth bass who lived there, but all I caught were a few little ones. My trouting experience had failed to prepare me properly for small-mouth fishing. It was a fair piece by bus so I decided to try some ponds closer to home.

From the bus on the way to Guines, I had caught glimpses of open water to the east of the road near a town named Cotorro. This town was only about a twenty-minute ride on the Guagua—this is slang for "baby" and is the nickname given the ubiquitous Ford buses. I took the Guagua to Cotorro armed with an uninflated one-man life raft Papa kept on the *Pilar*, which was left over from the Q boat days during the war. I also had an old fly rod and some trout bugs with which I hoped to catch some of the large-mouth bass I felt certain I would find in one of the ponds. A look at a fairly detailed map Papa had at the Finca showed a number of small ponds in a draw several miles long. They were connected by what appeared on the map to be channels. From town, I hiked down a cart track toward the depression where the ponds were and finally arrived at the closest of these, which was bordered with reeds. It was only about three or four acres in size and I rowed around for an hour casting my bugs. I would leave them still until the ripples had ceased and then give them just the slightest of pulls to disturb the water's surface. Since my efforts were fruitless, I finally decided "to hell with it" and pulled out at the south end of the pond, where the purported canal should have been. Instead, I found shallow boggy ground that could be negotiated quite easily on foot. Leaving the raft, but carrying the fly rod, I followed the bog all the way to the next pond, a distance of what seemed about a half mile. Looking across the second pond, which was even smaller than the first, I could see that the bog continued farther south. After a few desultory casts along the edge of the second pond, I decided to call it a day. Either there were no bass at all, or I was going about it all wrong. It was even possible mid-July was not the best time to be trying this.

Later, much later, after a return to military duties, a stint in Washington D.C. and an unpleasant assignment after the Japanese surrender as a camp commander of a German prisoner of war camp in Virginia, I was finally able to obtain my release from active duty. Since my only home was now in Cuba, I opted to return there. It was late November, and what passes for winter in Cuba was nearly in full swing. It can seem quite cold in a hilltop house open to the four winds and with no heating system of any kind except for lightweight blankets or sweaters. When it gets into the forties with a norther blowing, people suffer. In this instance, Papa being in residence with Mary, the weather made us think of bird shooting.

In the late twenties and early thirties, when it was still legal to shoot most species of shore birds, we used to hunt them regularly on the Keys. The ones we prized the most for their taste had always been greater yellowlegs, a medium-sized wader, which Papa had great success for calling back in after they had been initially disturbed. At that time, we tended to refer to all these wading birds as snipe, although true snipe were relatively uncommon along the Florida Keys. With this in mind, I suggested that we might try to have a go at some snipe shooting and mentioned the boggy marsh between the ponds at Cotorro. Since it wasn't far, Mary and Papa agreed to give it a try.

As so often happened in those latter days during the Mary regime, it became more of an expedition than it need have been, and there was a full picnic lunch with chilled wine for accompaniment. We brought 20-gauge ammo for Mary's Winchester model 21, which she had inherited from Marty who had inherited it from Pauline. Papa, as usual took his 12-gauge model twelve pump, and I took the Duke of Alba.

Juan maneuvered the station wagon down the cart track to the edge of the first pond and then Papa, the General, took over and assigned me to go around the opposite side of the pond while he and Mary would work their way down along the near side to the south end. There we would join forces to walk in line along the boggy depression to the second pond. Being the junior member of the expedition, I had the most ground to cover but actually put up a few birds along the shore in those areas where the scrawny local cattle had grazed the marsh grass along the water's edge. Being as yet unfamiliar with true snipe, I was caught by surprise in nearly every instance as the swift dodgy little birds took off with their *scaip* sound and whirr of wings. When I got to the meeting point, I had only fired twice and killed nothing. Papa had two birds for four shots fired. Mary had not gotten off a shot. She was a novice at this too. We formed a line with Papa in the middle, Mary on the right flank, and me on the left. We were about ten yards apart, and Papa had admonished us to stop after every shot to see if there was a bird down and, being without a dog, to retrieve any downed birds before continuing. None of us were to proceed as long as there was a bird down anywhere until it had been retrieved.

We each had a box of shells, not nearly enough as it turned out. The marsh was alive with birds. It was a snipe paradise on that particular day, and our progress was unbelievably slow as we stopped to find downed birds. I learned a lesson that should have stayed with me but, like so many learned for the first time, was soon forgotten. That was that without a dog, you should forget attempting doubles where the birds are not going to drop on clear open ground. It is difficult enough to mark a downed bird, and almost impossible when you are concentrating on shooting a second one. All too often, neither is found in the confusion. Papa's basic law of hunting, which was that nothing must ever be shot that is not going to be consumed, precluded any attempt to give up the search for a downed bird in order to continue shooting. So we advanced slowly. We must have put up well over fifty birds in the first hundred yards, and all our shells were gone shortly thereafter. I don't remember how many we ended up bringing home to Finca, but it was not an impressive number, probably between ten and twenty altogether. We had expended seventy-five shells in all. Papa had the most birds, and I had only a couple. Mary had one but was credited with several that Papa had actually shot. Lèse-majesté.

The snipe—cleaned, plucked, and pan-browned in bacon fat before a five-minute stint in the oven at its highest heat setting—made a mouthwatering feast. Unfortunately, Papa and Mary were off shortly thereafter for a two-week expedition up the coast in the *Pilar*. After their departure, I went back alone only once to the marsh and while my shooting improved, the birds were never as numerous as that memorable first day. I couldn't take the gun traveling by Guagua, and as the car continued to be mostly unavailable to me, I reverted once more to my despicable nocturnal pursuits which, at age twenty-two, suited me just fine.

13
A Pre-Castro Cuban Dove Shoot

We were a real mixed bag of shooters heading out from Havana and the Finca Vigia. We were to meet up in Colon, where we would spend the night before the next day's dove shoot. It was during the Christmas season of 1940, and I had the treat of two weeks in Cuba with Papa. Howard Hawks and his beautiful wife Slim were visiting, and I was driving the Buick station wagon with them and Elicio Arguelles as passengers, while Juan, the chauffeur, drove Papa, Marty, and Charlie Lombillo, who happened to be the Marques de Villamayor in his other Spanish life.

We stopped in Matanzas at the old hotel where they still served fresh-caught freshwater crayfish. They came from the river that flows down from the low range of limestone hills, which the highway crosses and then parallels all the way into the harbor at Matanzas. We splurged on giant plates full of the delicacies, and it was late when we finished. Juan and I were the only sober citizens present. The wine had flowed freely and, as usual, had been preceded by drinks on the road. It was still a couple of hours drive to Colon, and the truck and bus traffic remained heavy on the Central Highway, at that time the

237

only mostly paved link between Havana and the eastern provinces of Cuba. I was having trouble with the bright lights of the oncoming traffic when Howard kindly explained how I could avoid being blinded by concentrating on a point well to the side of the oncoming lights. Howard had not only piloted airplanes but also racing cars. His advice served me well and still does to this day.

The old style colonial hotel in Colon had the usual high ceilings and transoms above high, narrow doors. The windows were louvered to catch whatever cross breeze might be blowing up, and the utilitarian furniture was dark and heavy. We had a four o'clock wake-up call which allowed us about four and a half hours sleep. We had coffee and pancitos on the road to the shooting fields, where we were led by the local guajiro, who had been engaged to organize the boys for picking up and to coordinate with the owner of the land, a friend of Elicio's.

While it was still only faintly light, we were lined out across what would become the flight path of the birds from their roosts to a feeding area. Elicio and Charlie had brought proper shooting sticks, but the rest of us were equipped with folding canvas stools. Guns were spaced about forty yards apart with a bag full of 12-gauge shells and a young boy of indeterminate age. For about a quarter of an hour, there was an uneasy silence somewhat like that before a firefight in wartime. Then the first shots were fired, and the doves started flying toward us in increasingly large numbers, occasionally interspersed with the odd bobwhite quail. The din from the firing line was practically nonstop. My old Duke of Alba was so hot I could barely hold the barrels. This lasted for approximately an hour and a half before the number of birds lessened to a trickle. The bird boys picked up those birds that they had been unable to recover during the shooting, and all the shooters gathered together for the count and a cold beer or some iced wine.

The bag was over two hundred and fifty birds, including some two dozen quail. Papa, who liked being the general officer in charge of such proceedings, persuaded the rest of us that we had plenty of birds for the pot and to give to the guajiro. Furthermore, it would permit us to have a leisurely lunch and an unhurried drive back to Havana and environs.

We returned to the hotel in Colon, where they arranged for an asado of Lechon (roast piglet), and the usual accompaniments of fried plantain, black beans and rice, and boiled yucca (not the cactus but a long root vegetable with a consistency not unlike potato) invariably flavored with garlic. We were a merry but sleepy crew when we got into the cars for the drive back. Everyone had shot well, and when I remember how happy both Marty and Slim seemed and how beautiful, I can't help but feel sad that neither of these women would remain much longer with the men who had brought them to shoot.

14
Partridge

After losing my dog Basil but before sympathetic friends were able to advise me that I shouldn't hurry into replacing a recently lost dog, I contacted a serious local owner of Brittany spaniels. He kindly gave me the most recent issue of a magazine devoted exclusively to the breed. I perused it carefully with particular emphasis on the ads for puppies and found what I hadn't dared hope for. There was a litter of liver-and-white Brittany pups in Troy, Idaho, a small town in the northern part of the state near Moscow, the location of the University of Idaho. I called the phone number and was speaking to the owners of the breeding kennel within minutes, and we arranged for the air shipment of the last liver-and-white puppy left in the litter, most probably the runt. The last one chosen usually is.

While it may well be advisable to wait a couple of months before replacing a lost dog, there's no doubt in my mind that a new puppy will get your mind off the loss speedily, if for no other reason than you're too damned busy to keep thinking about it. I decided to call him Partridge and filled in the registration form from the American Kennel Club with the imposing name of Loudeac Chocolate Partridge.

241

Loudeac was for a place in Brittany I remembered from my child-hood. Chocolate came from his father, Chocolate Dandy, who was a dual champion field-trial dog who loved to hunt. This heritage would, with a little luck, give me a big running dog when the need arose, but one that could be trained to work closely in thick cover.

The primary difference between the puppy Partridge and his pre-decessor in our household, the puppy Basil, was that Partridge was much wilder by nature. I spent almost every waking moment of the following two months with him, and he slept in a box next to my bed so I could get him outside at any sign of stirring so as to housebreak him. I set up a training bench and taught him "whoa" as soon as he was ready for it, and walked and cross-country skied with him every day. He came to me in January, and I arranged for him to go to a trainer for two months starting in late April, his only preparation being basic obedience training and the limited work on the bench.

I called the trainer fairly often during Partridge's stay and was as-sured the pup was coming along fine. I then arranged my plans to be able to spend the last few days of his training with Partridge in central Washington, where the trainer had his operation. On the morning of my arrival, we went out with the pup, and he pointed a pigeon, which had been put out in some clover. I flushed the bird and shot it. The pup stayed on point, steady to shot, and then retrieved the bird on the trainer's command. I wish I could say that everything in Par-tridge's life went as smoothly.

Brittany spaniels are not simple creatures. My experience of them is that each has a mind of its own and Partridge was certainly no ex-ception. It sometimes seemed we were engaged in a test of wills. His trainer had used an electric collar, and I learned to use it too. While these are marvelously useful for correcting errors in a dog's behavior, they must be used judiciously and not as an instrument of revenge or anger. This can ruin a dog forever.

That first hunting season with Partridge was truly special. We started in southeast Washington, where the season opened on the first of September, and then moved to northern Idaho and western Mon-tana before heading up to British Columbia, where I could combine steelhead fishing with grouse hunting. The daily grouse limit there was ten birds. I don't remember ever shooting the limit of ruffed grouse but did get a combined limit of ruffs and blues once. My best take of ruffed grouse in a day was seven. Half the birds I shot in those glorious ten days were off Partridge's points, and he retrieved most of them, saving a good many that I had not killed cleanly and had flown on into deep cover before dropping out of sight. These were birds I would never have even thought to have been hit.

After the ten days in British Columbia, we headed back to eastern Montana, where I met up with my brother Pat to hunt sharptail grouse, sage grouse, Hungarian partridge, and pheasants. Partridge proved his mettle on all species, and we departed for a return to Sun Valley via the Clearwater valley, where I was again able to combine steelheading and bird shooting. This time there were chukars added to the mix, as well as valley quail in the willow bottoms late in the evening. I have never again enjoyed such an orgy of shooting as I did that first autumn with Partridge. We finished the season over in the Snake River country around Brownlee reservoir, hunting both in Idaho and Oregon. The final count of birds shot over his points in that season was more than two hundred. Had I been able to repeat the same itinerary, I'm sure he would have beaten his own record. It was not to be. Such are the realities of life.

Partridge has held his own over the years, often showing up fine dogs of great reputation. He was almost twelve when I started this writing and has slowed down considerably. Nevertheless, his reliability factor remains extraordinary, and he has become a surefire retriever, especially when his new young partner, Basa, the Gordon setter, shows a certain disdain for such mundane activities while there are still live birds about to find and point. They make a fine team, and I feel blessed to have been so fortunate in having these dogs in my life. Partridge has been special from the beginning. He filled a void I had thought impossible to fill and is still my best friend.

Two years later Partridge is no longer with us. He suffered from cancer and became totally incontinent. Angela gave him a special feast of his favorite foods—a whole raw filet mignon, a slice of Camembert cheese, and a pint of Häagen–Dazs vanilla ice cream—before we put him down. He died without pain and what looked like a smile on his face.

This book is, in essence, the repayment of the enormous debt I owe to those who came before me and who, through their writing or by their good example, taught me those things that made my life what it became, a life worth living.
                                                                    —Jack Hemingway

THREE

SOME TRIBUTES

A Tribute to
Jack Hemingway

By Tom Brokaw

As delivered on Saturday, December 9th, 2000, at the Explorer's Club in New York by Tom Brokaw, NBC Anchor, ASF National Council member, and longtime friend.

On behalf of Angela and other members of Jack's family, I am happy to welcome you to what is a celebration of a life lived large. Indeed, a life so robust and so memorable it cannot be stilled by a stopped heart or a flat line. It goes on in another dimension here today and forevermore.

Angela has asked me to open and close this service, and when we were puzzled by how I should be described, I suggested "guide," knowing that these would be the only circumstances in which Jack would accept me as a guide.

Howell Raines and I are here as co-chairs of the New York branch of the Jack Hemingway fan club. It is a measure of this generous and gregarious man that while we didn't know him long, to our regret, even an abbreviated relationship with Jack was as treasured as a long-life friendship.

Others will speak of his unslaked appetite for life, his passion for the rod and gun, the environment in all its forms, and the great wild things, large and small.

I would like to ask you to remember Jack from another angle. He was a quintessential member of a unique generation, one that so shaped the world we enjoy today.

He might have started life in the golden glow of celebrity and in what seems to the rest of us an impossibly romantic time, but he wore that lightly. I remember asking him, as I uncorked a bottle of vintage brandy, what his father was doing the year it was bottled. Jack thought for a moment, roared with laughter, and said, "He was leaving my mother!"

No, what Jack did was take his place alongside the ordinary Americans of his age who had no famous fathers or celebrated godmothers. He joined them in the fight for the survival of the world. He enthusiastically described parachuting into France with a fly rod in his pack, but he didn't dwell on being wounded or being captured. Typically, he preferred to discuss the heroics of others rather than his own.

It was not easy for Jack to return to civilian life, as it was not for millions of other young men. But like most of them, he refused a diet of self-pity. Nor did he later, when it became the fashion of the culture, go from talk show to talk show, lamenting the burdens of a famous and complex father. Instead he went fishing—or hunting—or to The Ritz.

He simply got on with life, literally whistling as he charged ahead, almost never looking back, laughing all the way, great bursts of laughter aloud and ever present in his eyes.

He was a man born in a time when the world was in the throes of great changes—the coming of age of radios, telephones, automobiles, manned flight—and also the coming great darkness: a world war fought on six of the seven continents and all the seas. He lived through the nuclear age and saw the end of the Cold War; men went to the moon and a president was assassinated. Species disappeared and the body's molecular structure was mapped. Prosperity spread and new technology empowered the least among us as well as the privileged.

But Jack's life was built not around these dazzling changes, but rather his passion for family and friends, the unalloyed joy of field and stream and, by God, no whining. He was put here to remind us that while all around us is changing, the pure pursuit of happiness is not selfish, but generous. It is noble for it lifts us all.

To be faithful to his life, we must continue the active pursuit of happiness—and ride the currents that carried our friend along on the slipstream of laughter, wild fish and birds, friends and family.

Eulogy for Jack Hemingway, December 9, 2000

By Howell Raines

When I was growing up in Alabama, there was a sentence of praise reserved for the kind of man who seemed to have realized his full potential in every way—physically, mentally, emotionally, and spiritually. "He covers all the ground he stands on," we would say of such a man. I thought of that sentence when I first met Jack out in Idaho and again when I learned of his death.

He covered the ground he stood on in a way that was totally, uniquely his own. By that I mean, Jack Hemingway filled places with his presence, and he had a great gift for making you feel lucky to be there with him.

Many others knew Jack longer and better than I. But I was fortunate enough to be included in the charmed circle of his friendship in three locations that he loved—Sun Valley, New York City, and Tierra del Fuego.

The first thing I learned about Jack was that he fit the classic definition of a gentleman. That is to say, he was a gentle man, a truly gentle man. I never saw him behave badly toward anyone under any circumstances. I've never even heard of him behaving badly.

251

The second thing I learned about Jack was that he seemed largely a self-defined personality. That seemed to me at the time, and it seems to me today, something like a miracle. For while Jack was born with the blessing and the burden of one of the twentieth century's most famous names, Jack was in no way derivative. He was so fully himself. In the rich autumn of his maturity, which was when I knew him, he had a kind of independence that let him rise up to greet each day with a shining enthusiasm, and he carried the fame that had come to him unbidden as if it were weightless and also something to be savored but not abused.

I admired the negotiation Jack seemed to have made with being Ernest Hemingway's son. We know from reading *Misadventures of a Fly Fisherman* that this was not always an easy assignment, and that no small amount of struggle went into Jack's success in finding his true métier as a leading figure in first the American and then the international conservation movements.

Very early in our friendship, Jack learned that my original ambition in life had been to be an English professor. He forgave me this. Yet he also knew I had more than a passing scholarly interest in his father's work, and in what it must have been like for Jack to have been dandled on Gertrude Stein's knee, to have watched the Fitzgeralds on their madcap ride, and to have known the great impressionists as guys around the neighborhood.

I never heard Jack name-drop about of any of this. I never pestered him with questions about this or that historical or literary detail. Jack was my friend because of who he was, not because of who he was kin to. Yet knowing my interest in literary history, Jack would answer any question that came up in the most relaxed, unflippant, expansive way. And my lasting impression from those talks was that Jack understood that he had grown up in an extraordinary time among magical, if flawed, creatures who put their stamp on the culture we have today.

In my life as a reporter, I have known many people who carried grudges toward famous parents or complained about this or that shortcoming that lay behind the curtain that separates the public and private personality of a great figure. But Jack, as I knew him, had a grown man's rounded, mature understanding of where he came from, of who he was as an independent person, and a healing love for his parents and the historic company into which they introduced him. I admired Jack's sense of balance so much, and I will never forget the generosity with which he shared his remarkable life with those of us born to a much smaller stage.

Now one thing that set Jack apart from every one of us here today was that the jottings in his baby album were composed by a genius. In the days since we lost Jack, I have been revisiting some of his father's writings about the small boy upon whom he doted.

This is from a letter written in Toronto to Jack's godmothers, Gertrude Stein and Alice B. Toklas—the "twin gargoyles of my childhood," as Jack once referred to them. It was written on October 11, 1923, one day after Jack's birth.

Ernest wrote: "The free time that I imagined in front of a type-writer in a newspaper office has not been. There hasn't been any free time or otherwise for anything. Young Gallito was born yesterday morning at two o'clock. No trouble. Only took three hours and the doctor used laughing gas and Hadley says the whole childbirth business has been greatly over-rated. Weight seven pounds and five ounces, which had a good deal to do with making it easy I'll bet. [This may tell us something about Ernest's understanding of childbirth]. I am informed he is very good looking but personally detect an extraordinary resemblance to the King of Spain."

Then this to William B. Smith, from Paris, on December 6, 1924. I have always remembered this letter because it confirms my suspicion that Jack's passion for fishing was as much an inheritance from his mother as from his father.

Ernest wrote, "[Hadley] fishes not with the usual feminine simulation of interest but like one of the men, she's as intelligent about fights as she is about music, she drinks with a male without remorse and turned out Bumby the boy spring off who is built like Firpo, sleeps all night and is as cheerful as a pup. Gee Boid the way he's built and the way he's coordinated, that guy will have a chance to step. Jack Pentecost [a boxer of the day] is a frail built one along side of him. [Bumby's] got a head piece so that when you tell him a thing once he does it."

To say that Jack's parents doted on him is an understatement. Their letters never fail to comment on his jolly nature, his robust physique and his precocious facility with languages.

This from a letter to Waldo Pierce from Gstaad in 1927.

"[Bumby] has fought every kid in town and learned German since coming down here. I asked him what he was going to do when he grew up and he said he was going to make whiskey for papa."

And finally this wonderful moment from a letter to Maxwell Perkins from Paris.

"I took my son, who is three years old, to the café the other afternoon to get an ice cream and while he was eating it and holding his harmonica in the other hand he looked all around and said, '*Ah la vie est beau avec Papa!*'"

From that we know that Jack was a man who found his motto at the age of three: *La vie est beau*. From that day on, whether he was waving ice-cream cones or jumping out of airplanes with a fly rod in his battle gear, Jack lived with infectious enthusiasm.

And in the end, Jack himself was the best literary witness to his own experience as a fisherman, soldier, and man of the world. He has left us a particularly fine account of the moment that shaped John Hadley Nicanor Hemingway into the man he would become.

I'd like to read that in closing. In this passage, Jack tells of the Sunday afternoons he was left to play on a dock while his mother went for a stroll in the French countryside with her soon-to-be-second husband, Paul Mowrer.

"There was a small dock extending into the water. From its outer edge I could watch the different kinds of minnows swimming in the current and among the waving strands of water weed. On this particular day I had fashioned a hook from the proverbial bent pin with pliers and a small hammer. Using some of the strong black thread Paul used to perform his marionette tricks for a fishing line, I fastened the line and the hook to a three-foot piece of willow shoot. With some of

Madame Fouk's bread—the part inside the crust—I rolled some tiny dough balls and impaled one on the barbless hook. I had a difficult time fastening the thread to the pin, but somehow I managed.

"I had no bobber, but the water was so clear I could see the minnows attacking my baited hook as it drifted in the current. I tried to imitate the style of the Seine fisherman I had seen. It worked. Not often, but often enough to excite and encourage me. I was able to time a strike *cum* heave and found a shiny minnow flipping and squirming on the dock beside me. Kimi took advantage of me and rounded out his already rotund shape even further with a feast of minnows, but I did manage to get some back to the kitchen in my pockets. . . . I was later admonished for using my pockets for a creel. Thereafter, I was provided with a cloth flour sack and my fishing forays became a regular feature of our Crécy weekends. I didn't know it, but a radical change had taken place in my life. I had become a fisherman and would never ever be quite the same again."

That little boy on the dock on the Grand-Morin river in France would turn himself into one of the world's great fly fishermen and a saver of the waters without which neither the fishes nor our own species will survive. Yet today we remember not the skill of the fisherman or the passion of the conservationist, but the great spirit of the little boy who announced *"la vie est beau"* and the man who lived every minute with the conviction that life is a precious and beautiful adventure. So it was for Jack. So it will be in days to come for us. But we also leave this place knowing that life was more beautiful when Jack was in it with us.

One Last Cast

A Tribute
By Dan Callaghan

J ack, we are the closest of friends who fished over 100 rivers together for 38 years after meeting at Steamboat Inn on the North
Umpqua River. There must have been over 1,000 good picnics
from the Madison River in Yellowstone National Park to the jun-
gles of Venezuela to the Wood River in Idaho. Now it is time to thank
you and to say, as we always did at the end of each day on the river,
"One last cast."

First, thank you for that big, booming, explosive, and happy
laugh. It was always like a burst of sunshine on a stormy day. It
brought warmth, joy, and happiness to all of us. I will always be able
to hear it. I don't think anyone has heard real laughter until they have
heard you and your brother Patrick laughing together.

Often, I just sat on the bank and watched you fish. I will always
see, especially when I am fishing, the powerful arc in your fly rod, the
way you would watch your backcast, the tight, close loop in your fly
line and how it would unfold, and just how you would put your hand
on your hip when your steelhead drift started. And I remember also

the beautiful, rhythmical tempo of your cast when you were dry-fly fishing.

There was the first time you took me to Silver Creek so many years ago, and long before you helped the Nature Conservancy obtain and manage a large part of it. As we waded in, the pale morning duns were hatching by the thousands. I had a bad time catching fish with so many naturals on the water, until you showed me what to do.

My first trip to Yellowstone was with you when we drove up from Jackson Hole with a bottle of gin. We woke up in the car in the old parking lot with Old Faithful erupting, and then we fished the Firehole River. And, while we were fishing, a herd of elk crossed between us, and there were buffalo on the banks.

One time, in June, in the Box Canyon on Henry's Fork of the Snake, the salmon flies were everywhere. I was waiting for you on the back of the tailgate. When I heard you whistling, coming up through the trees, I opened the Chilean wine we had. You sat down on the tailgate too, looked down, and said, "I think I will eat one of those salmon flies." You picked one up, and ate all 2½ inches of him. I can still hear the crunch. I handed you a glass of wine, you took a sip, looked at me dead seriously, and said, "The wine is wrong."

When we were in Paris we ate well. Very well in fact, and, of course, we consumed a great deal of fine French wine. This led to weight problems for both of us and to two nicknames I gave you. First you became "Hemingwaddle" and then you became the "Hunch Belly of Notre Dame." The nicknames stayed in France. In the south of France, after forty-five years, you drove up an old road and found the exact spot where you had been shot and captured by the Germans. Their machine gun pits were still there. A few days later we had a party, in an old café, with about twenty French Resistance fighters. I remember well how much they cared about your help to France during the war. Everyone had more to say as the wine flowed, and thank you for being my interpreter.

When you married Angela in Ketchum, I handed you a Hemingway Caddis Fly instead of the ring. After the most surprised look I ever saw on your face, you quickly recovered, hooked the fly in your lapel, laughed, and held out your hand for the ring.

You taught me to tie steelhead flies in Mill Valley when you lived there before moving to Ketchum. More importantly you taught me that, at the end of the day on the river, it was not how many fish you caught but what you saw and, even more importantly, what you felt.

There were other things too. Celebrating our October birthdays together. Martinis on the back porch of Cabin 1 at Steamboat while watching the river. Good talks on many things. All the times before dawn on the North Umpqua. Barbecues on your deck at Ketchum and fishing the Wood River behind your house. Serving as fish and wildlife commissioners in Idaho and Oregon at the same time in the early 70s, and that's when the wild trout programs got started in earnest in each state. Racing down the gravel bar in our waders on the Salmon River to see who could get to the steelhead pool first. Buying barbecued chicken from the Round Up Market in West Yellowstone for our picnics on the Firehole. The time you left the Hen Caddis fly in your ear for five days just because you liked it there. Driving through Norway from Oslo to the coast for salmon fishing. Buying that terrible wine from the little monastery in the mountains of France. The bland chicken with the red hot sauce and horrible beer in that isolated jungle village in Venezuela. When you released what we thought later was a world-record peacock bass. How proud you were when Mariel caught her first trout off my shoulders in the Metolius River. Drinking vodka in tin cups made from beer cans while driving back to West Yellowstone from the Firehole River. These are the things that memories and friendships are made of.

You and I both loved our friend Roderick Haig-Brown and his writing. Here is something you especially liked from his book, *A River Never Sleeps:*

"I still don't know why I fish or why other men fish, except that we like it and it makes us think and feel. But I do know that if it were not for the strong, quick life of rivers, for their sparkle in the sunshine, for the cold greyness of them under rain, and the feel of them about my legs as I set my feet hard down on rocks or sand or gravel, I should fish less often. A river is never quite silent; it can never, of its very nature, be quite still; it is never quite the same from one day to the next. It has its own life and its own beauty, and the creatures it nourishes are alive and beautiful also. Perhaps fishing is, for me, only an excuse to be near rivers. If so, I'm glad I thought of it."

You are my hero and my mentor. Most of all you are my best friend. So, Jack, one last cast. I won't say goodbye because you and your memories will always be with me. I will just say I love you, old friend.